LIGHT AND COLOR IN THE
WATERCOLOR
LANDSCAPE

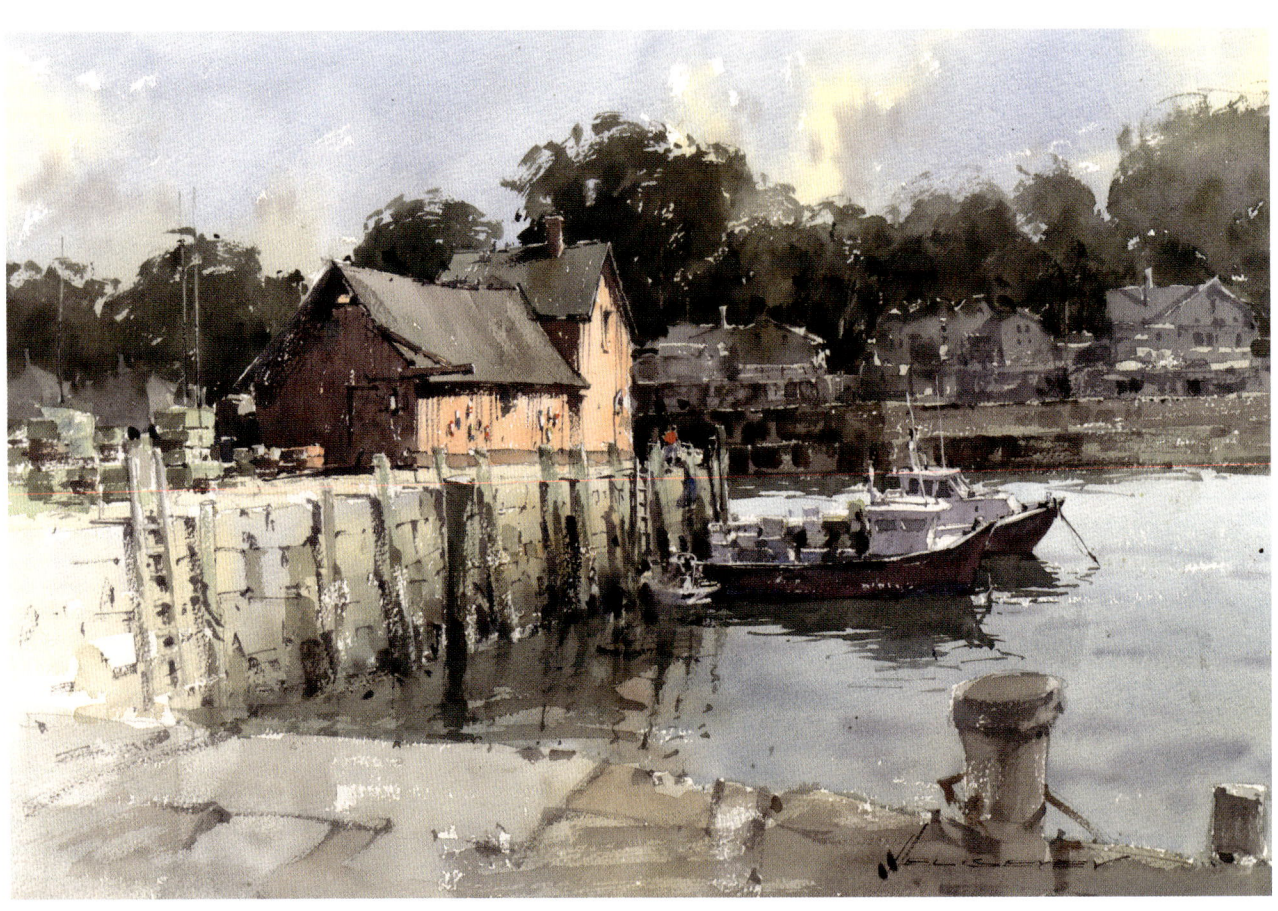

Rockport barn, watercolor, 14" × 21½" | 36 × 55 cm

LIGHT AND COLOR IN THE
WATERCOLOR LANDSCAPE

Essential Principles and Techniques

VLADISLAV YELISEYEV

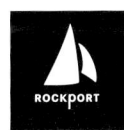

ROCKPORT

This book is dedicated to my father, whose influence has been fundamental to the person I am today.

Quarto.com

© 2026 Quarto Publishing
Text and images © 2026 Vladislav Yeliseyev

First published in 2026 by Rockport Publishers, an imprint of The Quarto Group, 100 Cummings Center, Suite 265-D, Beverly, MA 01915, USA.
T (978) 282-9590 F (978) 283-2742

EEA Representation, WTS Tax d.o.o.,
Žanova ulica 3, 4000 Kranj, Slovenia.
www.wts-tax.si

10 9 8 7 6 5 4 3 2 1

ISBN: 978-0-7603-9925-5

Digital edition published in 2026
eISBN: 978-0-7603-9926-2

Library of Congress Cataloging-in-Publication Data is available.

Design and Page Layout: Megan Jones Design
Cover Images: Vladislav Yeliseyev
Photography: Vladislav Yeliseyev

Printed in Guangdong, China TT112025

FOREWORD

Claude Monet famously said, "Color is my day-long obsession, joy, and torment." Indeed, having a healthy obsession with light and color is part and parcel of being an artist. Anyone with an eye for beauty can't resist the splendor and drama of certain lighting situations. The shimmer of sunlight on a coastal harbor. A soft morning light breaking through trees. The play of light on the side of a time-worn building. These magical moments of luminous color simply beg to be painted, and—as Vladislav Yeliseyev demonstrates so beautifully—watercolor is a wonderful medium with which to render them. But, as Monet infers, the work isn't without some real challenge. And that is where this book comes in.

Over his more than fifty years as an artist, Yeliseyev has developed many well-tested methods and strategies for painting—approaches that encourage captivating outcomes. In this book, he shares from this wealth of experience, offering advice and insights to help watercolor enthusiasts who are eager to enhance their skills. His aim is not only to offer practical guidance on essential tools, materials, and techniques, but also to provide instruction around the *thinking part of painting*—those conceptual considerations and creative decisions that further expression and help artists communicate with intention.

Yeliseyev has put in a lot of brush miles over the years and has earned plenty of recognition for his mastery, but he has also picked up important experience as a speaker, paint-out participant, demonstrator, juror, and art educator. He knows the common trouble spots for painters and which bits of knowledge often hold the key to creative breakthrough. This is the expertise that he has brought to the informative articles he has written for me, at *Watercolor Artist*, one of the publications that I work on. But here, in these pages, rather than presenting a single lesson, Yeliseyev shares a whole lifetime of acquired knowledge. With his encouragement, and this book as a guide, readers are sure to develop new capacities for painting, creating watercolors that capture color and light, and the very essence of a scene.

—Anne Hevener

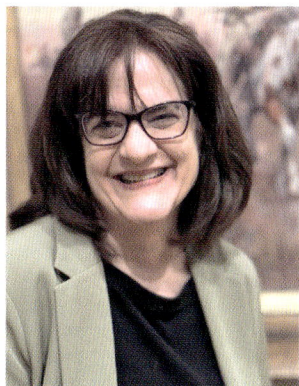

Anne Hevener is the Editor-in-Chief in the Fine Art Community, at Golden Peak Media, where she works with artists and writers to create content for *Watercolor Artist*, *Artists Magazine*, and *Pastel Journal*, and develops articles for artistnetwork.com.

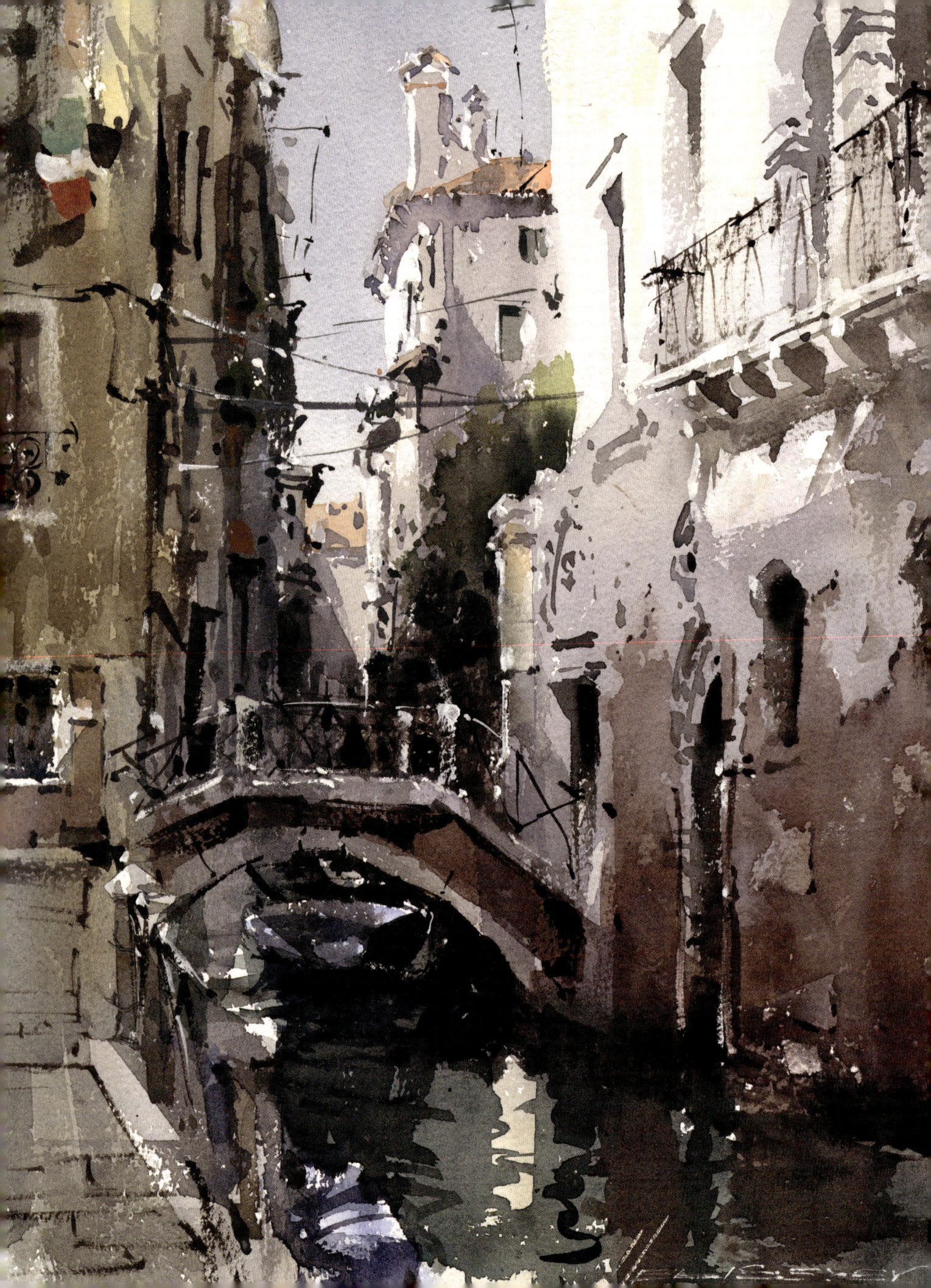

CONTENTS

◄ *Bridge*, watercolor, 14½" × 10½" | 37 × 27 cm

INTRODUCTION

This book is designed to assist artists who wish to embark on watercolor painting or enhance their watercolor skills. The information presented here may also be beneficial for artists working in other mediums, such as oils, acrylics, or black and white graphic arts. Readers seeking useful information here should bear in mind that all the content is based on my personal experience, spanning over 50 years of working with drawings, watercolors, and oils.

After many years of practice and teaching the fundamentals of watercolor and drawing, I came to the realization that my knowledge is deeply interconnected with various aspects of the theory of light and color.

The style of painting is unique to each individual, much like one's handwriting style, which would be nonbeneficial to anybody to learn regardless of how aesthetically pleasing it is. The purpose of this book is to provide artists with the tools and knowledge necessary to comprehend the fundamentals of various aspects of the artistic profession and to gain a better understanding of how these elements of artistic knowledge are interconnected.

If readers feel the content is somewhat advanced, I encourage them to start from the beginning, since each chapter builds on the concepts introduced in the previous ones.

This book, as you may have already gathered, is a study guide with a singular goal: to enhance the reader's proficiency in watercolor or any other artistic medium. I firmly believe that simply painting a lot is not enough for improvement; targeted exercises are crucial.

My hope is that this book will make it easier for readers to form a comprehensive understanding of the artist's profession and acquire a set of tools necessary for creating professional and captivating paintings along their artistic journey.

▶ *Old Cars*, watercolor, 20" × 16" (51 × 41 cm)

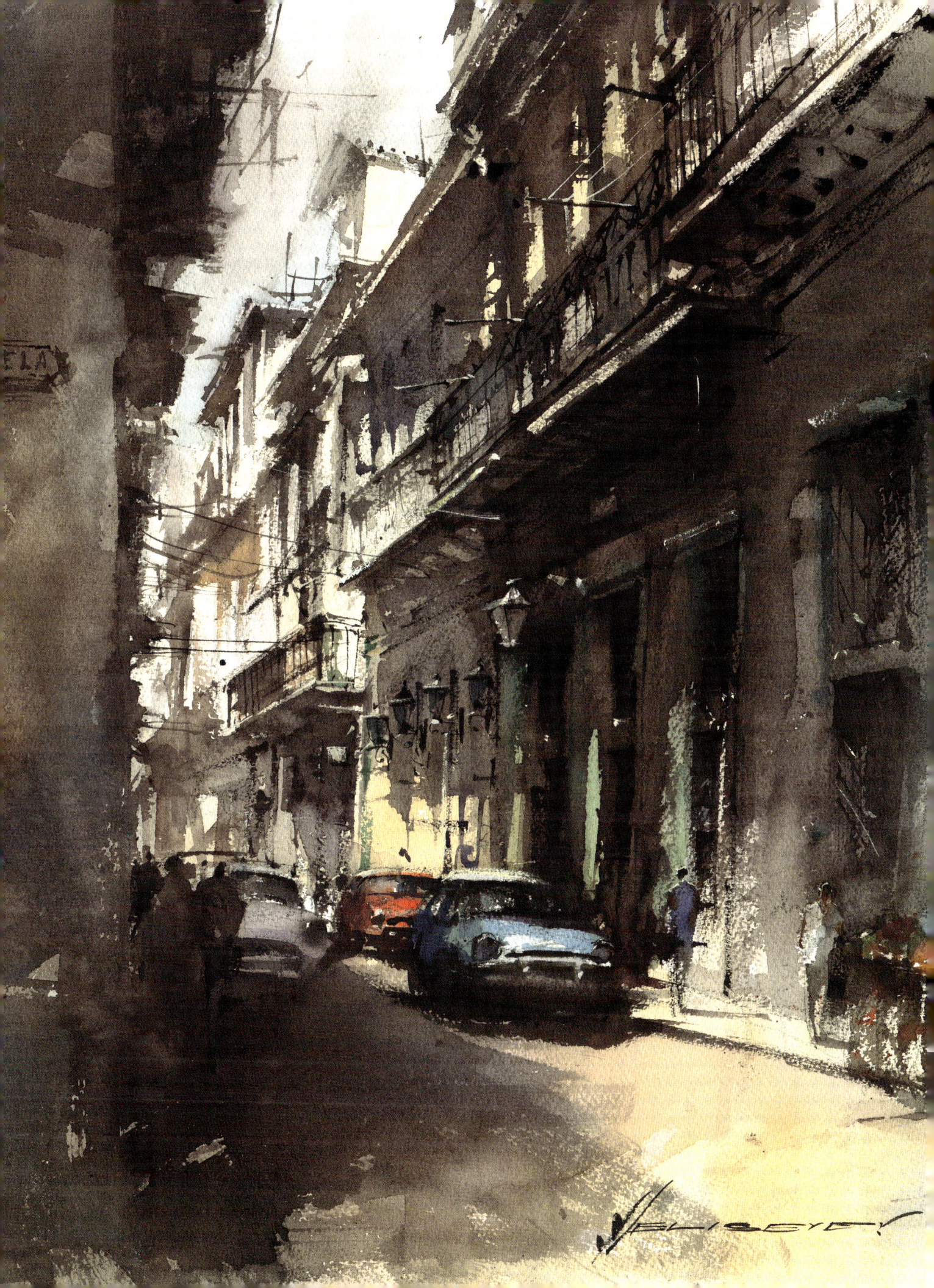

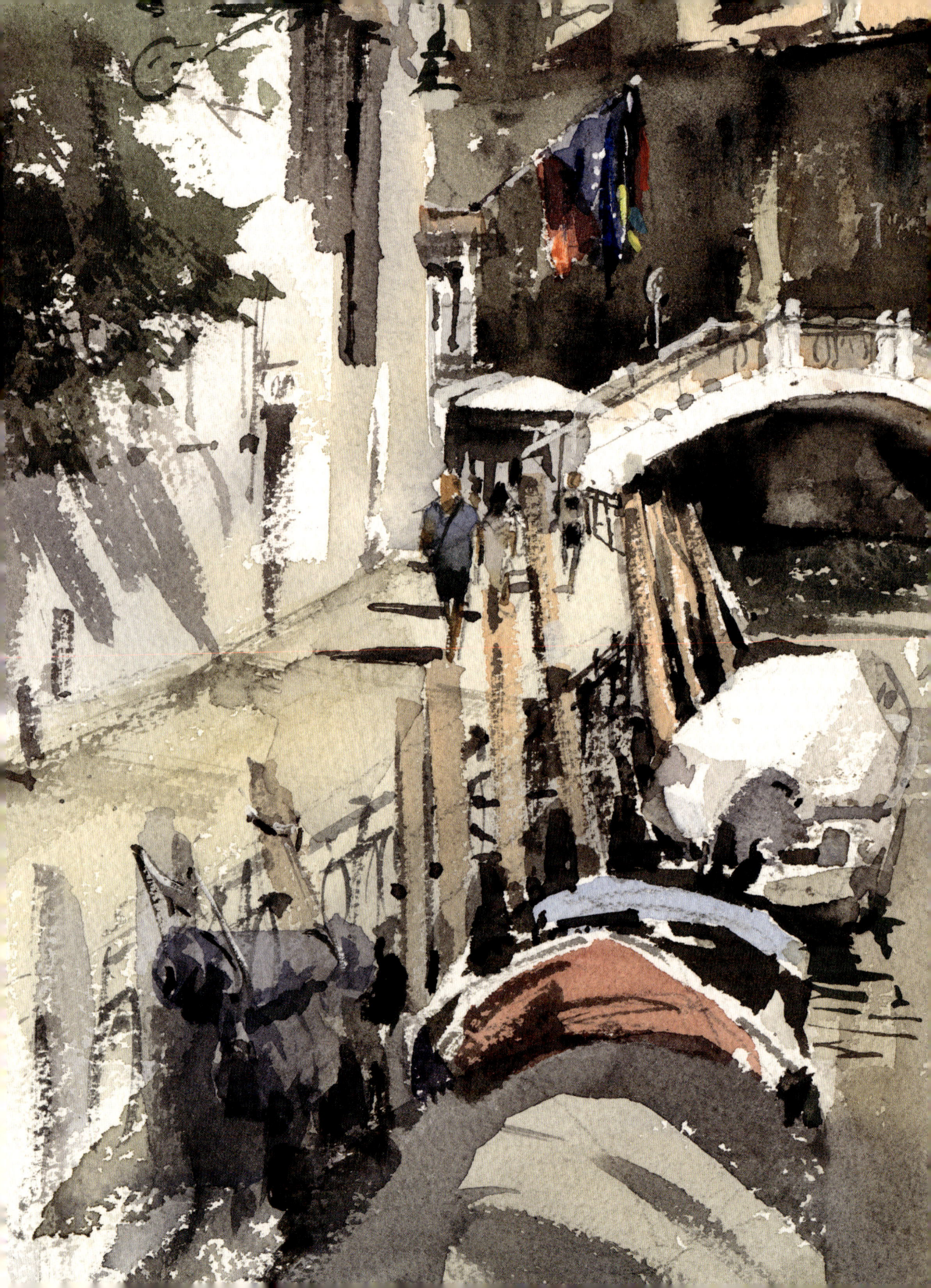

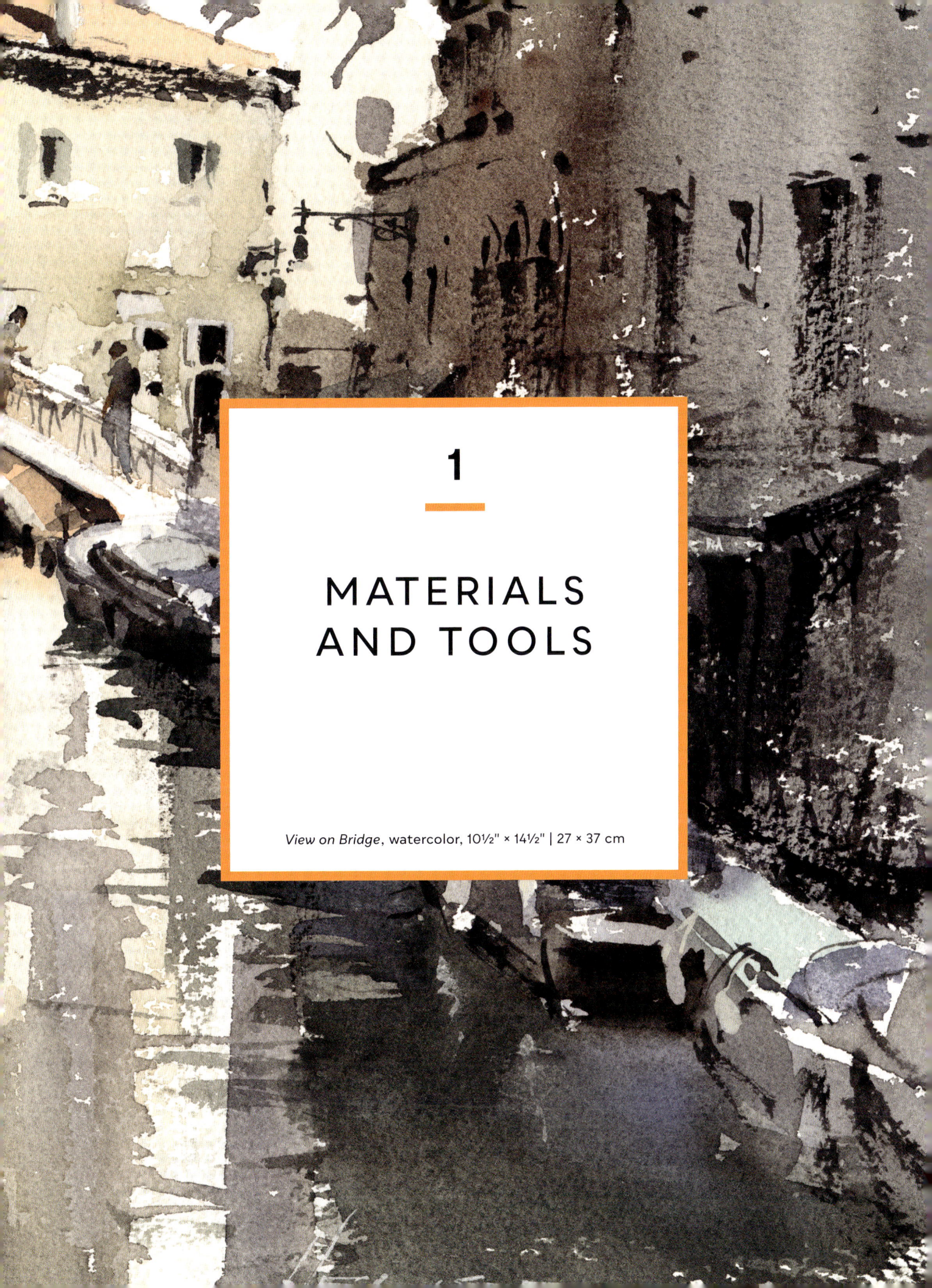

1

MATERIALS AND TOOLS

View on Bridge, watercolor, 10½" × 14½" | 27 × 37 cm

SETTING UP YOUR PAINTING WORKSPACE

Given the vast number of tables and easels available, here I focus on the setup that has served me well over the years. This setup has been instrumental in maintaining proper posture and ensuring convenience while painting.

When selecting a table or easel, the first consideration should be your preferred working position: seated or standing. Personally, I prefer to stand while working on my art. Standing allows me to quickly step back and view my work from a distance, which is essential for assessing progress. The height of the table is crucial—it should be adjusted to allow the painter to work comfortably in an upright position without needing to bend. Ideally, the angle of the table's surface should be adjustable, allowing it to incline between 0 degrees and 45 degrees. This range provides full control over watercolor washes.

While it's convenient to adjust the tabletop angle, I typically use two specific angles: about 10 degrees for large washes and around 25 to 30 degrees for finer details. Over time, each watercolorist will discover the angles that work best for them and stick to those. The angle of the working surface significantly impacts how beads form, how long the wash remains on the paper, and how it interacts with adjoining areas of still-wet paint.

CONFIGURING YOUR OUTDOOR EASEL

For outdoor painting, I prefer tripod-mounted boxes because they allow for quick height adjustments, making it easy to switch between standing and seated positions. Using a carbon fiber tripod greatly reduces the overall weight.

For information on outdoor gear, see page 19.

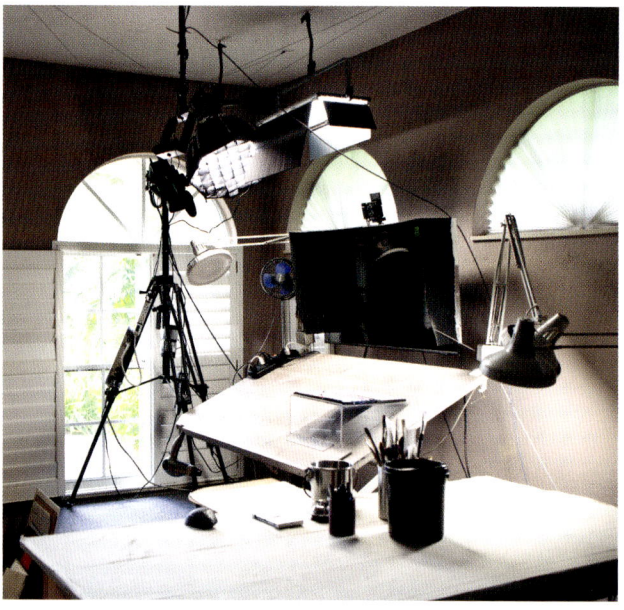

Studio workstation.

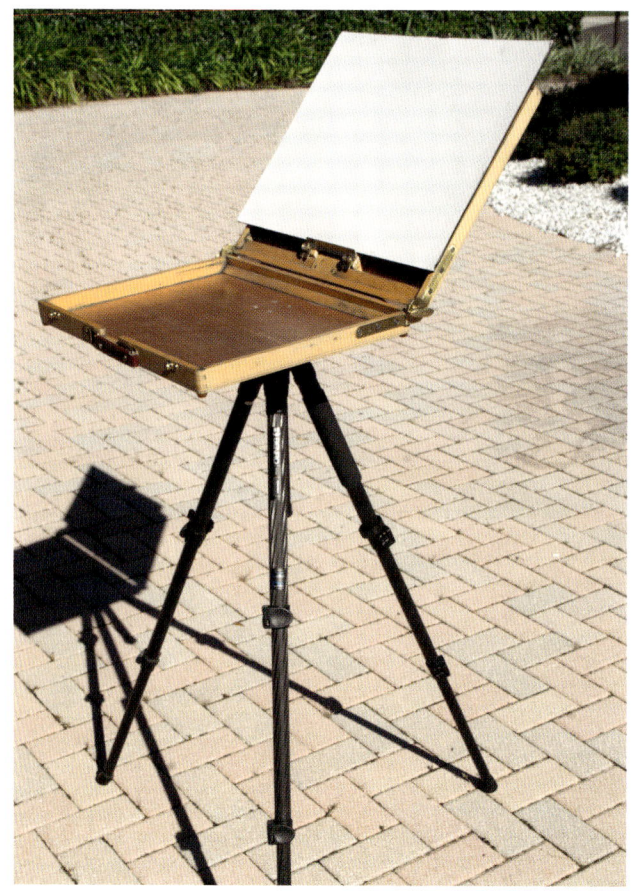

Outdoor easel.

OPTIMAL STUDIO LIGHTING

The most crucial aspect of setting up a painter's studio is the lighting. Natural light, though difficult to replicate with artificial sources, is indispensable for accurate color perception. However, achieving even and consistent natural light is nearly impossible, since its intensity and direction change throughout the day. Each painter has their most productive hours, which may not align with the availability of natural light.

For the best results, natural light should be diffused, with no direct sunlight hitting the workspace. Direct sunlight can bleach out colors, distorting the true appearance of your work. Ideally, windows in the studio should face north to capture consistent natural light. If this isn't possible, large overhangs above the windows are essential. Translucent curtains can be used as long as they don't alter the light's color.

To maintain consistent lighting throughout the day, I supplement natural light with artificial sources, such as LED lights with adjustable intensity and color temperature. Above my worktable, I've positioned a light panel with barn doors to prevent intense light from entering my peripheral vision while I work. Since I'm right-handed, another continuous light source is placed to the left to avoid casting shadows on my workspace. This light has a diffuser and grid to minimize glare.

It's important to note that each artificial light should have a high color rendering index (CRI), with a minimum of 95 out of 100 to match the quality of natural light as much as possible.

Ultimately, studio lighting is a combination of natural and artificial sources tailored to your specific needs. Positioning your workspace near windows to maximize natural light is always advisable, regardless of the number of artificial lights used.

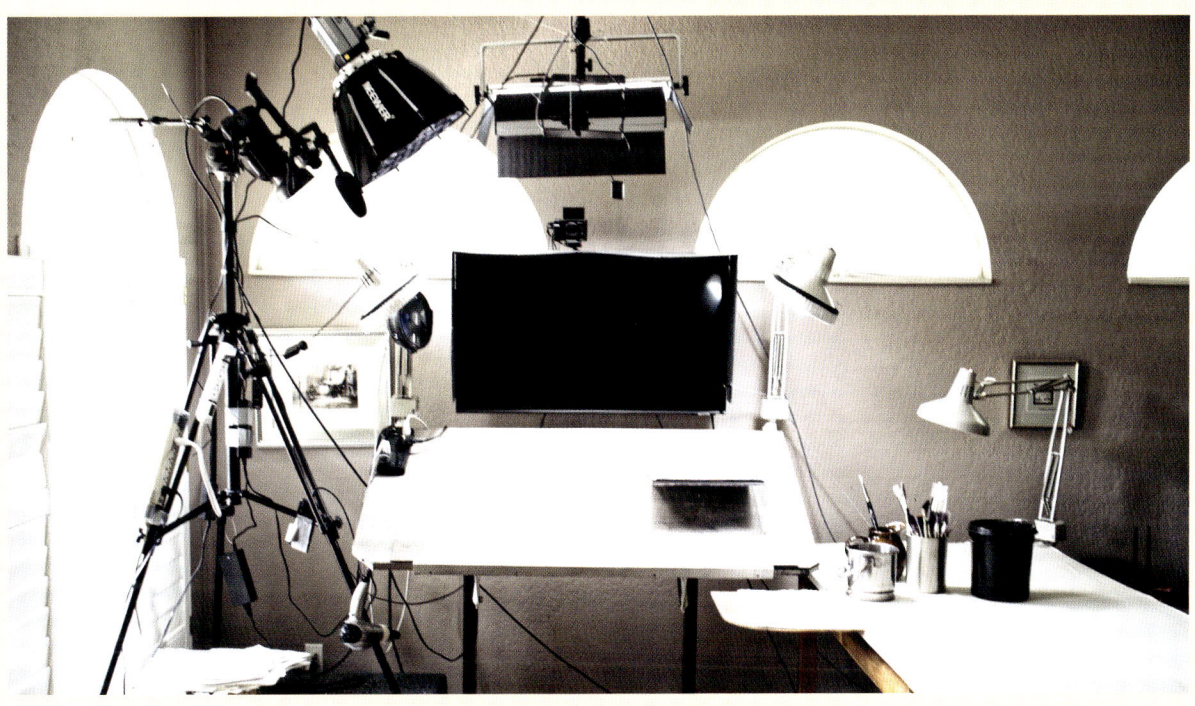

Studio light.

CHOOSING PENCILS AND SKETCHING PAPER

For graphite sketching, I prefer to use letter-sized laser jet paper attached to a plastic clipboard. This paper is bright and has a texture well-suited for pencil work. When sketching outdoors, especially in the rain, it's convenient to replace damp sheets with new ones. The paper is easy to find and restock, making it a practical choice for sketching on the go.

I rely on two specific mechanical pencils for sketching and creating layouts on watercolor paper. For general sketches, I use a 0.7mm mechanical pencil with 2B lead. I keep another 0.7mm mechanical pencil, deliberately different in appearance, loaded with HB lead for watercolor layouts. The harder HB lead minimizes smudging on rough watercolor paper when overworked. The 0.7mm lead is sharp enough to eliminate the need for a sharpener, yet thick enough to resist breaking during energetic sketching. The 2B lead, being the softest available, allows for deep, dark shades when needed.

When sketching, I attach a few sheets of paper to the clipboard to soften the pencil strokes, as a single sheet can be too thin. For ink and watercolor work, I switch to sketching albums specifically designed for those media.

A word about erasers: I use a white plastic eraser cut into a triangular shape to create finer, pointier edges for detailed erasing work. This plastic eraser is gentle on the watercolor surface which is important for consecutive watercolor washes.

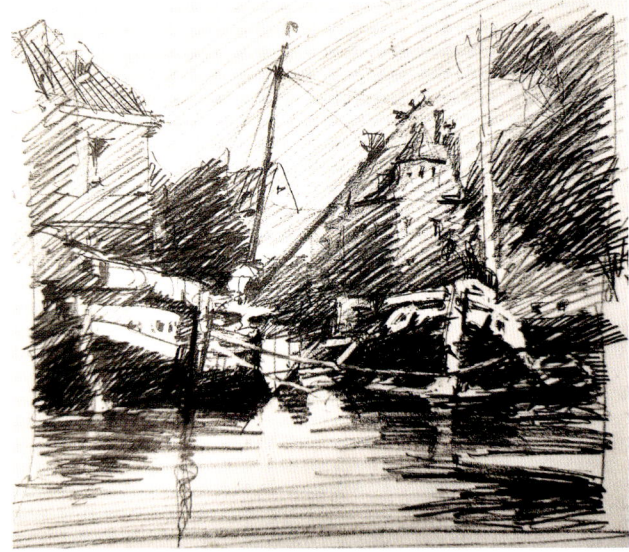

Leiden, graphite sketch, 8¾" × 10" | 22 × 26 cm

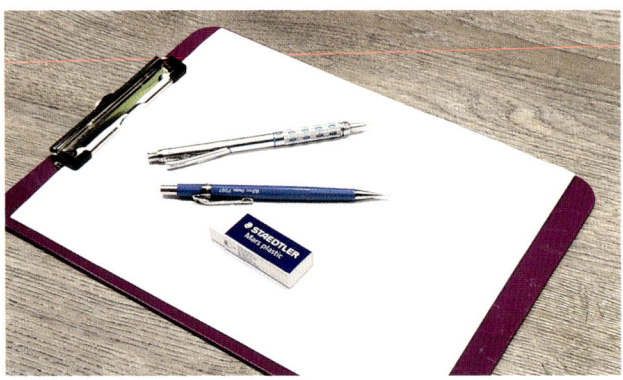

Paper, eraser, and pencil holders.

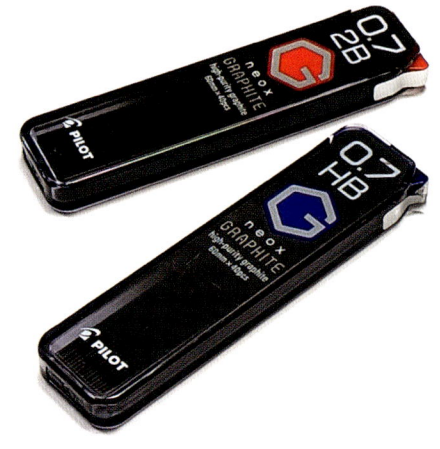

Pencil leads.

EXPLORING
WATERCOLOR PAPER

There are three common watercolor paper surfaces and three primary weights, with the added option of bleached or ultra-white watercolor paper. I won't delve into specific paper manufacturers, as it's possible to create magnificent artworks on paper from various manufacturers.

BLEACHED VS. UNBLEACHED

First, let's talk about bleached paper. Personally, I don't use it. If I need to define lost highlights or distinguish them, I leave the paper unpainted or I use bits of white gouache. Unbleached, natural-colored watercolor paper actually helps create contrast between ultra-white gouache highlights and the darker natural surroundings, making it easier to isolate them.

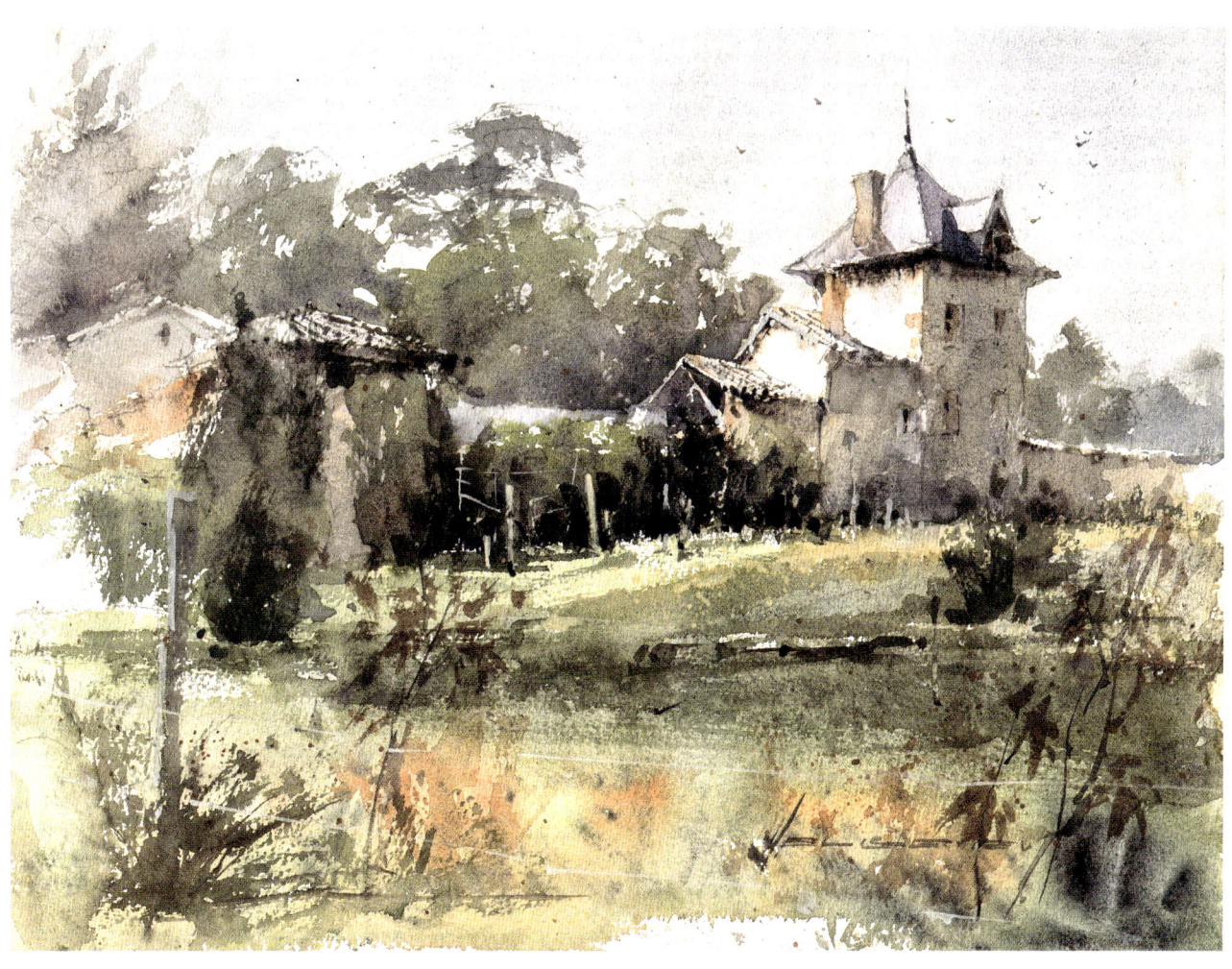

Vineyard, watercolor, 11½" × 15½" | 29 × 39 cm

WEIGHT

The weight of the paper can affect the intensity of color. When I used 90-lb (185 gsm) paper, I noticed slightly better color intensity retention. Thinner paper absorbs pigments to a lesser extent, allowing more pigment to stay on the surface. However, not all manufacturers produce thin watercolor paper.

On the other hand, heavier paper, like 300-lb (640 gsm), feels and weighs like a piece of cardboard. It's particularly useful when trying to prevent the surface from buckling after applying water. This weight is ideal if you need to frame the artwork and display it immediately after completing the watercolor. However, I don't use it for everyday work, since colors tend to tone down a bit after the washes dry. Mostly I use 140-lb (300 gsm) for my day-to-day paintings.

SURFACE TYPE

Lastly, the most crucial characteristic for me is the surface type. Hot-pressed watercolor paper has a smooth appearance and is ideal for working with pen and ink or creating ultra smooth washes, as shown in **A**.

The second type of paper is known as cold pressed. It features a medium-sized surface tooth, making it well-suited for larger sizes and capable of displaying the dry brushwork, as you can see in **B**. It's essentially a versatile paper that can accommodate the needs of most watercolor painters.

That being said, it's essential to note that to fully harness the drybrush capabilities of the paper, it should have a rough surface. When paired with synthetic brushes, it becomes easier to paint just the surface bumps and leave the "valleys" unpainted, resulting in distinctive bold and loose brushstrokes where needed. It's worth mentioning that, in practice, 300-lb (640 gsm) paper exhibits more pronounced bumps and is easier to work with compared to 140-lb (300 gsm) paper, as shown in **C**.

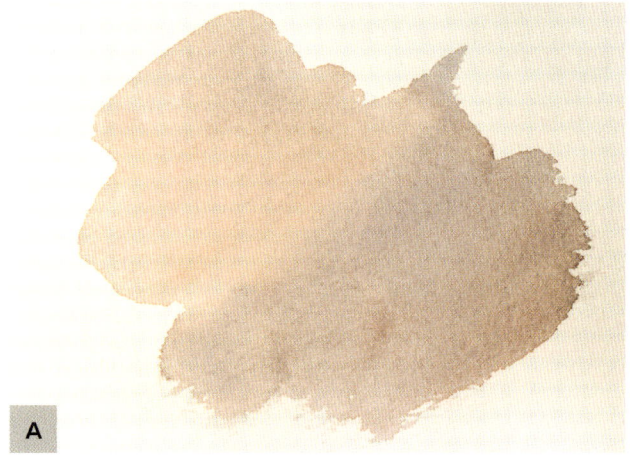

A

Hot-pressed paper.

B

Cold-pressed paper.

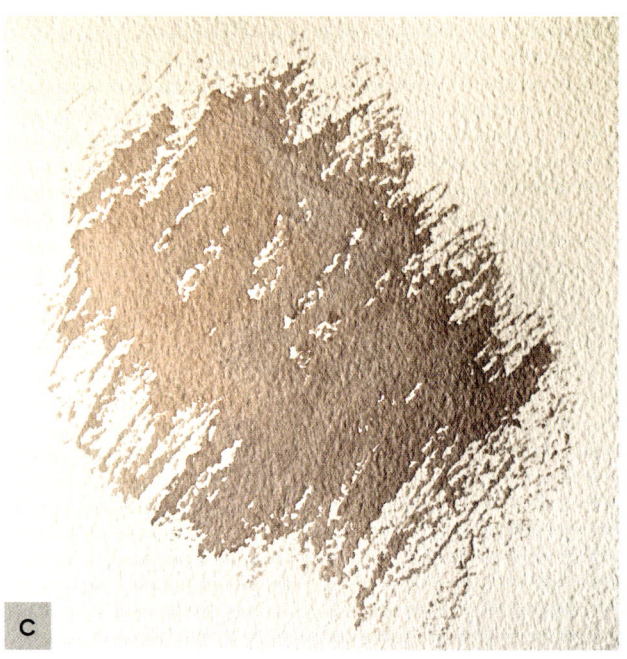

C

Rough surface paper.

UNDERSTANDING WATERCOLOR BRUSHES AND PAINTS

BRUSHES

There are numerous types of watercolor brushes on the market, but here I focus on those that I find most valuable in my daily work.

MOP BRUSHES

It's hard to imagine covering a significant amount of watercolor paper with synthetic brushes. For this purpose, I prefer mop brushes with natural fibers, such as squirrel or sable. The choice of brush size depends largely on the size of the watercolor paper I use, so I keep a few options on hand.

When I begin a watercolor painting, I rely solely on these mop brushes. Their key feature is their ability to hold a substantial amount of watercolor mix, far more than synthetic brushes. I prefer short handles for mop brushes because I hold the brush almost vertically relative to the paper, making it easier to manipulate.

SYNTHETIC BRUSHES

Synthetic brushes are good for fine calligraphy work. To create longer fine lines, I often use a sword liner brush, which is a versatile calligraphy tool capable of adjusting line thickness on the fly. A sword liner brush is particularly useful when painting tree branches (bottom right).

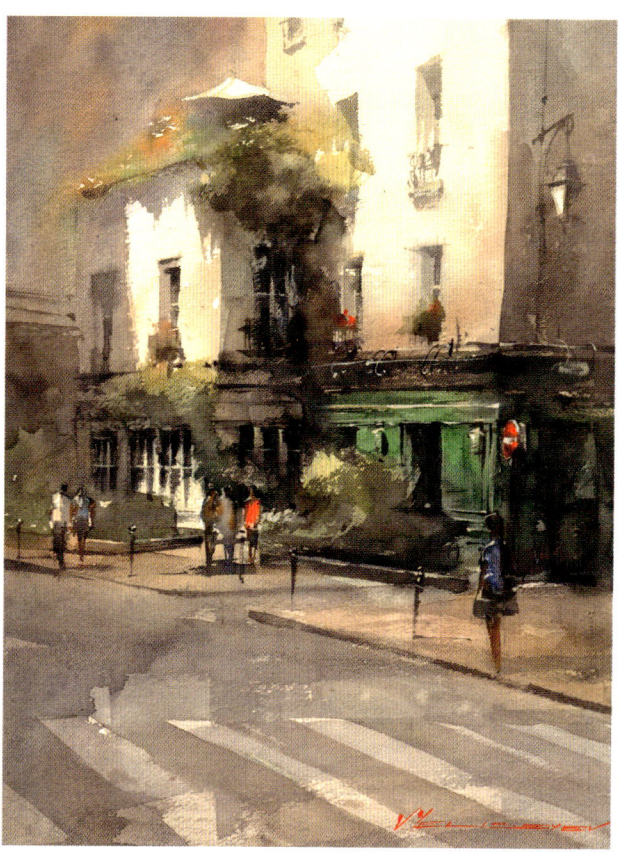

Rue Montmartre, watercolor, 16" × 12" | 41 × 31 cm

I've found that I don't need a large variety of brushes, as long as they remain in good condition and can perform the tasks I require of them.

Squirrel hair mop brush.

Synthetic brushes.

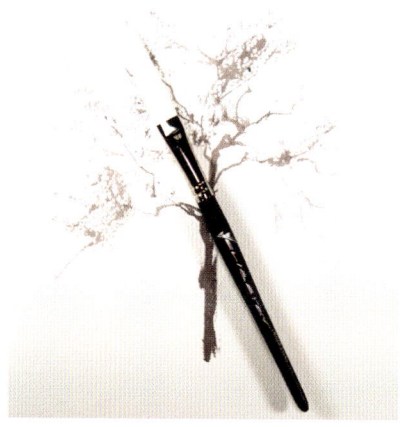

Sword liner brush.

PAINTS

When it comes to watercolor paints, I prefer to stick to a single brand whenever possible.

I tend to avoid mediums and other additives in my watercolors because they can lead to inconsistent results among paintings. However, these additives aren't inherently bad—they can be useful for extending drying time or introducing granulation effects. Ultimately, choosing whether to use them comes down to personal preference and requires experimentation to achieve the desired outcomes.

I prefer to buy my watercolors in tubes, which allows me to refill individual plastic containers in a small metal box palette for travel. I won't delve into individual colors here, as I cover color theory later (p. 106).

The main mixing palette I use is a simple aluminum box with three large, flat mixing areas, making it convenient for both studio work and travel. I organize my paints into clear sections for yellows, reds, and blues, which makes navigating the palette much easier.

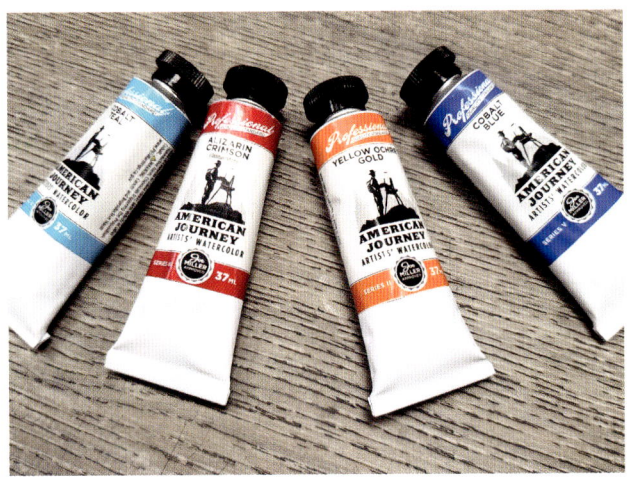

Watercolor paint tubes.

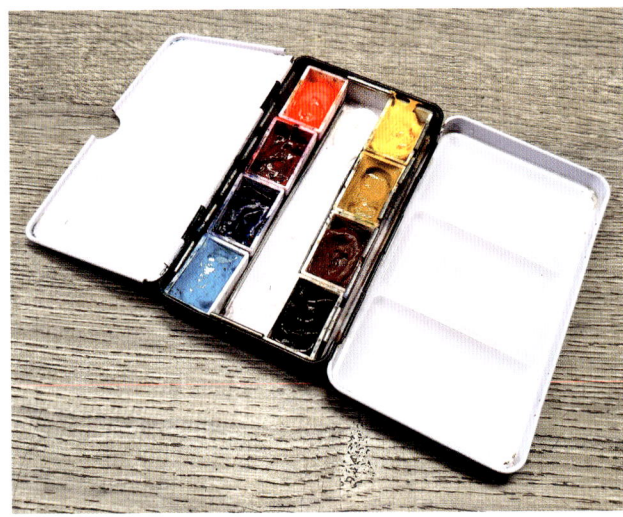

Small travel palette.

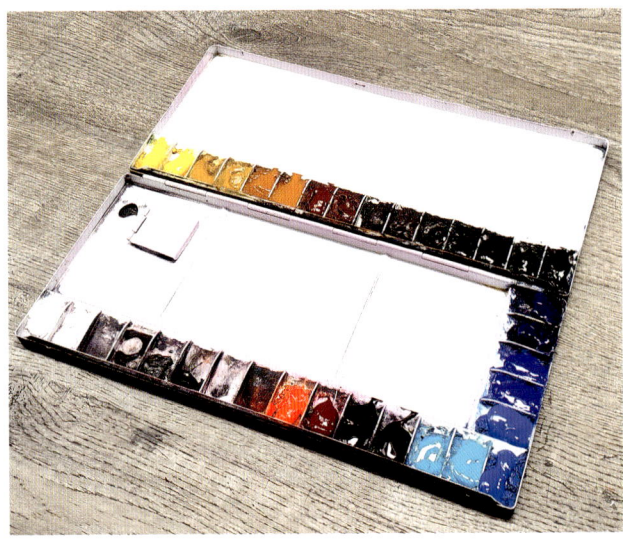

Studio watercolor palette.

OUTDOOR PAINTING GEAR

When it comes to outdoor painting, two essentials come to mind: the bag to carry everything in, and the easel and the art supplies themselves.

When selecting a bag, I look for ones with special fasteners that allow me to attach a tripod. Outdoor photography bags often meet these needs; many are wheeled and can also be carried as backpacks.

Instead of traditional French easels, which are designed primarily for oil painters, I prefer a pochade box attached to a tripod. This setup should be large enough to hold your largest watercolor paper or block and accommodate a palette, either inside or on a side shelf. The tripod's adjustable height ensures a comfortable painting position, and its lightweight design—especially if made from carbon fiber—makes it easier to carry.

I highly recommend painting in a standing position so you can easily step back and observe your work from a distance. For those who find standing for long periods challenging, a small collapsible folding chair is essential.

Regarding umbrellas, I advise against attaching them to tripods with pochade boxes, as they tend to tip over in windy conditions. Instead, consider using umbrella stands with ground spikes when painting in the countryside. When working in urban environments, finding a shady spot is often the best way to avoid needing an umbrella altogether.

Water, the heaviest item you'll carry, is crucial for watercolor painting. I carefully consider my painting location, as there is often a water source nearby. In cases where water isn't readily available, a watertight, empty bottle—like a used juice bottle—can be handy for transporting water.

The good news is that outdoor painting gear is typically a one-time investment that lasts for years. It's important to invest in quality products that balance strength with lightweight design, ensuring they don't need frequent replacement.

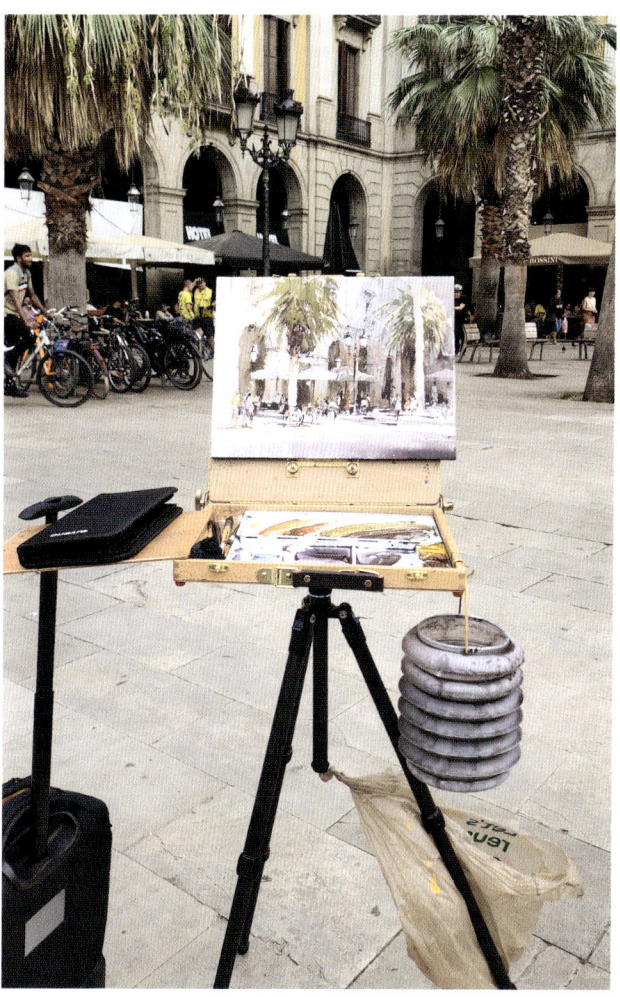

In Barcelona.

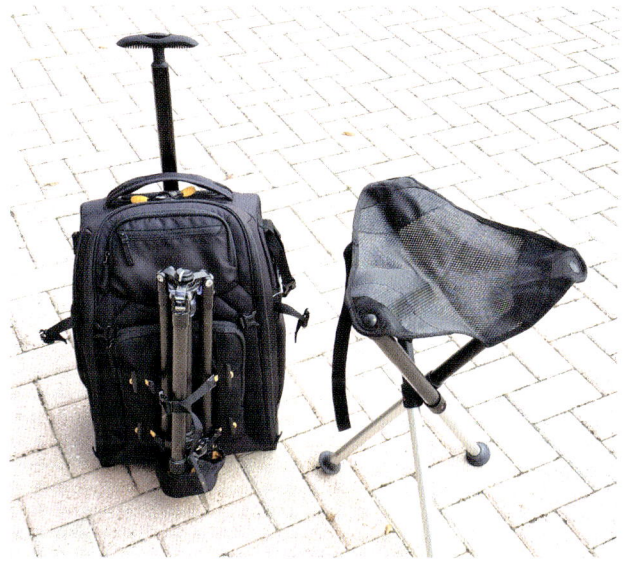

Backpack and folding stool.

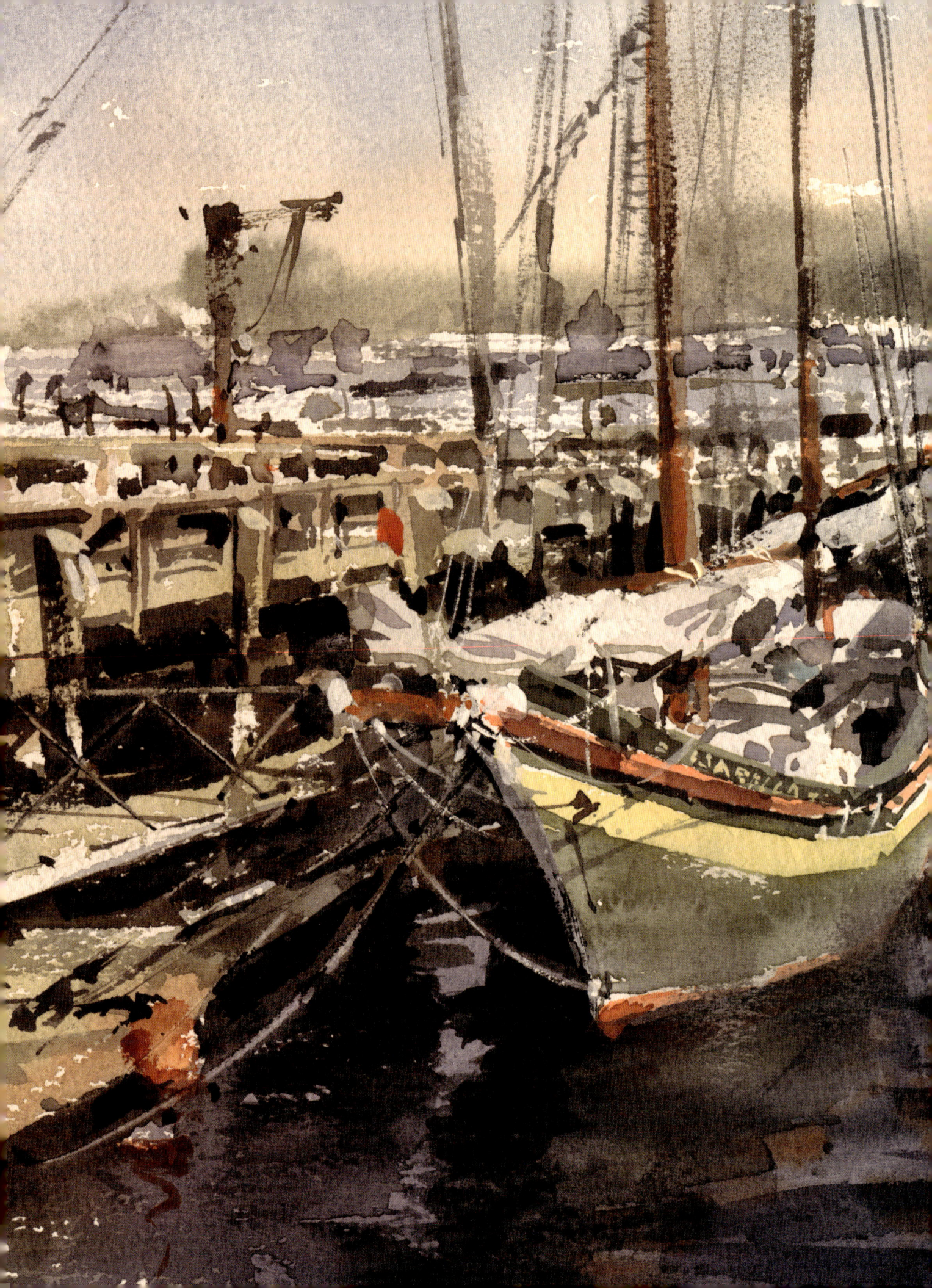

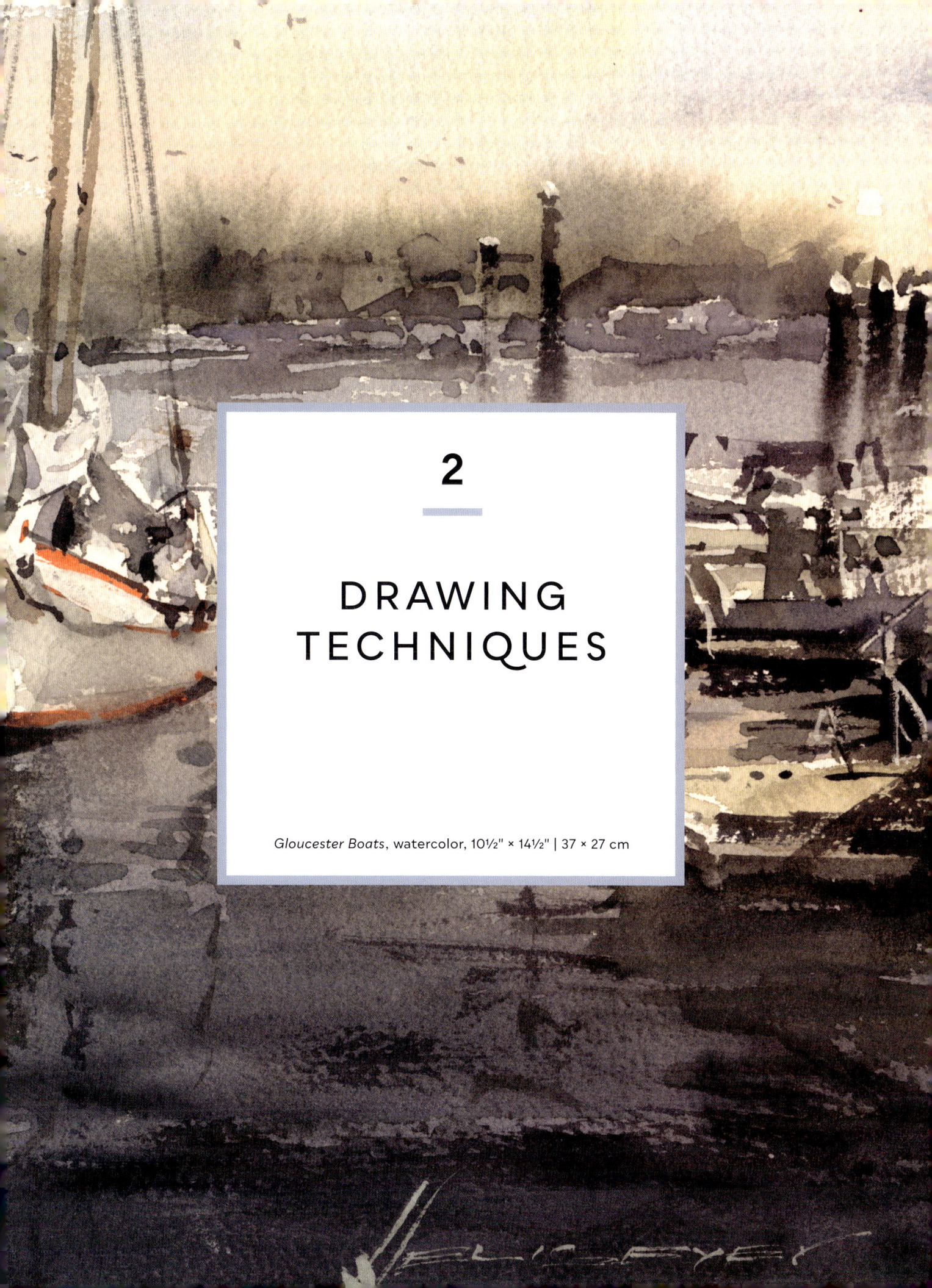

2

DRAWING
TECHNIQUES

Gloucester Boats, watercolor, 10½" × 14½" | 37 × 27 cm

MASTERING DRAWING FUNDAMENTALS

In planning this book, I made a conscious decision to emphasize drawing techniques because they form the foundation for serious work in the visual arts. While this book focuses on watercolor, it would be naive to assume that anyone can master this medium without proficient drawing skills.

A well-made drawing significantly impacts how viewers perceive a work of art. When viewers notice obvious mistakes, they often dismiss the work as amateurish within seconds and move on. It's important to note that while a drawing doesn't need to be academically precise in every detail, any deviations from the "correct" representation should be intentional, which, incidentally, can be even more challenging to execute.

Individuals who are unable to draw basic lines accurately will encounter challenges with these exercises. Drawing skills are a pure craft and don't require any inherent talent to master.

Another aspect of achieving realistic drawing involves composing elements within a painting. Often, beginner painters arrange people in a single line at equal distances from each other. While this might work for trees, it's rare for people to align themselves this way. Even when it comes to trees, I encourage diversity in their heights and placement to break the monotony of geometric uniformity. This practice is rooted in the fact that Mother Nature never repeats herself, and it's the artist's role to enhance these differences to bring out the individual personalities and unique characteristics of every object in our surroundings.

Some beginner painters might argue that tracing photographs is a simpler solution for their paintings. However, the task of creating a meaningful image from a traced photo is more complex than it may seem. To begin with, elements in photographs are often arranged haphazardly and far from ideal. Human poses can appear unnatural, trees may obscure important elements, cars might be in the

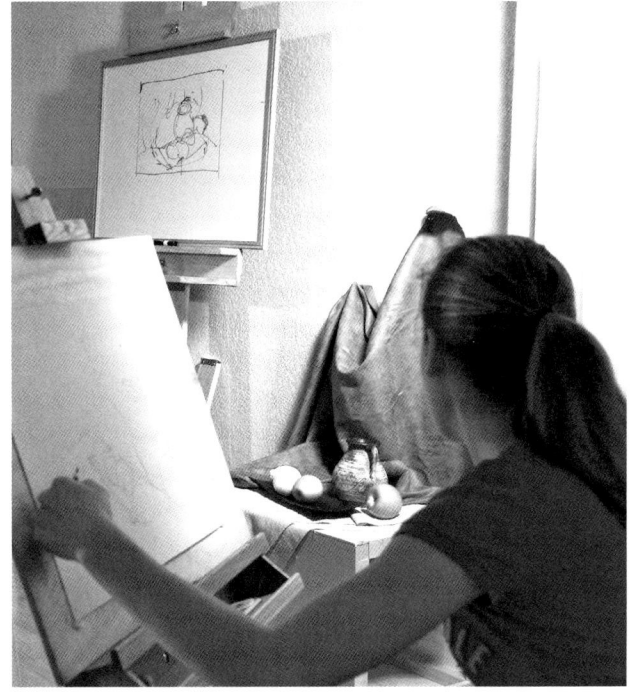

Drawing class.

wrong place, and buildings may not match our perceptions of them. The ability to rearrange and alter these elements is a formidable task. This process of rearranging and modifying elements at will is what we call "artist reinterpretation." Failing to fluently execute these changes can hold a subject forever captive without hope for release.

Another crucial facet of drawing involves comprehending how light interacts with objects' surfaces (see "Rendering Objects in Light," p. 30). Without a firm grasp of the physics of light, it becomes challenging to convincingly convey a realistic image to the viewer.

Once the artist gains a comprehensive understanding of how light operates on the surfaces of objects, it becomes evident that, rather than merely depicting the objects within a painting, the artist embarks on the journey of painting the light upon them. This shift in perspective elevates the artist's skill to an entirely new level.

COMPOSITION, PROPORTION, AND PERSPECTIVE

So, what exactly are drawing skills? When working with my students, I see three essential areas: composition, proportions, and perspective skills.

COMPOSITION

Let's begin with composition, which can be the most challenging area for beginners. It involves years of studying the work of masters, creating your own abstract compositions, experimenting with dynamics balance, focal areas, color, and the rhythm of the painting's parts, among other aspects.

In *Havana Street* (below left), one can easily notice strong diagonal movement, creating a very dynamic composition.

I won't delve deeply into this intricate subject in this book because it's complex, partly psychological, and could fill a volume of its own. However, there are some aspects worth mentioning. The concept of the rule of thirds is highly effective when dealing with composition. It's relatively easy to grasp without diving deep into the complexities of composition. These lines essentially suggest what not to do when composing an image. They encourage artists to avoid placing their focal areas in the center of the image and to move them closer to where the lines intersect. This deviation from the static and sometimes mundane image helps create more dynamic compositions.

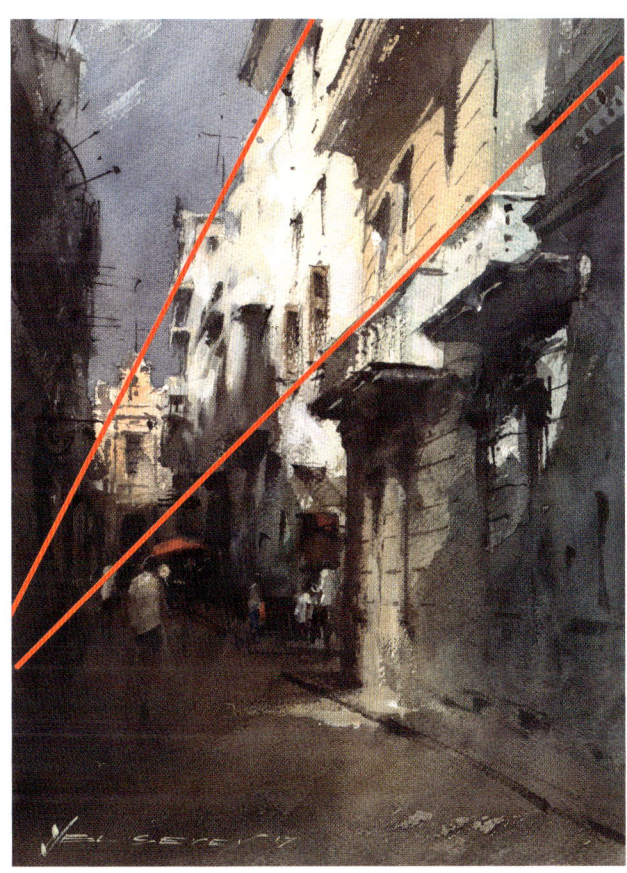
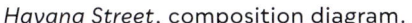

Havana Street, composition diagram.

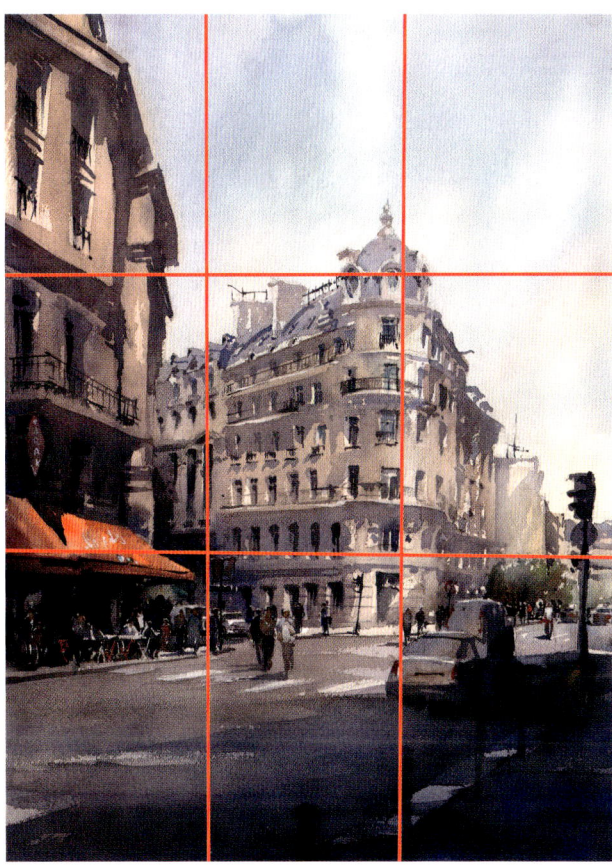

Paris Red, composition diagram.

PROPORTIONS

Moving on to proportions, the concept is much clearer and easier to understand. Just as one might go to the gym to tone their muscles, an artist can train their eyes to see proportions correctly by drawing more often with a pencil from real-life subjects. Painters can use the pencil not only for drawing but also as a measuring instrument to check angles, vertical alignments, and compare proportions. The key is to recognize that accurately drawn proportions in the image lead to a resemblance to the depicted object, whether it's a simple rectangular prism or a portrait. Illustration **A** shows how to use a pencil to measure proportions in any direction.

Keep in mind that this method provides approximate information about how one dimension differs from another, rather than exact measurements. In real-life experience, I've often been amazed at how proportions are often whole numbers, such as 1:2 or 1:4, for instance.

One of the most common mistakes I've noticed when working with my students is the inability to see angles correctly. I've already mentioned that the pencil isn't the only drawing tool, that it can also be a valuable instrument for measuring sometimes challenging-to-discern angles. By using the pencil as a vertical or horizontal plumb line, we can avoid errors (**B**).

I employ this method frequently when working *en plein air*. The trick is to place the pencil against the sharper angle (the more acute angle) because our visual memory can better handle these angles. For instance, I can easily distinguish between a 5-degree and a 10-degree angle, but not between 45 and 55 degrees.

At times, you might intentionally deviate from correctness, and this deviation is very welcome in fine art. Artists intentionally break away from correct and often dry presentations. Much like a caricaturist who exaggerates specific features to convey an object's character fully, fine artists can see and enhance these features, breaking away from conventional "correct" academic presentations.

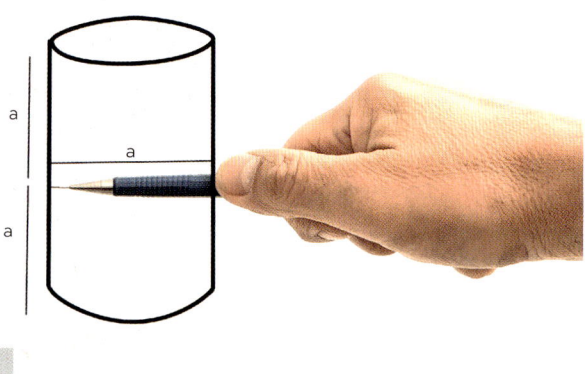

A

Measuring proportions.

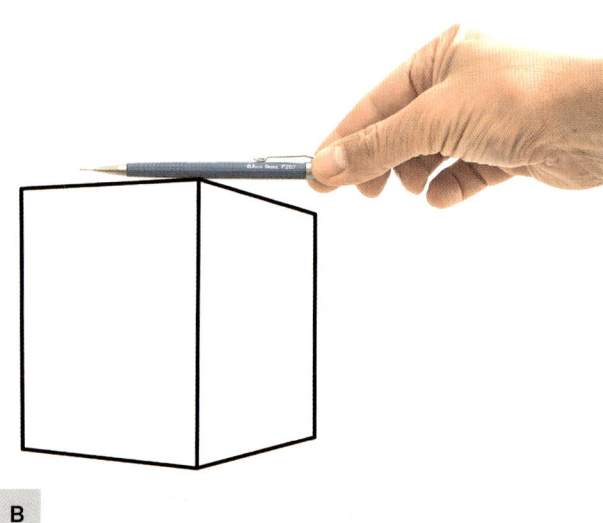

B

Measuring angles.

In the case of a painter with a well-trained eye, knowledge of perspective can sometimes be overlooked because the artist can capture correct relative sizes. However, it's essential to mention that perspective knowledge can also save a lot of time and frustration for most painters. In fact, it's so useful that I decided to address perspective later in this section (p. 27).

UNDERSTANDING BASIC FORMS

When I draw objects, I find it very helpful to see them as a combination of simple forms that, when joined together, can create a compelling and realistic appearance on a flat drawing surface. Using this method makes it relatively easy to draw virtually any object around us, no matter how complicated. I urge you not to confuse this with the blocking method of drawing, which we will cover later.

GEOMETRIC SOLIDS

So, what are the simple forms we use to achieve the desired appearance? They include objects such as spheres, cones, various prisms, pyramids, and so on. The immediate advantages of using them as underlying wireframes are that it's easier to capture the correct proportions of the whole object and its parts, place the object in the correct perspective, and, most importantly, as I mentioned before, convey real-world depth into a convincing, professional-looking drawing. This method also assists when applying tonal values to the drawing or painting, as the artist can see the forms clearly and judge the light on their surfaces easily.

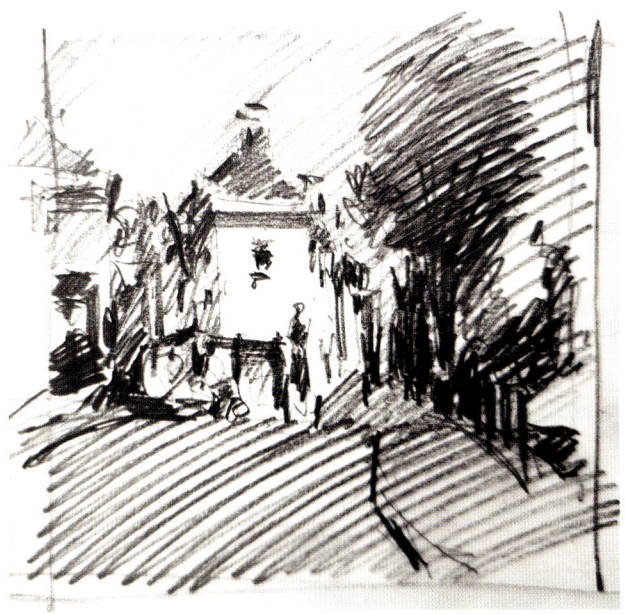

In Amsterdam, graphite, 37" × 38" | 93 × 96 cm

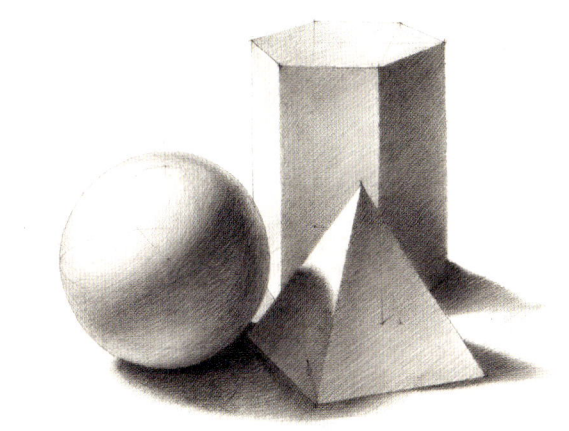

Primitive Forms, graphite, 12¼" × 14" | 28 × 35 cm

Scan to view a
video tutorial

DEMONSTRATION: BASIC FORMS DRAWING METHOD

The example below uses a common water bottle as a model for this step-by-step drawing process.

While the copying method may yield acceptable results for a painter with a trained eye, when using the contour copy method, an initial line drawing ultimately lacks three-dimensional structure, making tonal value studies much more challenging later in the painting or shading process.

The images below significantly reduce the mindless copying method that beginner painters sometimes employ and forces the painter to relay all information observed to the brain before sending signals directly to the hand with a pencil. There's an almost infinite number of details that can be applied further, such as minute details on the body of the plastic bottle. Usually, I stop there and implement them during the painting process using a paintbrush. This chain of command is broken from the beginner's methods of drawing and painting, and takes time to master and implement.

This method is applicable to virtually every subject matter the artist may encounter, from simple ones to complex subjects like animals, portraits, and the human body. One important thing to mention here is that this method of drawing can be considered a

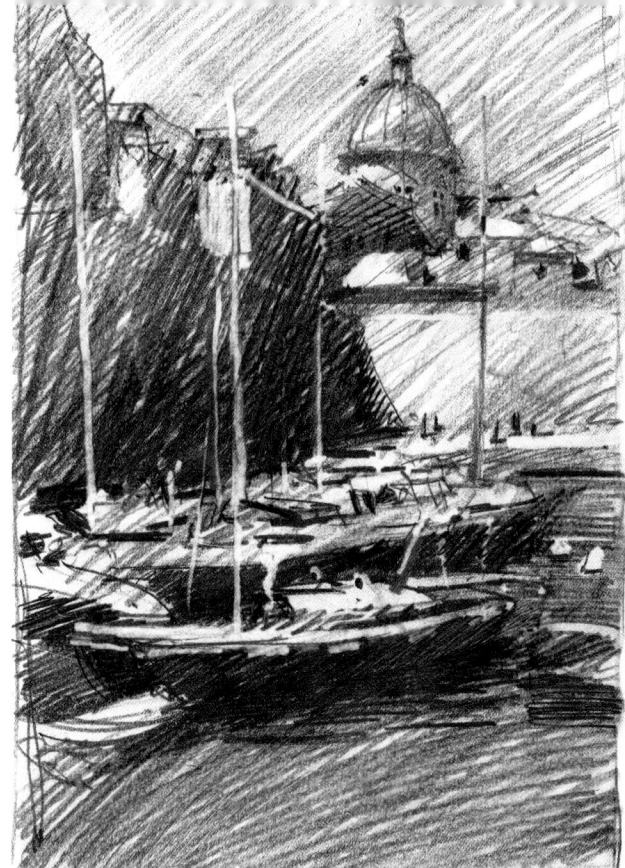

Dubrovnik Boats, graphite, 9" × 6½" | 24 × 16 cm

craft, which means that anyone can master it without needing exceptional talent. Just as an excuse for the inability to read and write due to a lack of talent doesn't make sense, the same applies to drawing skills. Anyone can master them with enough persistence.

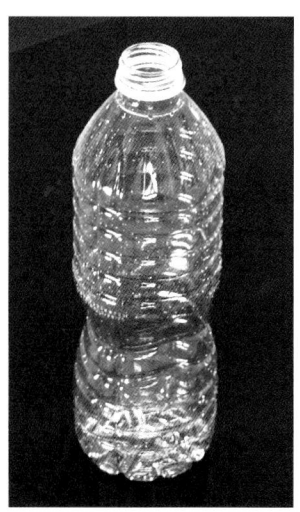

Reference photo.

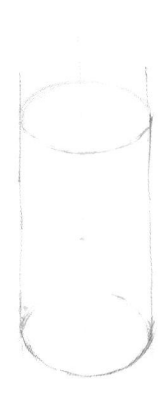

1. Basic form. Initially I draw the basic underlying cylinder in the correct proportion, as if it's an x-ray.

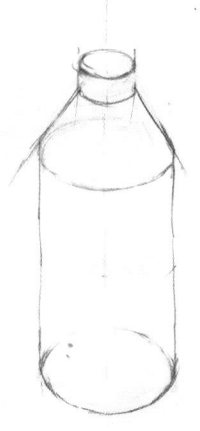

2. Adding extra forms. Then I add a cone at the top of it as a simple cone and a cylinder on top of the cone as a bottle neck.

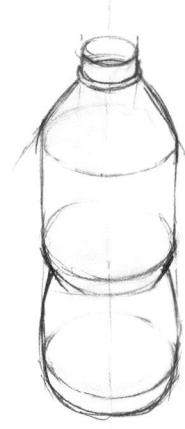

3. Detailization of forms. All of this signifies the basic form, which is ready for detailing.

INTRODUCTION TO PERSPECTIVE DRAWING

Perspective, often the most daunting of the three drawing skills, appears to be a common source of anxiety among beginner painters. However, in reality, it's perhaps the easiest to master. This is because it leaves little room for interpretation and is as learnable as geometry or math.

The concept of perspective emerged relatively late during the Renaissance, leading to more realistic three-dimensional paintings. If we visit an art museum, we can observe that paintings created before this era often lack a sense of depth and appear flat.

Linear perspective essentially boils down to two simple rules, with everything else following from these.

1. The first rule dictates that objects appear smaller the farther they are from the viewer—an idea easily comprehensible through our everyday experiences.

2. The second rule states that two parallel lines converge at a single vanishing point (VP) on the horizon line (HL) if they run parallel to the ground. To illustrate the second rule, imagine standing in a flat desert and gazing at railroad tracks (**A**).

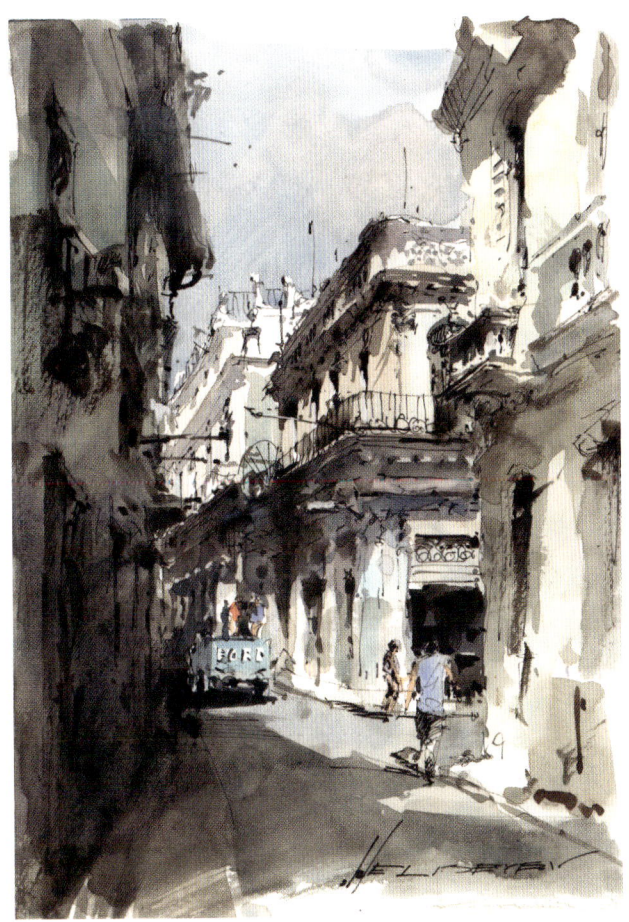

Cartagena Street, watercolor, 11" × 8½" | 28 × 18 cm

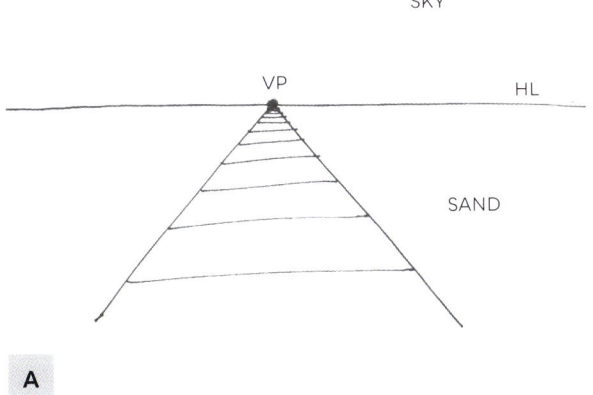

A

ONE-POINT PERSPECTIVE

This illustration clearly shows that the railroad cross-ties appear smaller in the distance, aligning with the first rule of perspective. In one-point perspective, every line in the scene converges toward a single VP on the HL. Lines parallel to the picture frame—those moving from right to left and vice versa—should be drawn parallel to the top and bottom of the frame. Another crucial aspect for painters to verify is that the heads of people in the drawing align with the HL, assuming that all individuals in the picture share the same height as the viewer. Realistically, this alignment is rarely possible, as depicted in illustration **B**, which features people of varying heights.

Drawing **B** also demonstrates that every element with lines parallel to the railroad tracks shares the same VP.

Drawing railroad stations is easier because they typically align with the tracks, and even rows of windows can be sandwiched between guidelines (the dotted lines shown), making the drawing process much easier and faster. It's important to note that while one-point perspective is common in paintings, it requires a specific viewing standpoint. In our example, that means staying in the middle of the tracks to experience the view. However, the picture dramatically changes when you step out of this specific vantage point, compelling you to employ a second VP for a more realistic portrayal of the scene.

TWO-POINT PERSPECTIVE

In two-point perspective (**C**), introducing a second VP allows for a more realistic description of both sides of a building adjacent to the tracks. In this case, all lines parallel to the viewer converge toward the second VP, which also lies on the HL.

Other aspects remain consistent, with human heads aligning close to the HL. Among my students, I've noticed a common challenge in distinguishing between lines going to the left (VPL) and those heading to the right (VPR). To facilitate this, I suggest associating the walls on the left (L) and right (R) relative to the center vertical edge separating them with corresponding left and right VPs. Smaller elements like windows, doors, and chimneys are also placed between guidelines, similar to one-point perspective. I typically envision these guidelines rather than drawing them to work quickly and maintain perspective accuracy.

Scan to view a video tutorial

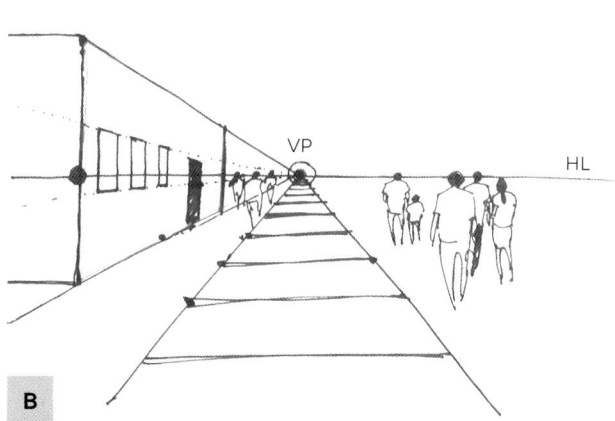

B

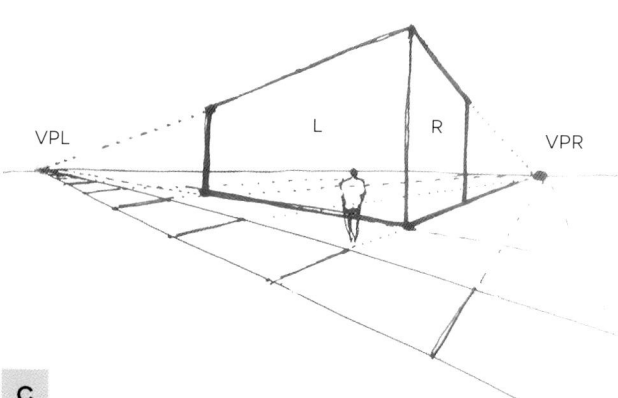

C

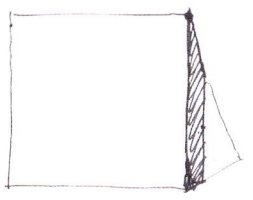

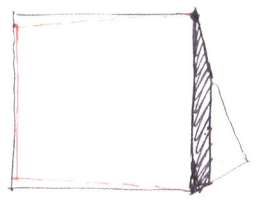

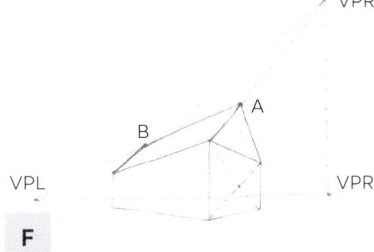

D   E   F

COMMON ISSUES

Numerous practical tips could be shared regarding perspective, but I will highlight the most common issues I've encountered with my students. One frequent mistake involves rendering both sides of a building using a two-point perspective view when the front is treated as a one-point perspective (**D**). The artist must correct the front facade, as shown in **E**.

Another significant challenge painters face is drawing buildings with sloped roofs (**F**). After sketching the basic rectangular prism using two-point perspective, locate the center of the front peak (point A) of the roof by drawing two diagonal lines. Then, connect point A to the corresponding VPL. To find point B, extend VPR into the sky to find the vanishing point for the inclined roof line (VPRs). Finally, connect the prism's corner to VPRs to complete the structure accurately. Please note that the dotted lines in the drawing represent guidelines, which I often visualize rather than draw.

It's important to mention that while artists must be familiar with these rules, they aren't obligated to adhere to them rigidly. Instead, artists can consciously bend them to fit their artistic vision, achieving the desired results in their paintings. I frequently use this flexibility to mask distortions in extreme areas of a picture, where they may be most noticeable. Another area of perspective adjustments comes in handy when the artist is specifically aiming at enhancing the character of the objects by creating the illusion of longer, shorter, or bigger specific elements in the picture.

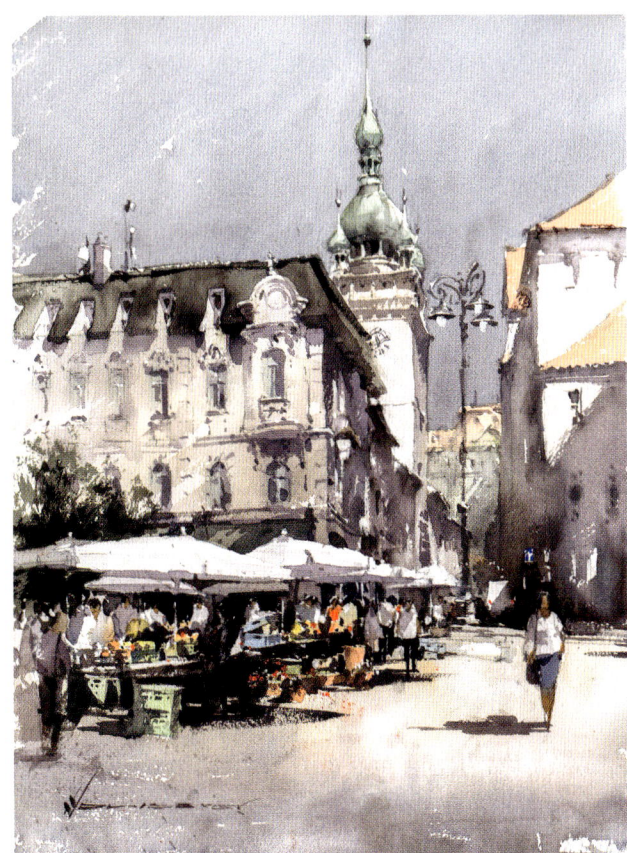

Sunday Market, watercolor, 19" × 14" | 48 × 36 cm

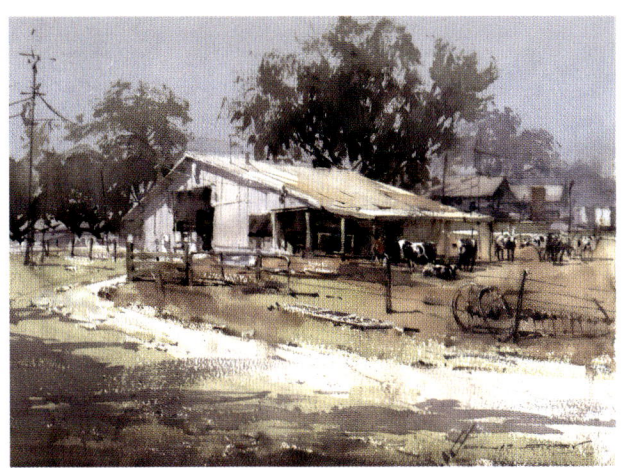

Cow Farm, watercolor, 14" × 20" | 36 × 51 cm

DRAWING TECHNIQUES

RENDERING OBJECTS IN LIGHT

Natural light manifests in different forms—diffused, direct, or in shadow—imparting diverse characteristics to subjects. Since the sun is the sole light source during the day, we can easily understand how that light interacts with objects' surfaces under almost any conditions.

Artificial studio lighting endeavors to emulate natural light, aspiring to replicate its full spectrum and color accuracy. In contrast to natural light, there can be multiple sources of artificial light, each requiring separate consideration. A simple approach to illuminating an indoor still life involves using a single or dominant light source to replicate the qualities of natural light.

Regardless of its source, understanding the principles of light is fundamental for any artist seeking to create a convincing three-dimensional illusion on a two-dimensional surface. The images shown in (**A**) illustrate the transition from a basic line to a three-dimensional effect that avoids the use of line, a creative exercise I encourage my students to replicate for the entire alphabet so they can explore the potential effects of light on basic forms.

THE THREE ESSENTIAL TONAL VALUES

To help identify the areas on an object illuminated by the sun, let's look at a white cube placed on a white surface. Only three surfaces are illuminated while two remain dark. Note that the cube itself obstructs the sunlight from reaching the surface it rests on, creating a cast shadow. Thus, we observe three distinct areas: *lit area*, *midtone* (the dark surfaces of the cube), and *cast shadow* (**B**). These three fundamental tonal values are essential

considerations whether painting outdoors or from photographs, especially for beginner painters dealing with complex scenes.

Emphasizing the importance of the darkest value—the cast shadow—and rendering it accordingly is crucial. The cast shadow always aligns with the midtone because it projects the midtone onto the illuminated surface on which it sits. The boundary between the midtone and cast shadow demarcates two distinct areas. Instead of replicating minor nuances, I advise painters to identify the midtones, the darker cast shadow next to them, and proceed to painting.

It's vital to understand that the overall shape of the cast shadow projects the midtone's shape onto the illuminated area, but duplicating its precise shape is less important than capturing a shape that enhances composition and aesthetics. Maintaining reasonable and mutually realistic proportions among these shapes ensures a cohesive and visually believable artwork; for example, when a larger object in an image casts a larger shadow than a smaller one (**C**).

REFLECTIONS AND HALFTONES

Two critical factors regarding secondary light effects should also be acknowledged. One is *reflections*, which can manifest anywhere, most pronounced on surfaces like glass and water. Light rays bounce from illuminated areas, scattering into dark areas. Even cast shadows gradually lose their intensity as they

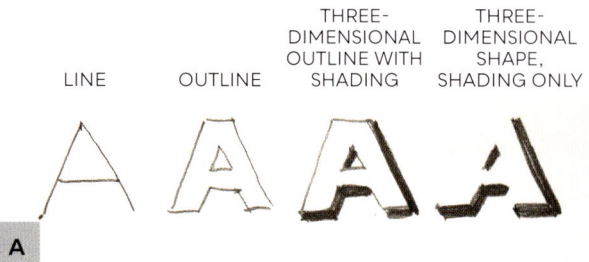

LINE · OUTLINE · THREE-DIMENSIONAL OUTLINE WITH SHADING · THREE-DIMENSIONAL SHAPE, SHADING ONLY

A

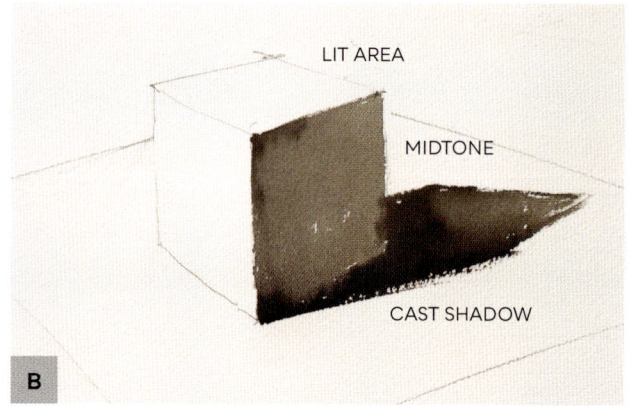

LIT AREA

MIDTONE

CAST SHADOW

B

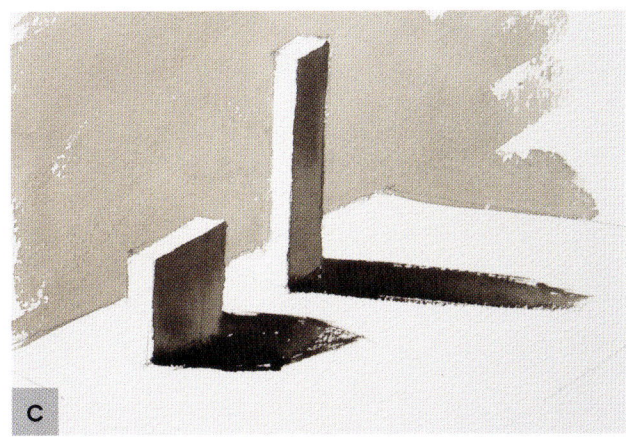

C

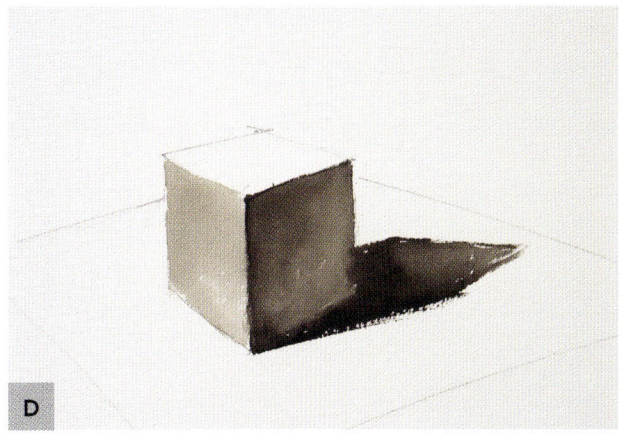

D

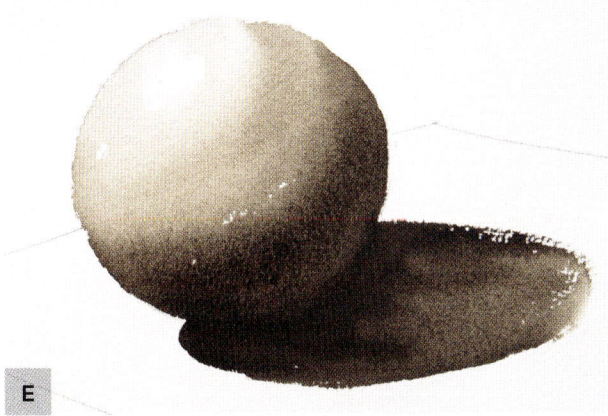

E

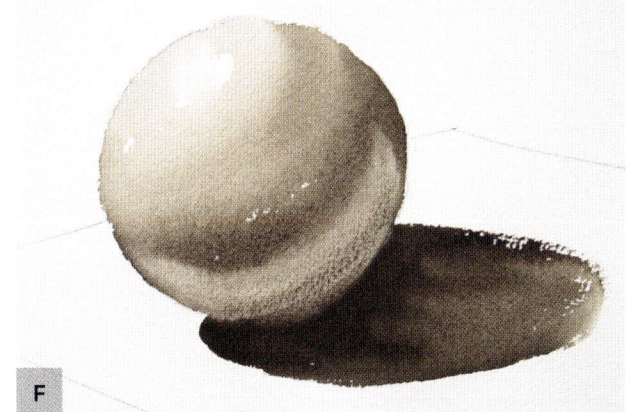

F

move away from the midtone due to the increasing prominence of reflected light. The midtone area receives a notable amount of reflected light itself, especially when approaching the white surface it rests upon, resulting in a lighter appearance (**D**).

Another aspect to consider is the presence of *halftone areas*. One point on the sphere is brilliantly illuminated, receiving light rays at a right angle, making it the brightest area on the sphere's surface. Other surrounding areas remain under direct light but at receding angles, causing them to appear darker. These areas, though darker than the hot spot, are still considered lit and hence are brighter than those in reflected light and midtones (**E**). It's crucial not to exaggerate reflected light, unless the object's material is highly reflective, as it can create an unnatural "hollow" effect (**F**).

▸ When painting objects under diffused lighting conditions, the direction and intensity of light must still be considered, even though the object may appear flattened and two-dimensional. This effect is advantageous when using objects, such as distant mountains or large buildings, to frame the scene.

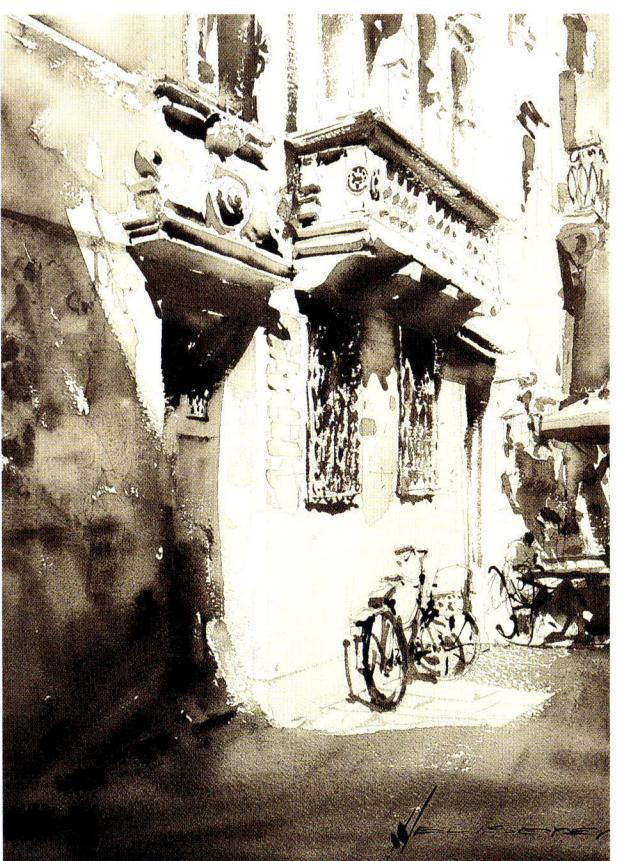

Venice Light, watercolor sketch, 20" × 15" | 51 × 38 cm

DEVELOPING SKETCHING TECHNIQUES

Sketching is a fundamental skill that every artist should master in order to create quick and effective visual references for developing larger, full-color paintings.

TWO TYPES OF SKETCHES

Pencil sketches. I typically carry in my backpack a simple clipboard with regular letter-size white laser printer paper, which is easy to replenish and whose texture is excellent for shading. I use a soft graphite lead for drawing; with the aid of an eraser and masking tape, making corrections and adjustments, including adding or removing elements, becomes quite manageable.

Watercolor sketches. Another approach to sketching involves using monochromatic watercolors. The properties of a watercolor sketch closely resemble those of a final painting, making it a superior reference in terms of presentation looseness. I frequently use sepia (see *Venice Bridges in Grisaille*), though indigo has also yielded successful and pleasing results (see *Venice sketch*). Watercolor sketching has some disadvantages; most notably, the challenge of making corrections and the slow drying process.

The sketch preparation process is highly creative, and speed and immediacy are its advantages. I usually spend no more than 20 minutes on a single sketch. I make my sketches somewhat smaller than letter-size paper and ensure they're centered, which allows me to add space for refining the composition (see *Cashiers*).

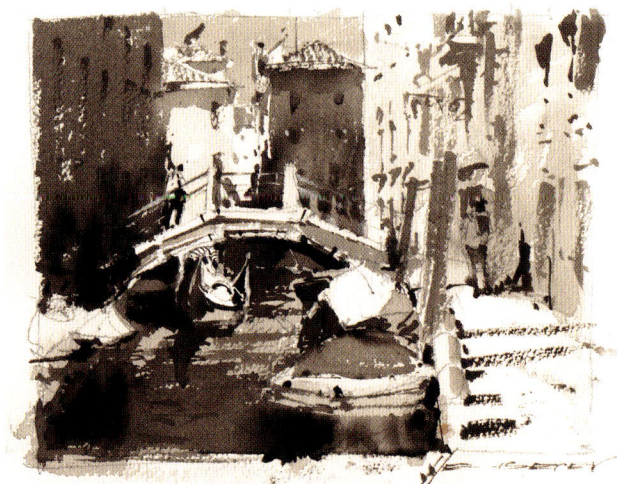

Venice Bridges in Grisaille, 9" × 7" | 23 × 18 cm

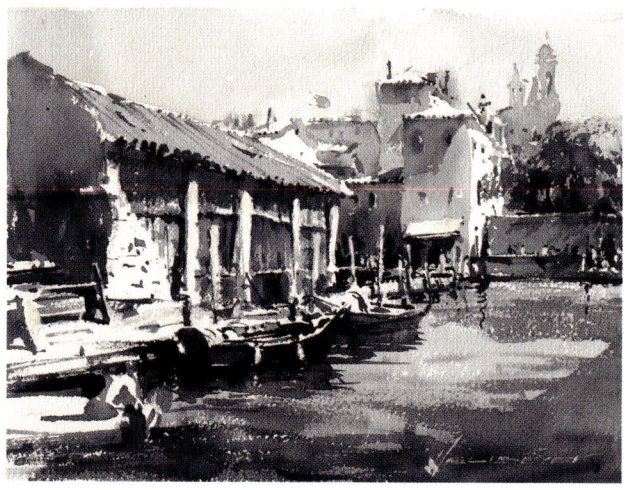

Venice sketch, 7¾" × 10½" | 20 × 26 cm

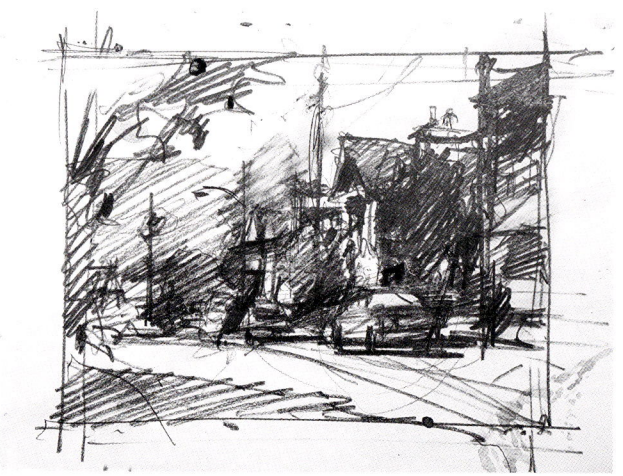

Cashiers, graphite, 6½" × 9" | 17 × 22 cm

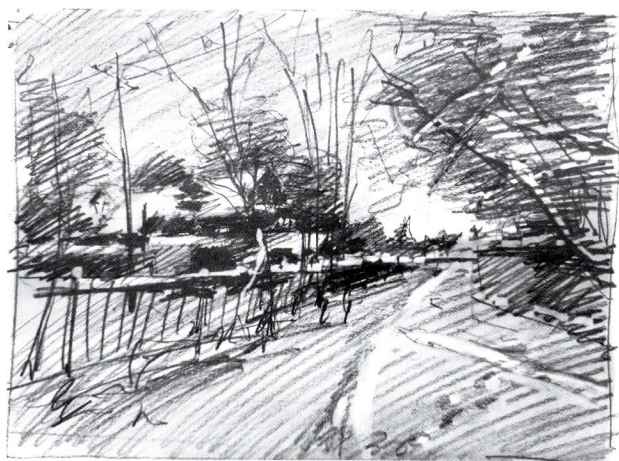

Winter Path, graphite, 8" × 11" | 21 × 27 cm

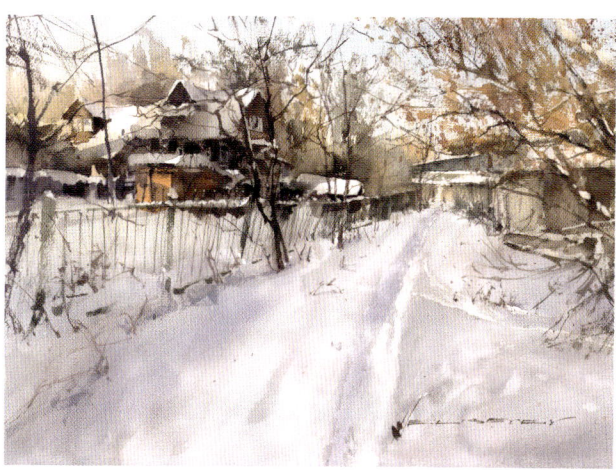

Winter Path, watercolor, 15" × 22" | 38 × 56 cm

WHY START WITH A SKETCH?

If the sketch doesn't resemble a small, monochromatic, loose version of the envisioned painting, I won't start the larger piece. During the sketching phase, I usually examine three key areas in the following order to make necessary adjustments: overall composition, focal areas (p. 122 for more details), and the relationship between lights and darks. In rare cases, the subject matter may need to be abandoned as uninteresting or because it depicts disadvantageous light.

Before starting the sketching process, I keenly observe the landscape and visualize the future painting in detail (p. 56). If I'm satisfied with these crucial aspects (see *Winter Path*, graphite), I proceed with the final, large, full-color painting using the small sketch as a reference.

A crucial aspect of the sketch is its actual looseness of presentation. Quickly drawing or painting helps capture the essence of the scenery boldly, disregarding insignificant details. I've found this approach invaluable and incorporate it into the final painting as much as I can. The sketch often contains subtle hints that prove useful, especially in the secondary areas of the painting.

I suggest covering every part of the sketch with a wash or pencil shade. Every single element should fall into the right tonal value in relation to its adjacent areas (see *Old Boat*). I only leave untouched white paper at the focal areas to express brightly lit areas or *hot spots*, which are reflections of light on metal, glass, or water.

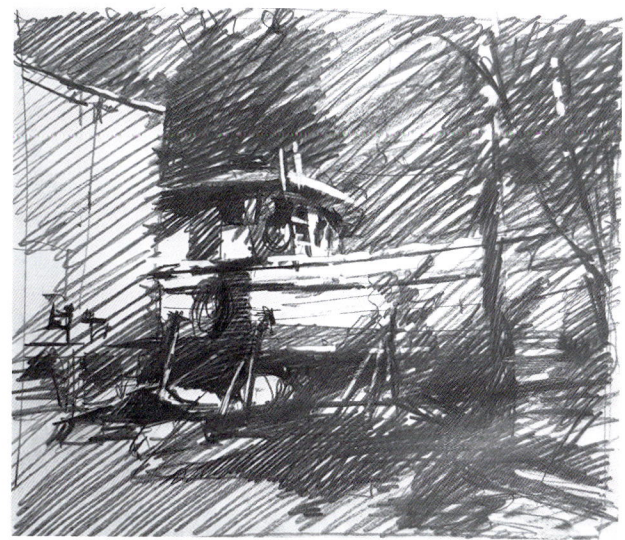

Old Boat, graphite, 8" × 10" | 21 × 25cm

How far can your sketch veer from the original view? I usually reinterpret the scenery to align with my intended ideas for the final painting. During the sketching stage, I can identify and relocate intended focal areas, add or eliminate a scene's details, and adjust sizes of elements at will. I do strive, however, to adhere to my initial overall impression of the scene, its mood, and its dynamics. Changing these fundamental aspects would negate my intended purpose in selecting the subject matter.

REINTERPRETING THE SCENE

It remains a captivating phenomenon that, even if multiple artists were to paint the same scenery, the resulting outcomes would exhibit striking and delightful variations. In fact, this diversity in interpretation is not only intriguing but also serves as a testament to the richness of artistic expression.

You might ask, "Can I simply replicate what I see in real life?" Most likely, the answer is no. Objective scenery reproduction on a two-dimensional surface, such as paper, is akin to looking at a photograph. While photographs excel at preserving memories, they often lack the emotional impact we experience in diverse environments. In my opinion, evoking these emotions is the ultimate goal of fine art.

COMPOSITION

The most important area of reinterpretation lies in composition, wherein artists have the power to change the arrangement of elements in their work, significantly impacting the viewer's experience. For instance, focusing on the sky area in one painting and the water in another transforms the paintings into distinctly different creations (see *Cortez Boats* and *Fishermen's Boats* at right).

Additionally, the choice of areas of interest in the scenery varies among painters, affecting the overall perception. Altering tonal values allows us to manipulate these areas to suit our artistic intentions. After compositional decisions, this manipulation has the most significant effect on the final appearance of the artwork. Most often than not, contrast lies elsewhere in the real scene, prompting adjustments to highlight the intended focal area in the painting. Focusing on specific objects in the scenery often leads to a reinterpretation, diverging from reality and thus giving a different look and feel to the painting. In *After the Rain* (opposite, top), the contrast was intentionally brought into the water reflection area and the shadow above.

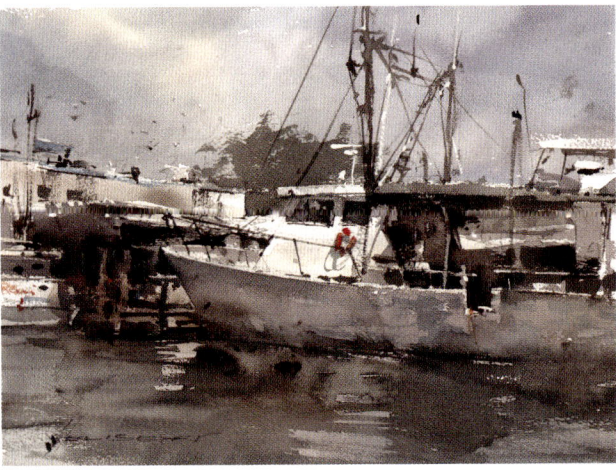

Cortez Boats, watercolor, 9½" × 13" | 24 × 33 cm

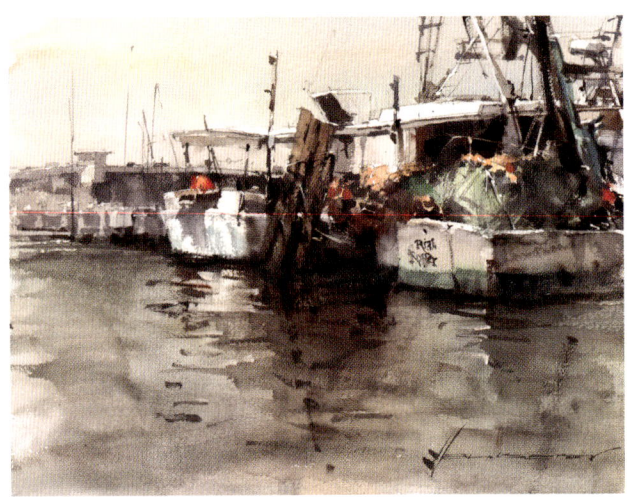

Fishermen's Boats, watercolor, 10" × 13" | 25 × 33 cm

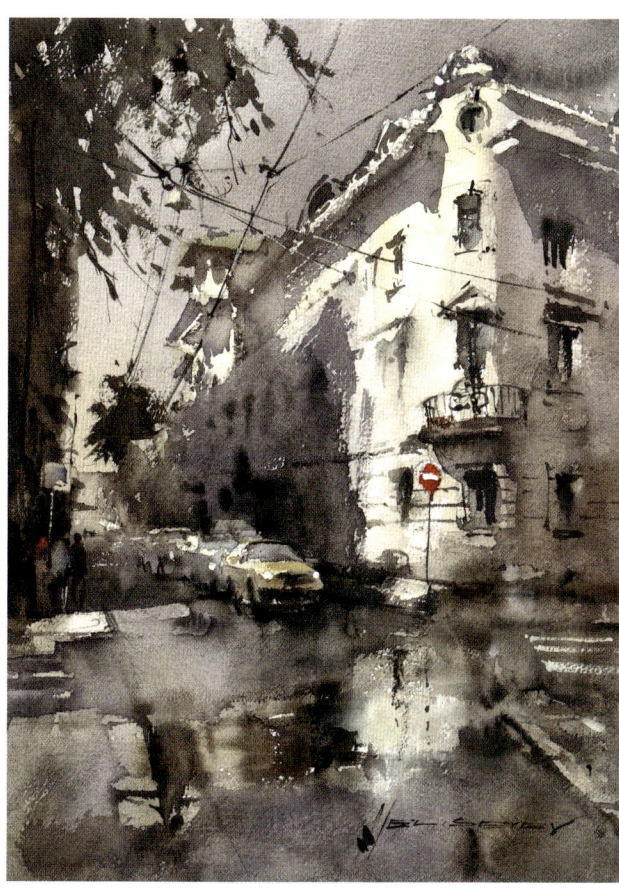

Another area where change is inevitable is the shape and size of the objects we paint. These changes, particularly with trees, shrubs, grass, barriers, and walls, aim to create a harmonious balance among various elements in *The Chateau* (below).

When dealing with items like cars, boats, and people, considerations of size and placement are crucial.

◄ *After the Rain*, watercolor, 14" × 10" | 36 × 26 cm

▼ *The Chateau*, watercolor, 14" × 11" | 27 × 37 cm

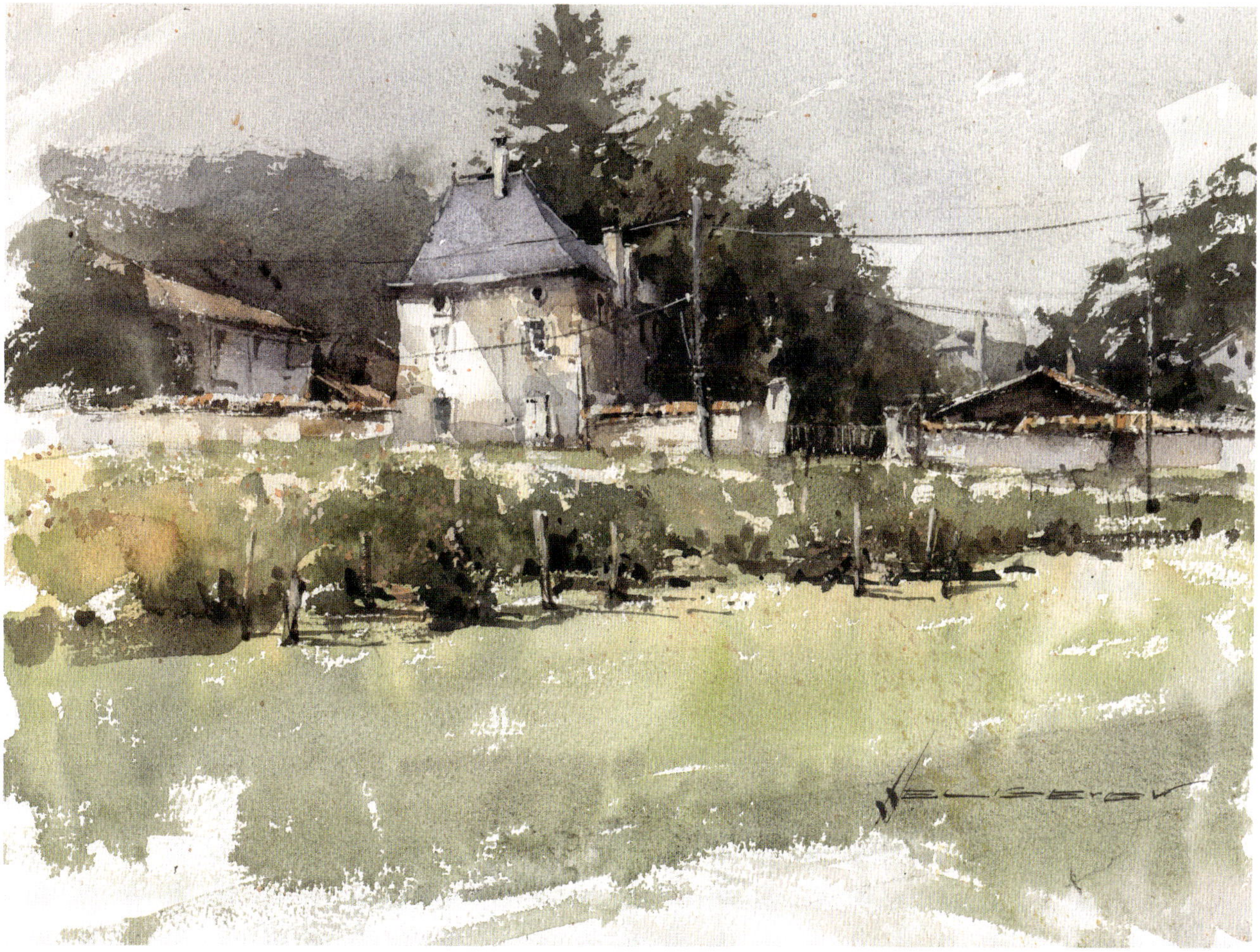

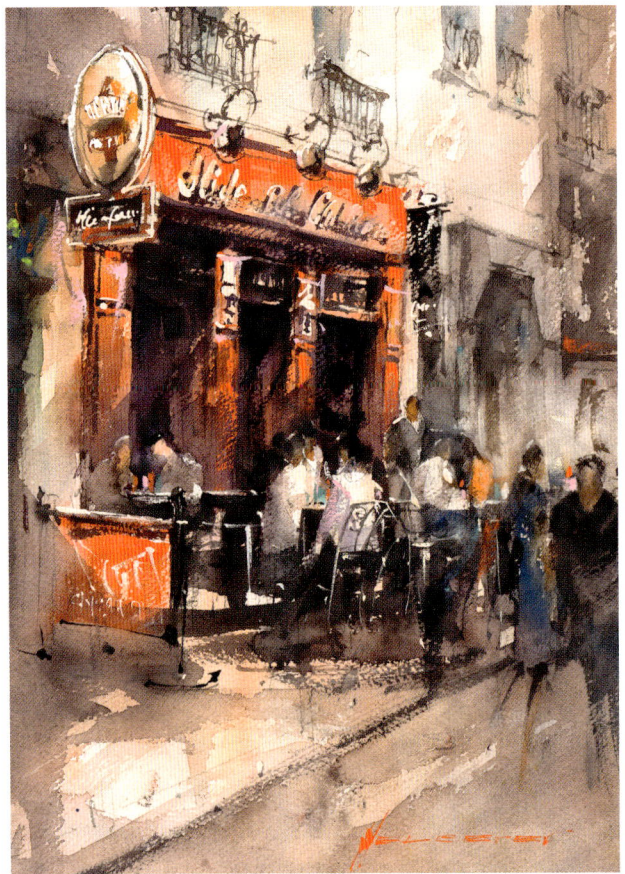

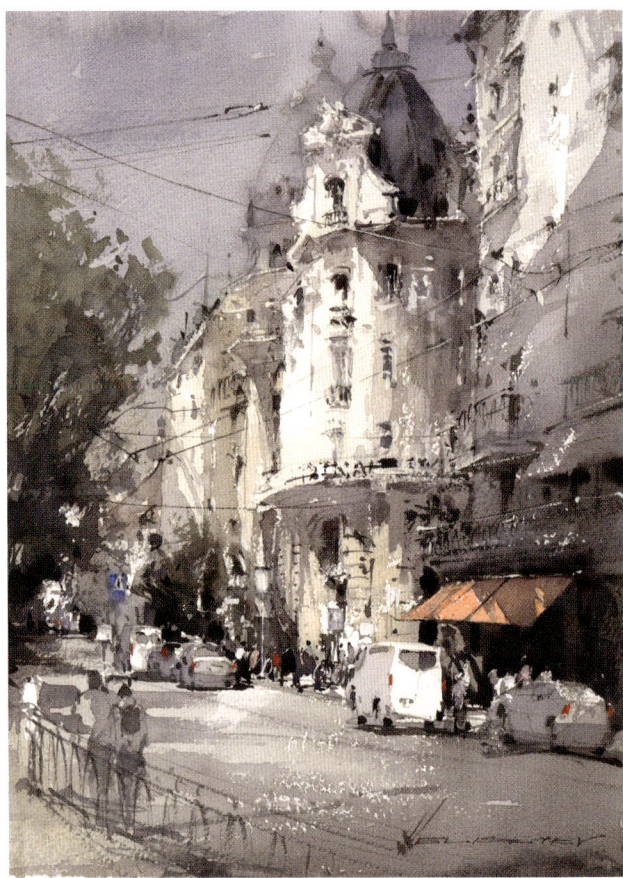

Paris Bistro, watercolor, 14½" × 10½" | 37 × 27 cm

Montreaux Street, watercolor, 14½" × 10½" | 37 × 27 cm

COLOR TEMPERATURE AND INTENSITY

Another critical aspect of interpretation lies in the use of color within a painting. Beginning with the broad spectrum of color temperatures, from warm hues to cool, we possess the power to profoundly influence the overall ambiance of the artwork, as illustrated in *Paris Bistro* (above left).

Another aspect deserving thoughtful consideration is the intensity of color within specific elements of the scene. At times, an excess of color can disrupt the intended narrative, becoming superfluous and obstructing the painter's unique vision. My approach typically involves employing more vibrant colors, strategically placed closer to focal points.

When a noticeable color competition arises between secondary and primary areas within the painting, a crucial decision-making moment is reached. It's imperative to discern which colors should be toned down or intensified and where these adjustments need to take place. Rather than meticulously resolving color equations at a granular level across the entire painting, I find it simpler to systematically reduce color intensity in the secondary areas (see *Montreaux Street*, above right).

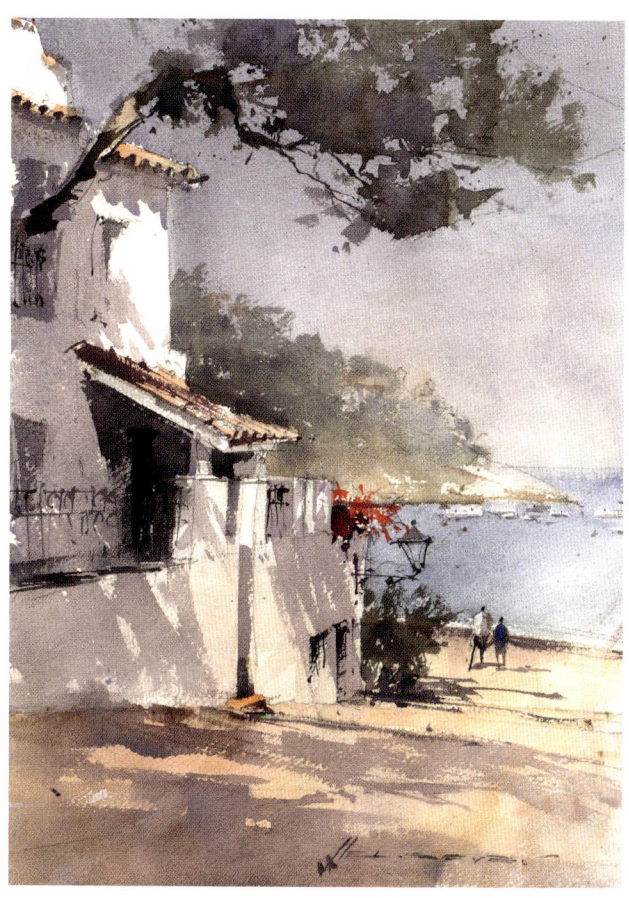

Palafrugell, watercolor, 14½" × 10½" | 37 × 27 cm

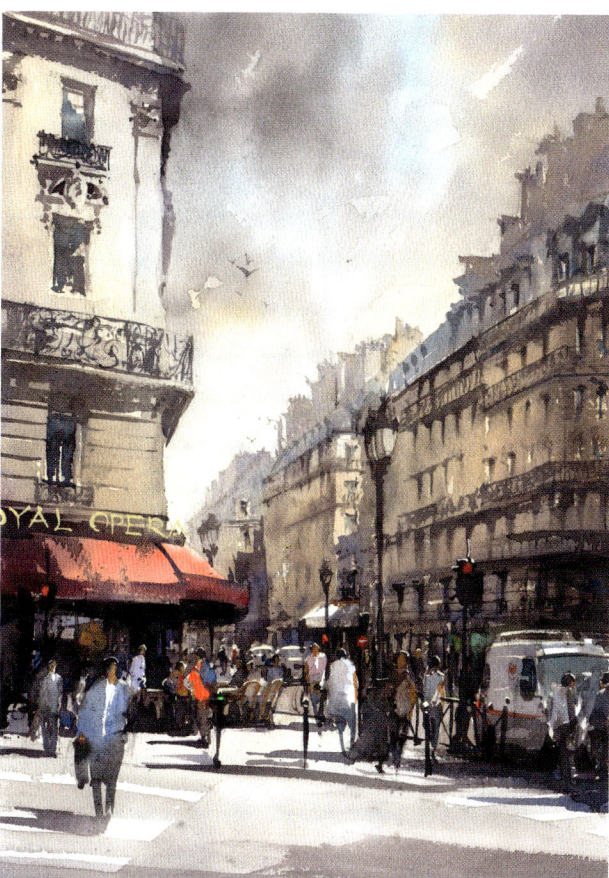

Le Royal Opera, watercolor, 21" × 14" | 54 × 36 cm

THE COLOR OF THE SKY

Delving into the specifics of individual colors, one key consideration frequently arises: the color of the sky. I often find myself pondering whether alterations to the sky's color are necessary. This decision involves meticulous assessment, from the adjustments in tonal values to the play of temperatures, each contributing to the painting's character. Furthermore, I question the need to modify the shapes of clouds, contemplating how their portrayal can impact the overall composition. Especially when confronted with a complex subject matter composing numerous elements, a fundamental query arises: Is it essential to include clouds in the painting, or might their absence better serve the artistic vision (see *Palafrugell* and *Le Royal Opera*, above left and above right).

Considering the looseness in interpreting the scenery itself is imperative. One fundamental rule I follow in the painting process is to embrace less detail whenever possible. In watercolor, materials like rough-surface paper and springy synthetic brushes are invaluable in achieving this effect. When a painting hints at detail rather than presenting it explicitly, it encourages viewers to engage longer, mentally completing the artwork to perfection. This interaction has dual benefits: involving the viewer in the artistic process and allowing them to reinterpret the piece to their liking, establishing a more intimate connection between the artwork and the viewer.

PENCIL LAYOUTS ON WATERCOLOR PAPER

When I create my pencil layout on watercolor paper, I simply observe the landscape and draw it lightly as a massing. Simultaneously, I refer to any previously done sketches, if available, and adjust my layout based on the sketch rather than the photo or the actual view. It's crucial to draw very lightly and suggestively to merely indicate the object locations and some essential details. The HB 0.7mm variety mechanical pencil I use for drawing on watercolor paper is much harder than the 2B I use for sketching.

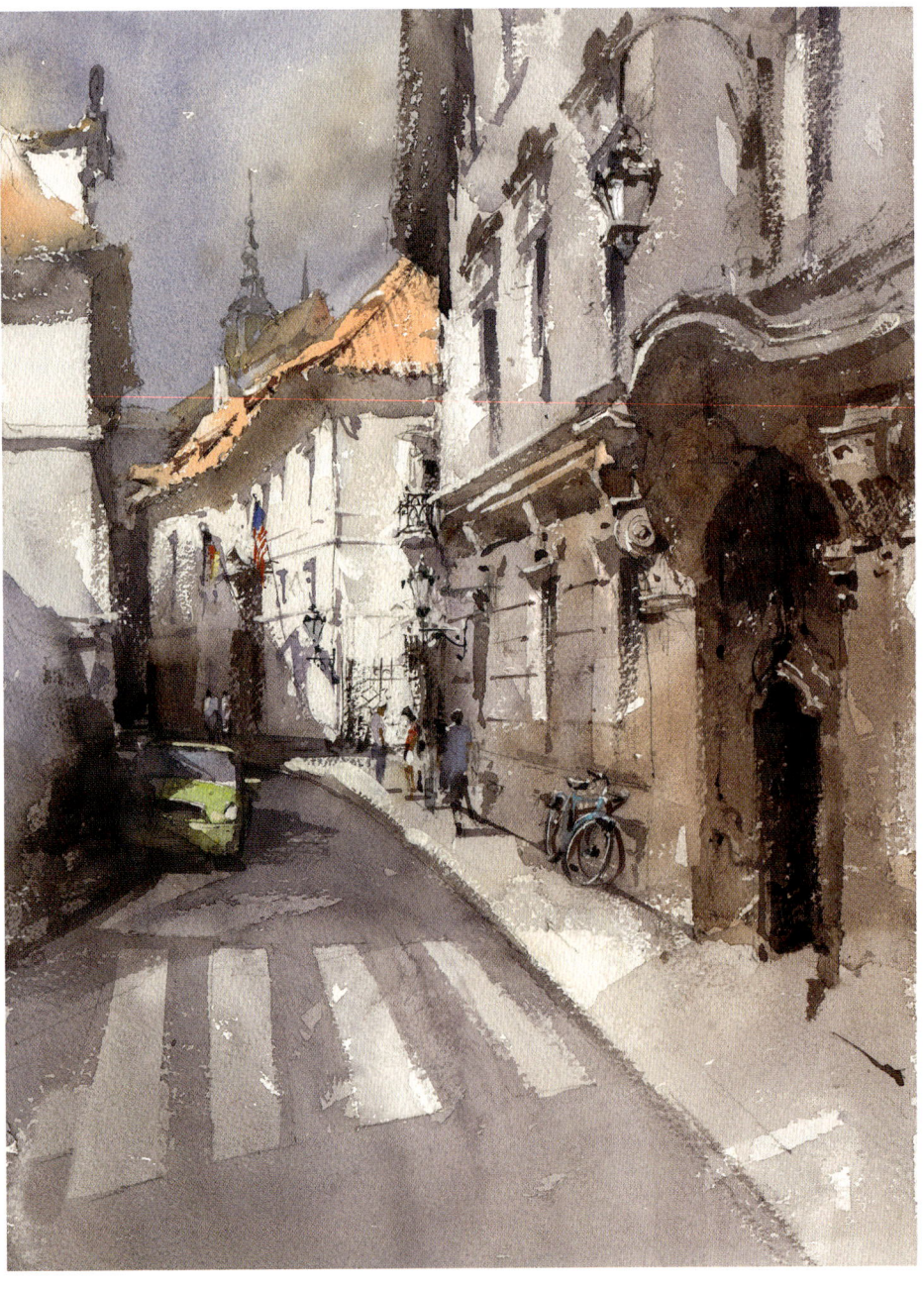

Prague, watercolor, 19" × 14" | 48 × 36 cm

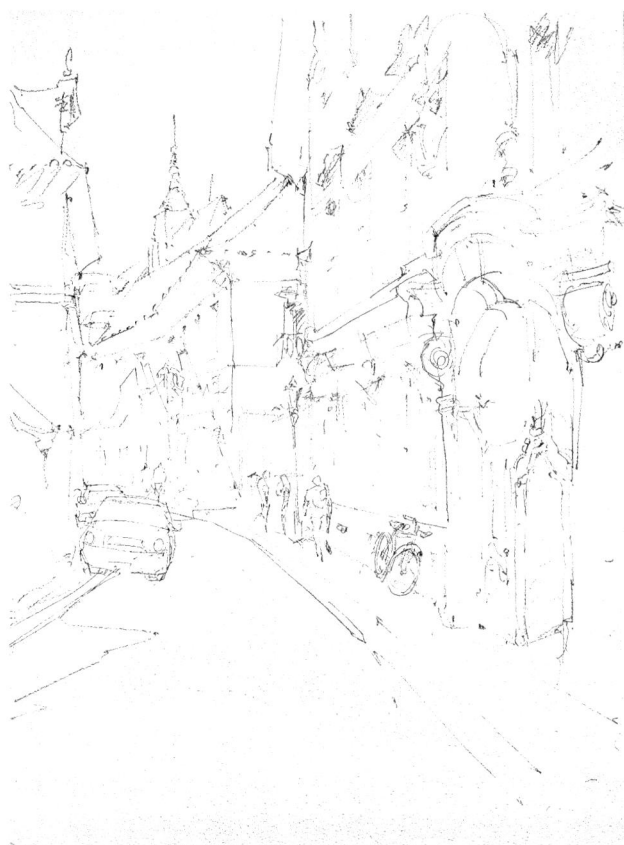

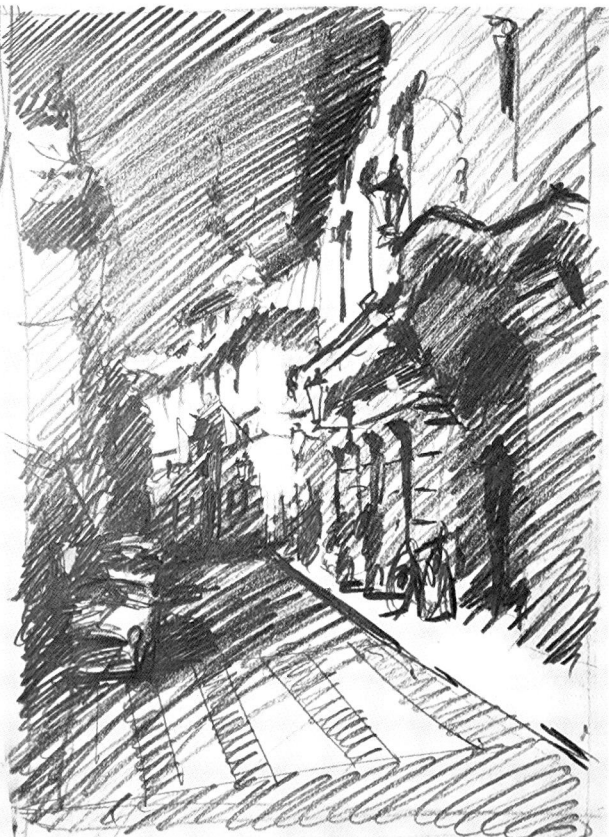

Prague, HB pencil, 19" × 14" | 48 × 36 cm

Prague, 2B pencil sketch, 8½" × 6" | 22 × 15 cm

As I mentioned, I aim to include only a bare minimum of details during this initial phase to keep the door open for interpretation and adjustments during the painting process. The order in which I draw doesn't matter as long as I move from big elements to small. An important technique I've learned is that if I draw a line incorrectly, I'll draw the correct one alongside it before erasing the incorrect line. The incorrect line serves as a guide to correct it afterward. This method has saved me a lot of time and frustration during the process.

I truly believe in the freedom of spiritual spontaneity, which can only be fully realized during the immersive painting process. If I draw everything in extreme detail, it may interrupt that process and risk making the painting feel more like a coloring book. Additionally, some watercolor papers don't respond well to plastic erasers, so I try to use them very

sparingly. When it comes to drawing people and cars, it's advisable to determine their locations during the sketch preparation stage. The fluent and gestural approach when it comes to people and cars is easier to copy from a sketch rather than laboring over them in the final drawing.

I'm often asked whether it's advisable to stretch the paper on a board before starting the watercolor application. I don't typically stretch my watercolor paper unless it's for a commercial illustration assignment. A bit of buckling doesn't significantly interfere with my painting techniques, and the minor inconvenience doesn't justify the effort of stretching the paper and waiting for it to dry for hours. When my goal is to produce a "clean" illustration, I'd say stretching is a must. I won't delve into the technicalities of how to stretch watercolor paper, as there is plenty of information available online.

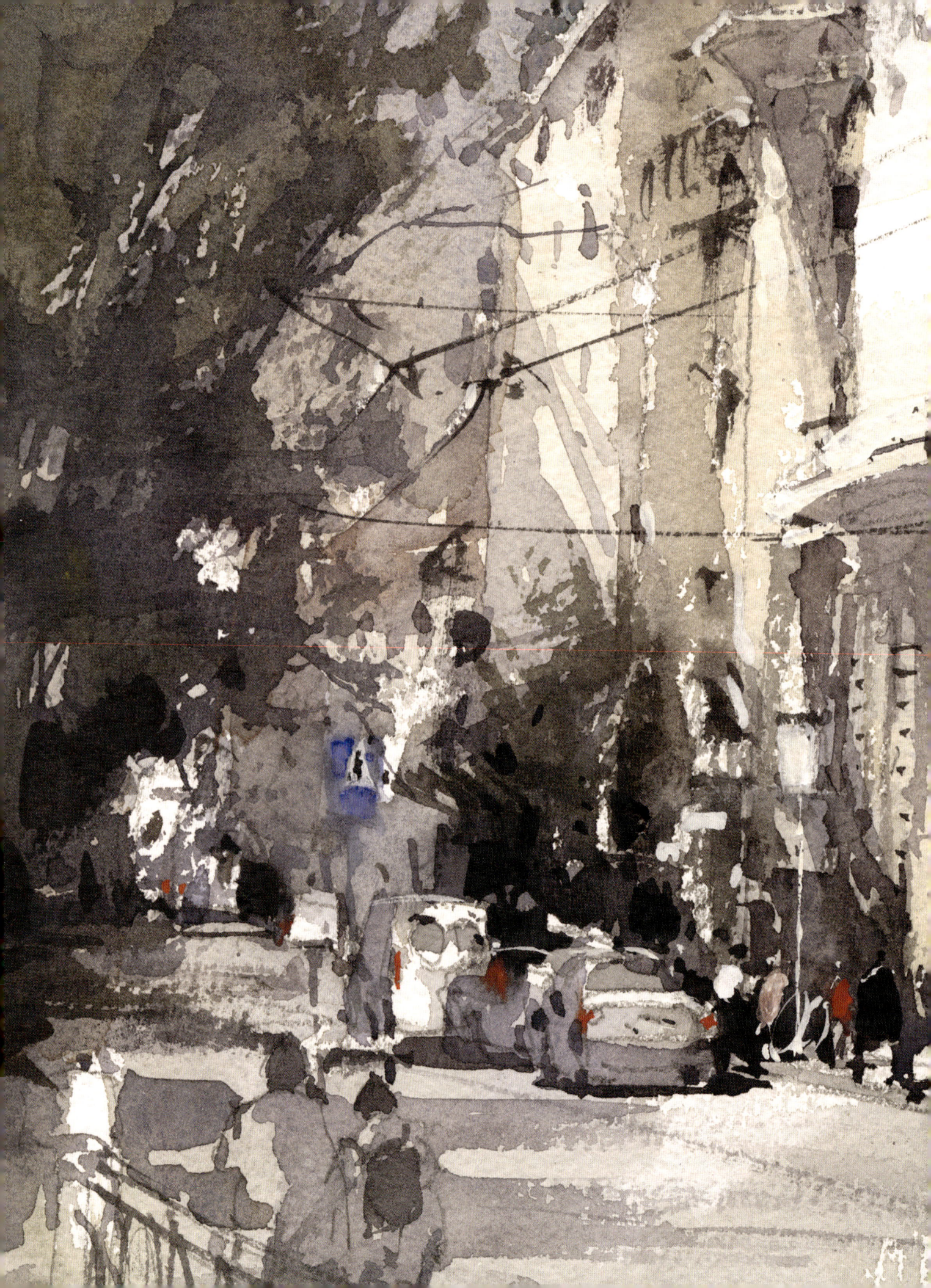

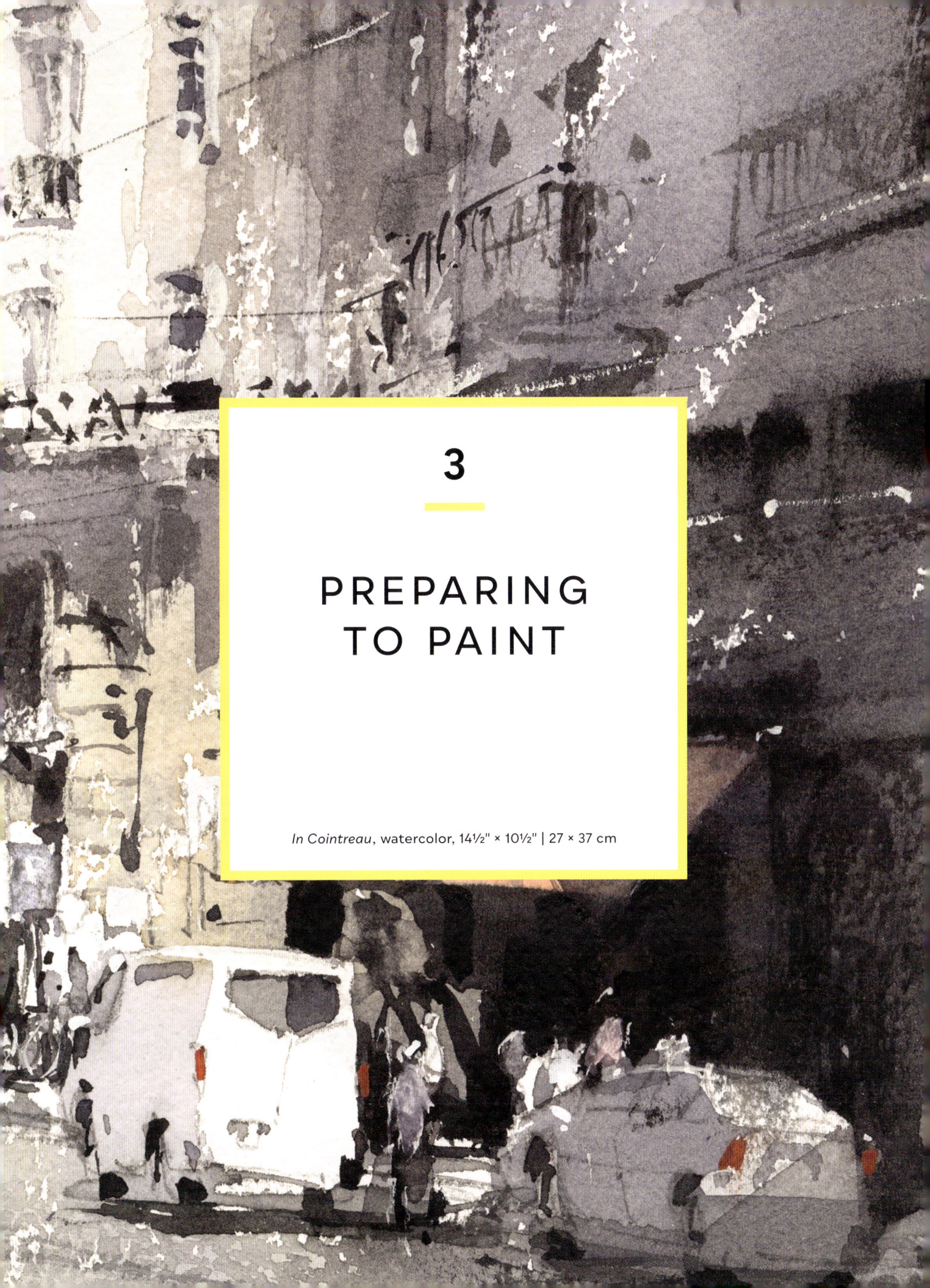

3

PREPARING
TO PAINT

In Cointreau, watercolor, 14½" × 10½" | 27 × 37 cm

COMPOSING YOUR WATERCOLOR PAINTING

As the viewer engages with the artwork, they virtually traverse toward a predetermined area intentionally created by the artist, usually situated in the midground plane (see "Navigating the Three Planes of Vision," p. 114). Along this journey, the artist should strategically place directional elements and obstacles to craft an interesting and engaging experience as the viewer approaches the main area of depiction. These elements can range from obvious to subtle objects gently guiding the eye toward the destination.

Skillful artists can achieve this without overtly pushing the viewer, employing a theatrically playful manner. Obvious guiding elements may include roads, plants along the way, or water edges. Stoppers, or obstacles, are particularly intriguing, as they offer a vast array of possibilities, ranging from direct barriers like walls and rocks to more subtle elements like standing people, cars, or trees. Since these elements are movable, it becomes the artist's responsibility to manipulate them effectively, creating an intriguing and compelling visual path leading to the focal point.

I view my scenery much like a theater stage, where the director strategically places elements not only to enhance the narrative but also to provide a sense of depth and, most importantly, relevance to the scenery. This approach enriches the viewer's experience, encouraging them to mentally engage with the narrative and, ultimately, capturing their attention for a longer duration.

I've already discussed the importance of the relevance of supporting elements in a painting to the main subject matter. It's quite straightforward to understand that objects should complement the central theme of the depiction. For instance, if the main subject is a boat, elements along the way could include ropes, old anchors, ladders, other smaller boats, water, birds, and so on. However, placing a tennis court nearby might seem out of place. In essence, ensuring the appropriateness of elements in the painting is a thoughtful approach to their placement.

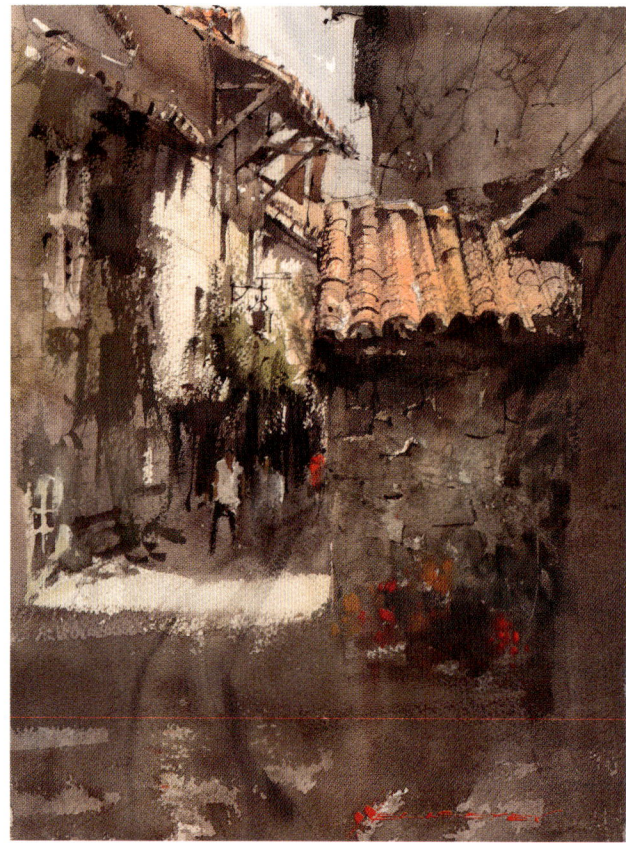

In Pérouges, watercolor, 14" × 11" | 36 × 27 cm

I prefer to stage my paintings with a prominent object in the foreground plane. In *Knoxville Farm* (opposite top left), the substantial tree acts as a barrier, complemented by the log on the ground to the left, guiding the viewer's eye toward the barn on the right. This setup also aids in perspective, given the tree's significant size. The rusting, abandoned farm equipment on the right serves as a natural stop, preventing the eye from moving further right. The large oak tree, logs, farm machinery, country path, and abundant grass are all fitting elements that contribute to the rural scenery. Introducing a children's playground into the picture frame, in my opinion, would detract from the overall expression and experience of the scene.

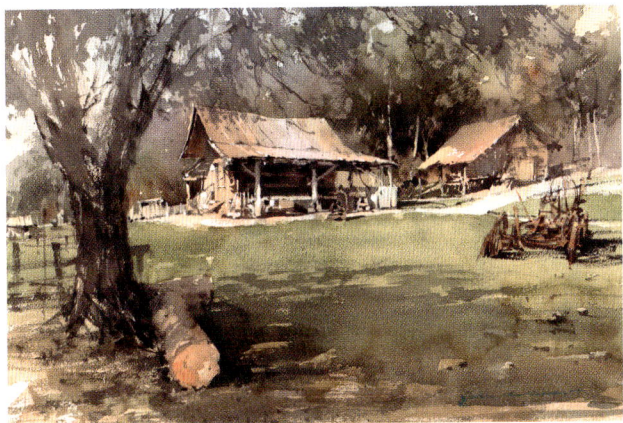

Knoxville Farm, watercolor, 14" × 21½" | 36 × 55cm

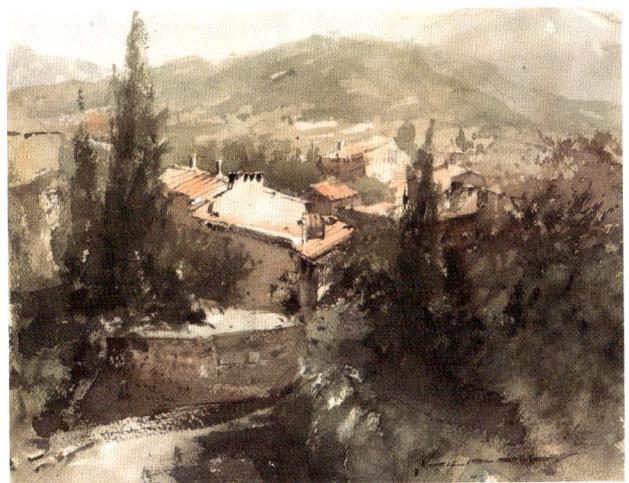

Bordeaux Village, watercolor, 10½" × 14" | 27 × 36 cm

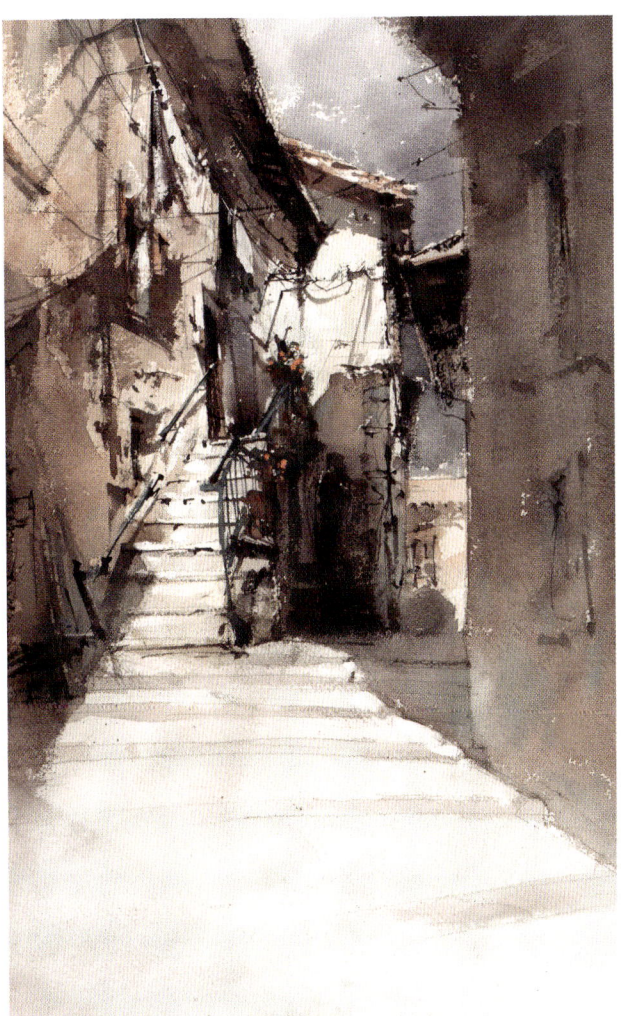

Stairway Stroncone, watercolor, 21½" × 14" | 55 × 36 cm

Bordeaux Village (above bottom) features strategically placed obstacles within the picture frame to guide the viewer's gaze toward the town. A substantial stone wall blocks the path forward, prompting the viewer to shift to the right along the dusty country path. Here, they encounter a tree that directs them both left and right, unfolding a zigzagging path in front of the house and ultimately leading them to the destination. Often, these elements are inherent in nature, and it's crucial for the painter to discover the right vantage point to faithfully capture them on canvas. These scenes may not always reveal themselves outright, requiring the artist's vision to discern what aligns with the desired composition.

In *Stairway Stroncone* (above right), an unobstructed path is evident along the road, leading upward with the assistance of stairs adorned with prominent green handrails and vibrant red flowers. A small object on the ground near the stairs serves as a minor obstacle, easily avoided and not impeding the forward journey. Upon reaching the top of the stairs, the viewer is greeted by a rewarding composition of large flowers, creating a striking contrast against the white wall in the background. This static image allows for observational appreciation, where all elements coexist harmoniously without conflicting with each other.

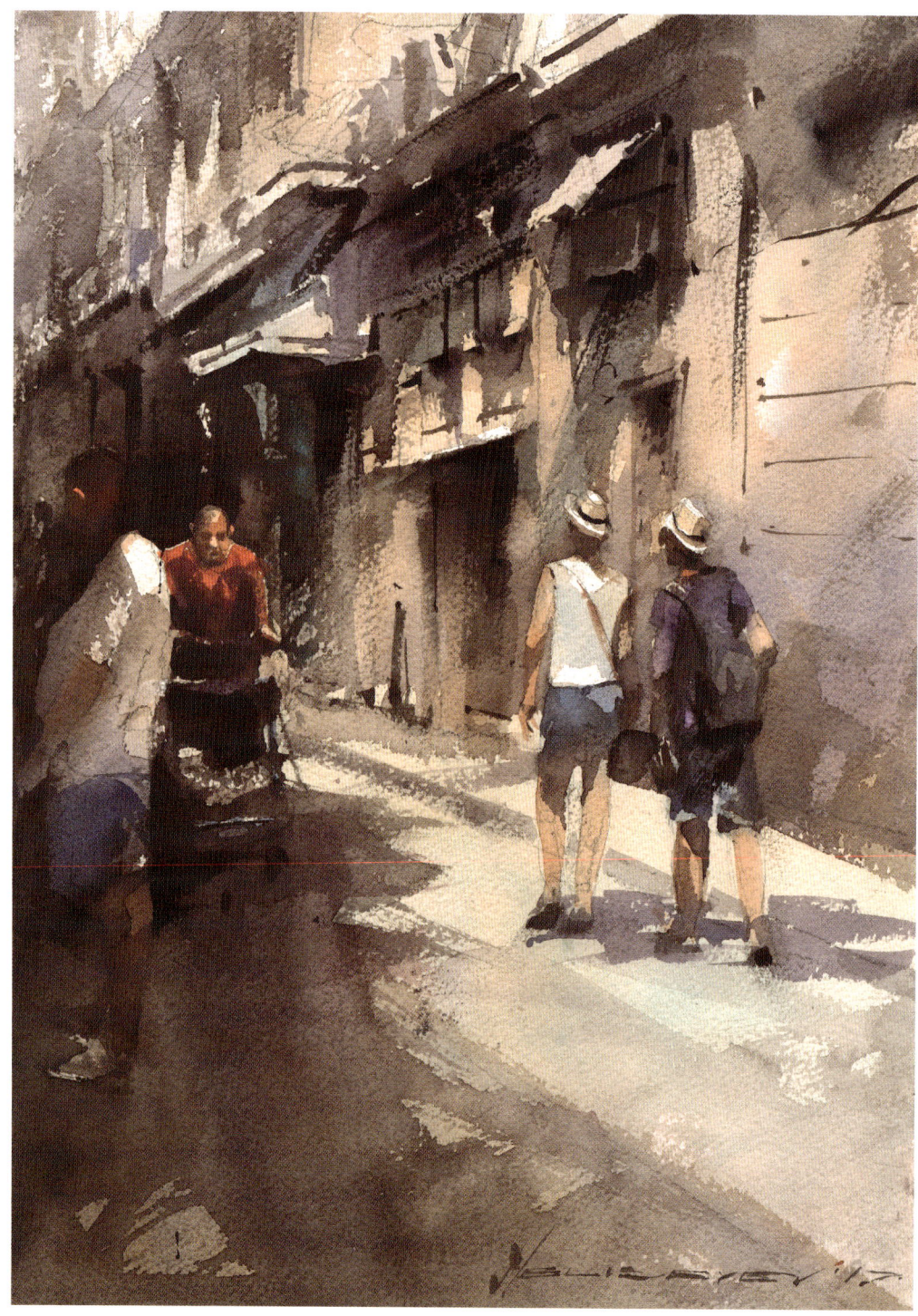

Tourists in Havana, watercolor, 14" × 10" | 36 × 26 cm

Another crucial aspect of composing an image involves the interplay between elements to enhance the perception of depth in the painting. Whenever possible, I superimpose larger elements on top of those in the distance. This technique becomes particularly effective when placing elements like people in a way that partially covers elements in the background. Unlike when people are arranged separately, this method intensifies the sense of depth, as illustrated in *Tourists in Havana* (above).

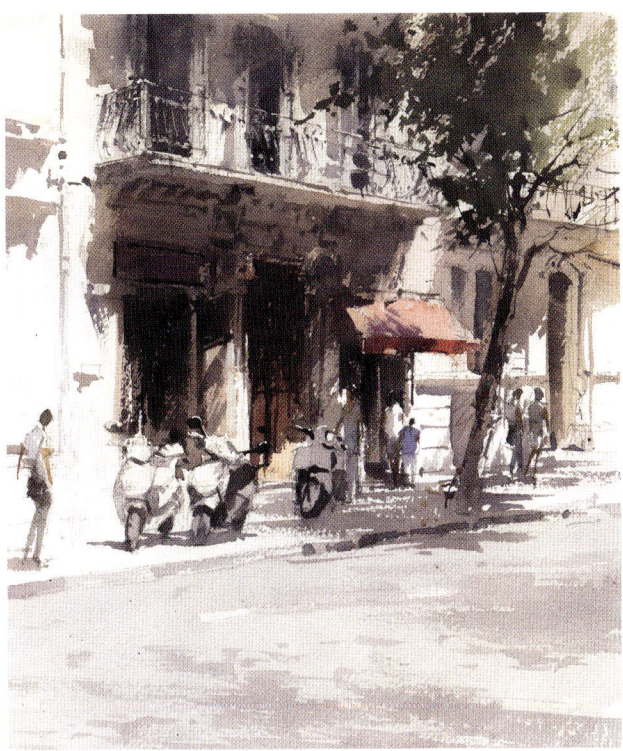

Barcelona, watercolor, 14½" × 10½" | 37 × 27 cm

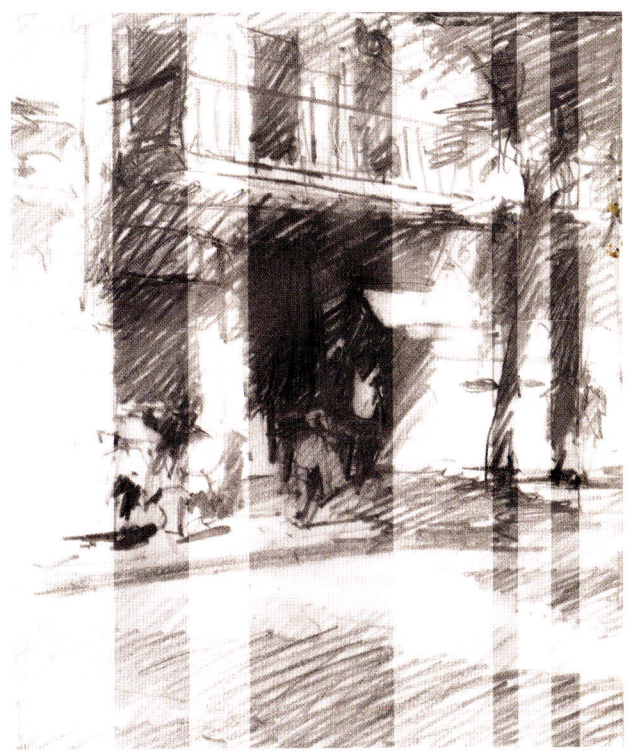

Vertical rhythm.

The interaction between elements in a painting is often an overlooked aspect. To better illustrate this concept, imagine the large cast shadow from one element falling onto another, as depicted in *Provence Tree* (below).

The cast shadow serves to unite the elements, forging a connection between the trees and the building behind, especially under specific lighting conditions. I often extend the shadows to reach another element, further enhancing this effect within the composition, as shown in the image.

Consider the sequence of lights and darks when composing the painting. If that sequence is not observed properly or not deliberately presented, some elements in the painting may lose their significance. It's especially important to address this in the sketch stage, where the artist can manipulate tonal values to enhance the overall presentation of the future painting. The illustration above right shows how the bands of lights and darks were preserved and enhanced.

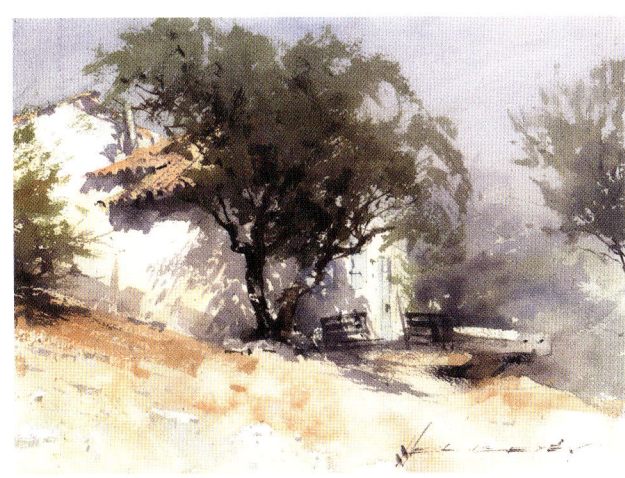

Provence Tree, watercolor, 10½" × 14" | 27 × 36 cm

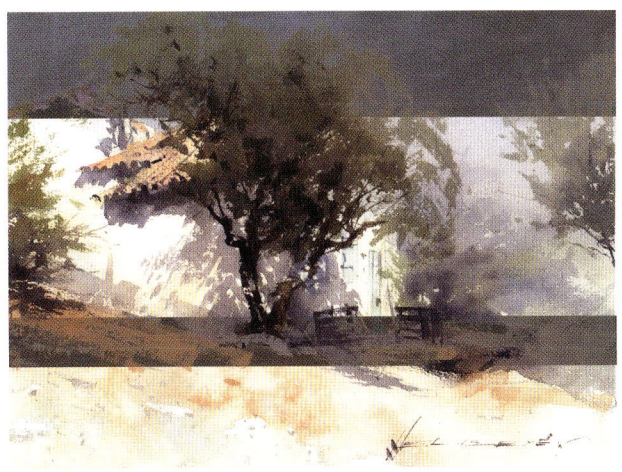

Horizontal rhythm.

SELECTING YOUR SUBJECT

Every painter seeks to capture something that truly speaks to them and holds a deep emotional connection. I often find myself in the same situation, but many times, after contemplating the scenery in front of me for a while, I choose to keep walking in search of a better view and there is why.

One type of subject I tend to avoid painting is artworks in the form of fountains and sculptures. Once a piece has been created, anything subsequent is essentially a copy. If I do decide to paint a fountain, I try to divert attention from it and focus on activities surrounding it—playing children, mothers with strollers, birds, and so on. Town squares with fountains are teeming with life and can be engaging to portray, especially if the fountain carries a historical patina. The same principle applies to landmarks. I often incorporate them in a secondary role, like part of the background, without singling out a focal point for their location in the painting.

This consideration extends to the setting in which the main subject is placed. Many beautiful objects become challenging to paint if they are situated in an artificial or inappropriate setting. For instance, an old locomotive might be ideally placed at a bustling railroad station, but nowadays, they are often displayed as relics in various parks without any connection to railroad activity.

Some states feature fascinating collections of old barn-type buildings in museum parks, aiming to preserve historic architecture and create a compelling rural atmosphere. The success of painting in such places depends on whether the setting looks authentic and resonates with the subject. Recently, I painted at a museum park in Appalachia, where the truthful setting and the barn itself impressed me with its naturalness (opposite center).

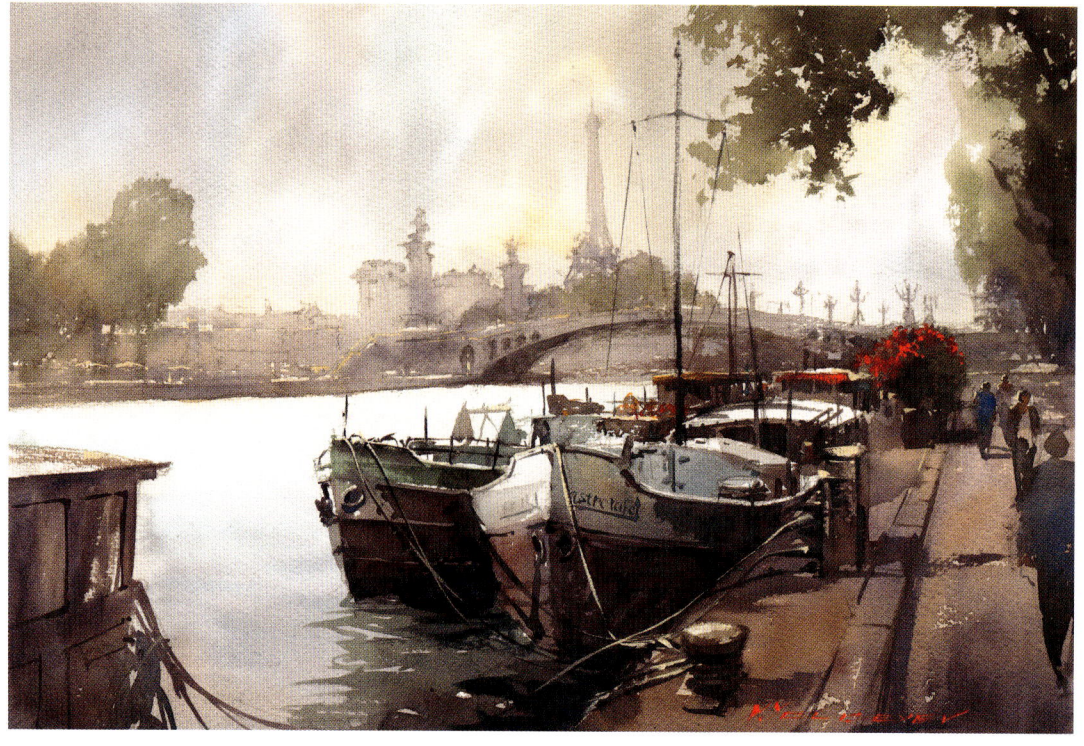

Seine Barges, watercolor, 14" × 21" | 35 × 53 cm

As you may notice, it may be simpler for me to identify what I wouldn't paint, rather than to guide you toward suitable subject matters. This is because there are numerous elements influencing the ultimate decision to paint, and explaining them all would require an extensive volume of information.

That being said, I will mention that visiting national art museums and studying the compositions and subject matter of masters can also be a fruitful starting point. Over time, I've developed a sense of harmony that I believe every painting should embody. It's akin to classical music, where even in the most complex passages, a sense of harmonic completeness is ever-present, even in what may initially seem discordant if intentionally designed.

Returning to subject matter, alongside the considerations mentioned above, personal experience plays a vital role. My upbringing in a large city has endowed me with an understanding of how big cities function, influencing my choice of subjects related to urban life. Similarly, individuals with backgrounds in farming, fishing, or other environments have a deep understanding and inner connection of those settings, giving their work authenticity and depth. This inherent, hard-to-explain understanding of our roots facilitates our work, making it more genuine and resonant.

Ultimately, achieving minute effects in your paintings is important, but it's equally crucial to be emotionally connected to the environment you're painting. Some individuals possess the remarkable ability to immerse themselves emotionally in the setting they paint, experiencing it on a deep, instinctive level. For instance, when I paint a fishing boat, I mentally become a fisherman, smelling like fish, feeling wet and tired, and sharing jokes with fishermen working nearby. This emotional involvement and cohesion with the subject are paramount (see *Dry Dock*, at right). Without it, the work may be visually appealing but lack depth, resembling mere illustration—a beautiful but shallow creation with a short-lived impact.

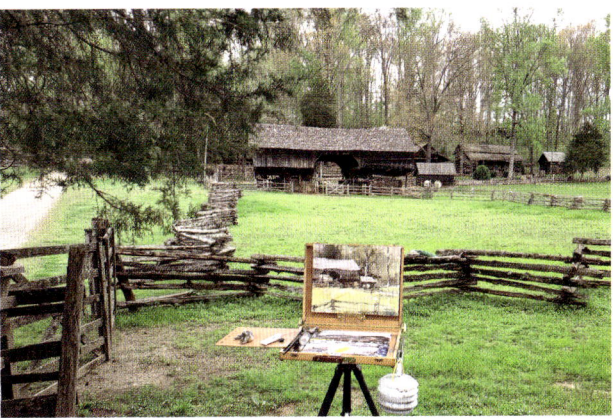

The Museum of Appalachia, Clinton, Tennessee

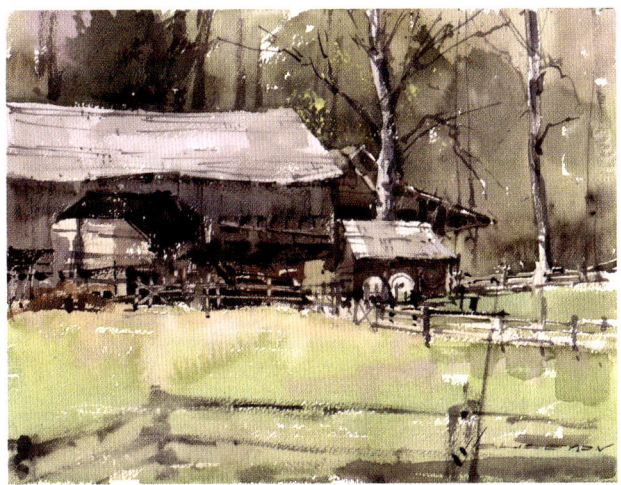

Appalach Farm, watercolor, 10½" × 14" | 27 × 36 cm

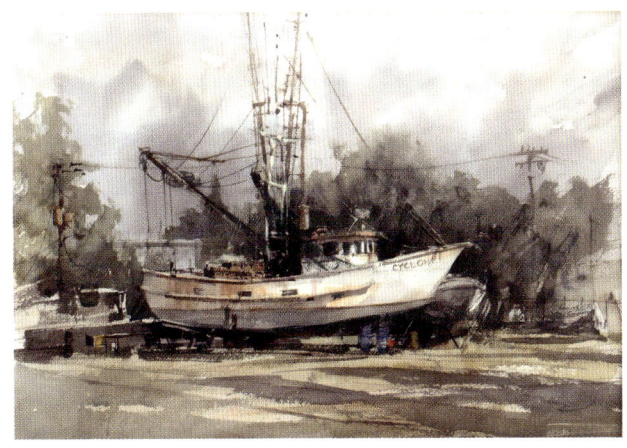

Dry Dock, watercolor, 20" × 13½" | 34 × 51 cm

CULTIVATING THE RIGHT MINDSET

In an era where virtually everyone can effortlessly capture a snapshot of any scene, the once alluring charm of the so-called realistic form of presentation seems to have waned. The contemporary audience seeks something beyond mere replication—a more personal, subjective essence in the artworks they engage with.

SPEED FOR SPONTANEITY

Addressing the insufficiency of merely copying reality or relying on photographs for creating a meaningful painting, it's essential to delve into the artist's mental state during the work in progress. Undoubtedly, almost every artist, regardless of intent, tends to slip into a copying state during this process. This tendency becomes more pronounced toward the end of the painting process, particularly when mental fatigue sets in, and sustaining a focused state becomes increasingly challenging.

The revelation that working at a faster pace enhances focus and results in bolder, more immediately appealing watercolors underscores the significance of a free-flowing process. This spontaneity in execution imparts a natural immediacy that surpasses attempts to fabricate a loose aesthetic.

This phenomenon is reminiscent of a learning stage in our lives—an almost inevitable phase where individuals are compelled to adhere to a meticulous approach. This period, analogous to the school-imposed method of slow and accurate handwriting, serves as a foundational experience. It lays the groundwork for later creative freedom, akin to the ability to write freely and express individuality in one's handwriting after mastering the fundamentals. Just as the rigid constraints of slow handwriting are eventually surpassed for more expressive styles, the artist's journey involves breaking free from constraints to embrace a liberated and spontaneous creative process.

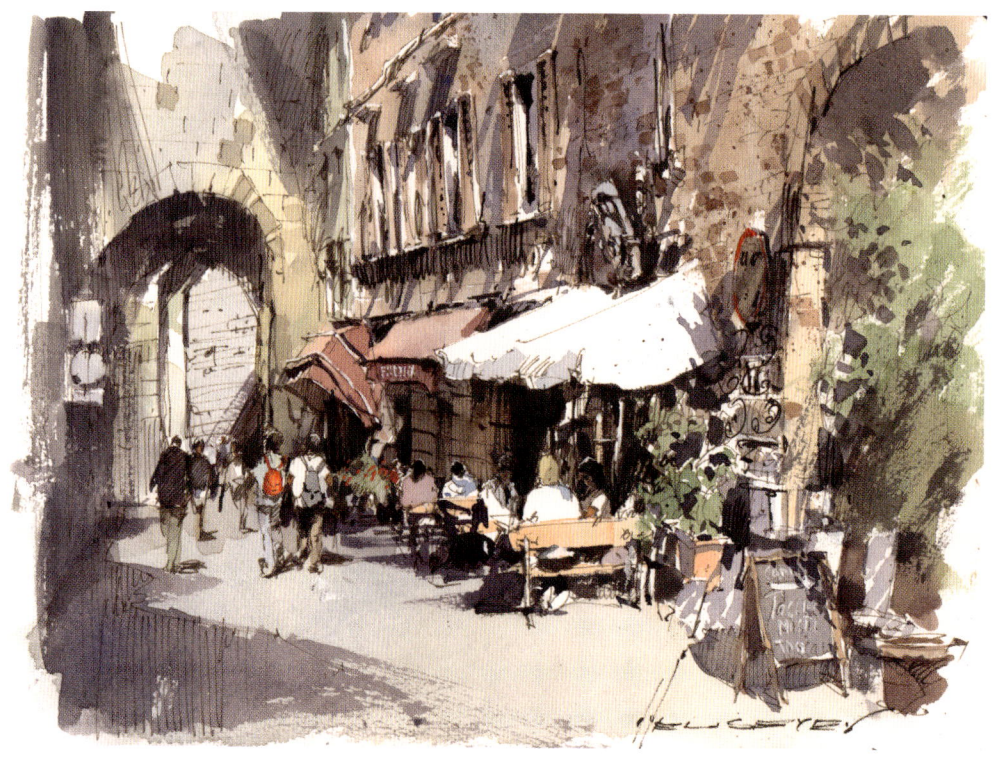

Montepulciano, watercolor and ink, 8" × 11" | 21 × 29 cm

LIGHT AND COLOR IN THE WATERCOLOR LANDSCAPE

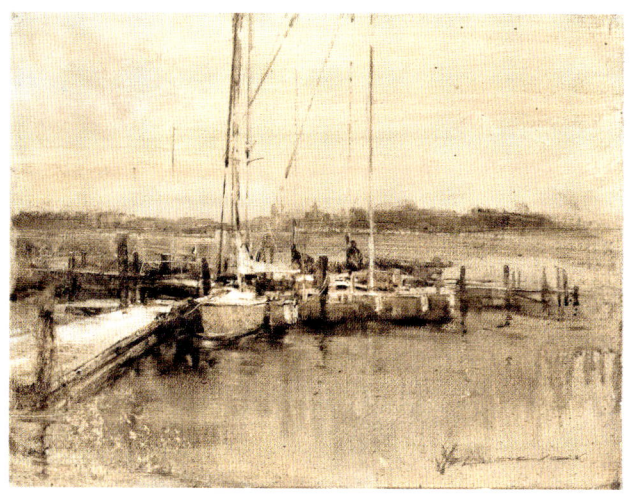

Sailing Club, watercolor, 9" × 12" | 23 × 30 cm

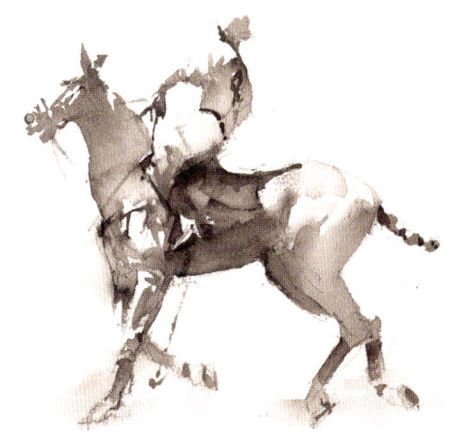

Polo Rider, watercolor, 9" × 11" | 23 × 28 cm

Also, color becomes a pivotal element. A proficient artist should possess the skill to mix any color rapidly, simply by observing the source. While this may sound straightforward, achieving mastery in these abilities requires time, practice, and a deep understanding of the medium.

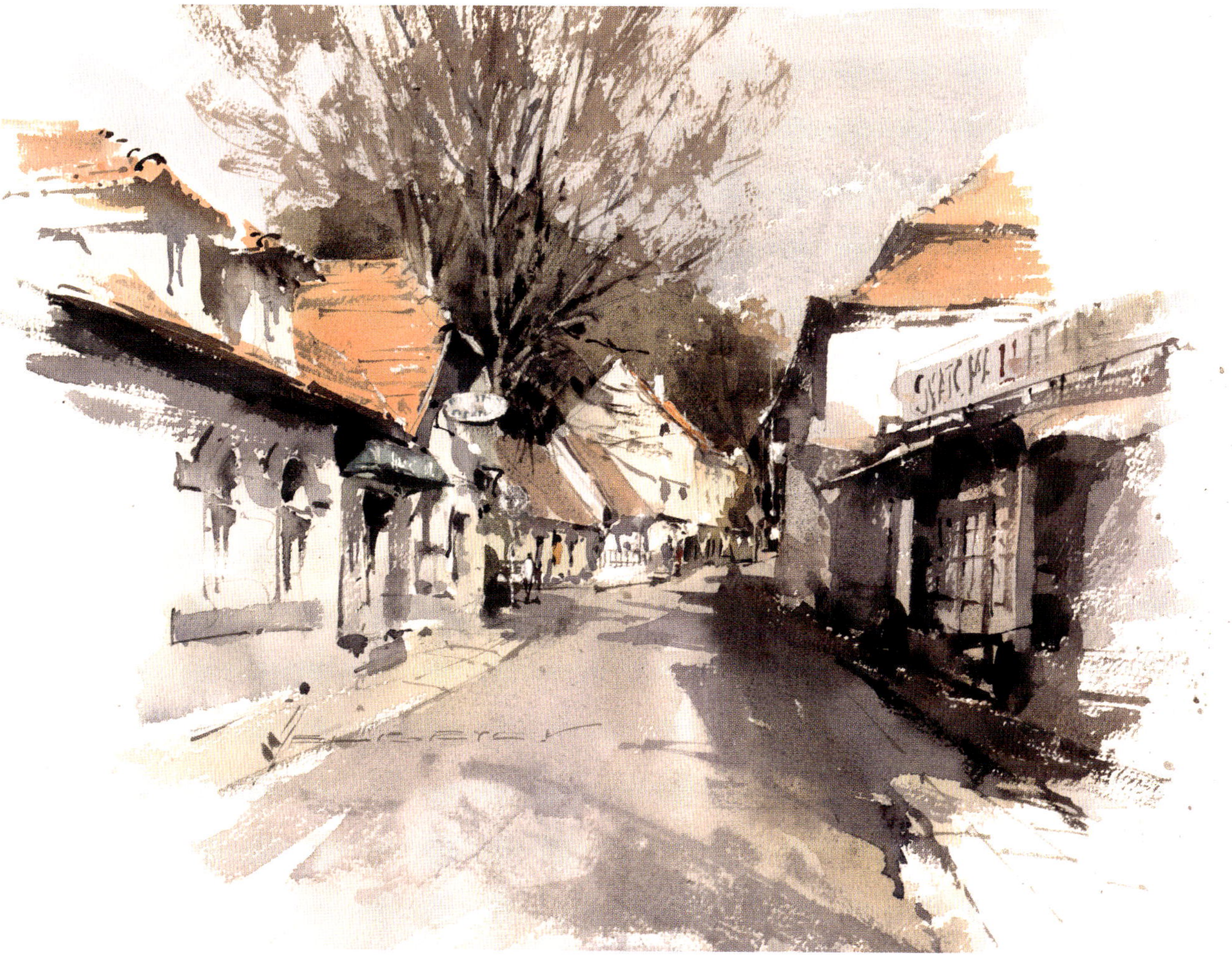

Carlstein, watercolor sketch, 12" × 16" | 31 × 42 cm

STRATEGIC MINDSETS

To navigate through the painting process and maintain a productive flow, I employ a few mindsets that effectively simulate a sense of urgency. One such strategy involves envisioning a tight deadline, as if I have a mere 30 minutes left before submitting the work to a client. This mental scenario compels me to execute the task with expertise within a short timeframe.

The key is to find a method that generates a sense of urgency and keeps the creative process dynamic and focused.

It's crucial to recognize that certain aspects of the artistic process cannot be expedited; they demand meticulous attention. Elements such as the accurate distribution of darks and lights in the painting, the preservation of focal areas, and the maintenance of overall color harmony fall into this category. The question arises: What elements can be shortcut? The answer lies in specific details within the view that beginners often fixate on, such as the number of windows, the intricate details within them, the exact placement of shrubs and trees—details that are seldom precisely situated in reality.

Why are these elements not considered as crucial? Because they contribute little to the character of the place and can be treated as fillers. As discussed later in "Achieving Realism in Watercolor" (p. 58), people often struggle to recall these exact details even moments after passing by them. The truth is, the vast majority of these minutiae hold minimal value for the overall impact of the painting. They are akin to the icing on a cake; easily perceived, yet often mistakenly prioritized by beginners who instinctively focus on the first visually striking elements. However, the true substance of the artwork lies beneath this surface allure, in the deliberate composition, the nuanced play of light and shadow, and the artist's ability to capture the essence and character of the scene.

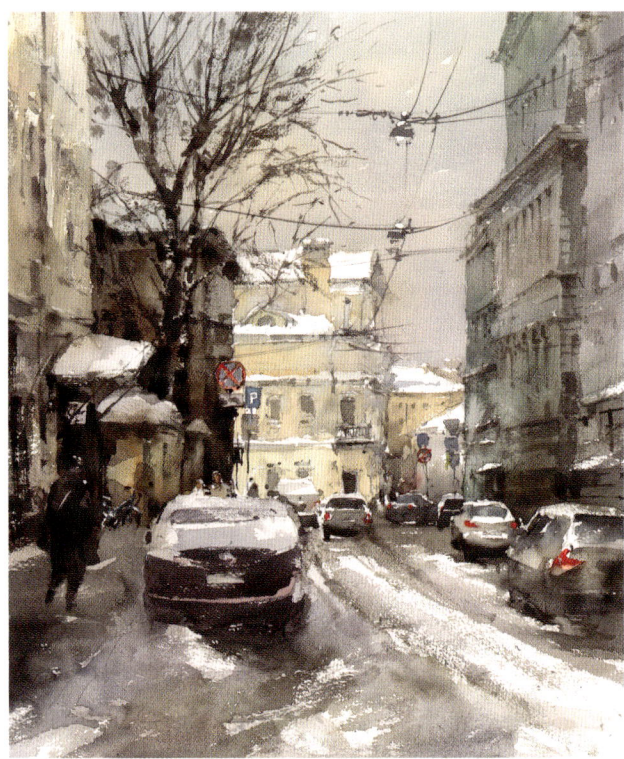

Wintertime, watercolor, 17½" × 15" | 45 × 38 cm

Personally, I mentally note how many people, trees, cars, and so on will complement the future painting, aligning them with the overall composition. This approach compels me to identify and prioritize the most crucial elements of light in the scenery, avoiding unnecessary details surrounding them. By painting only what's essential, progress becomes efficient and rapid.

STRATEGIC PLANNING:
BEFORE YOU PAINT

I've noticed that it's tempting to dive into the painting process without proper planning, particularly when the subject matter is exciting or time is of the essence. At the same time, through my participation in numerous plein air competitions, I've come to realize that a systematic approach from start to finish with rapid execution is essential for achieving meaningful and exceptional results.

The pivotal question often revolves around the choice of format for the painting. After careful consideration, I may initially opt for an obvious horizontal orientation, only to change my mind minutes later because the overall composition would benefit more from a vertical format, and vice versa. This is a crucial aspect, and it's challenging to provide a one-size-fits-all solution. A seemingly logical choice of a horizontal format for a vast landscape may prove inferior to a vertical presentation if it adds more drama compositionally, and vice versa, as in *Tile Roofs* (right).

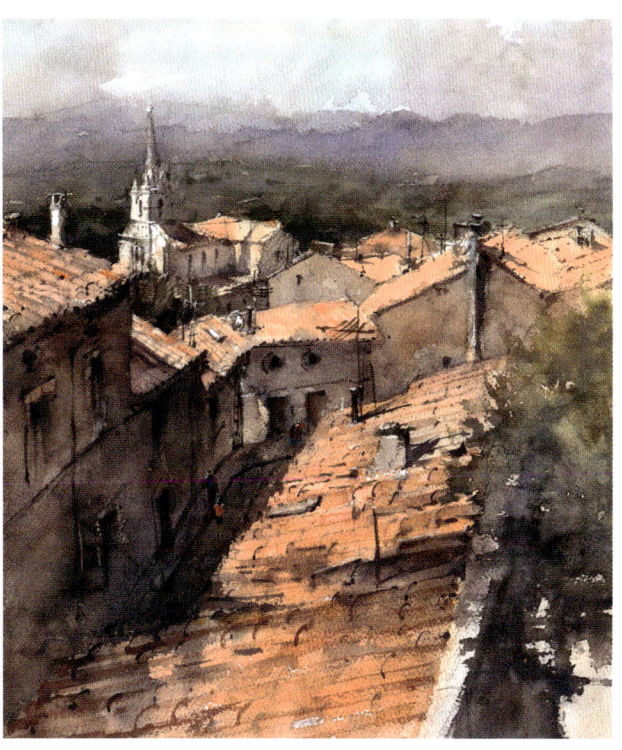

Tile Roofs, watercolor, 16" × 13½" | 39 × 34 cm

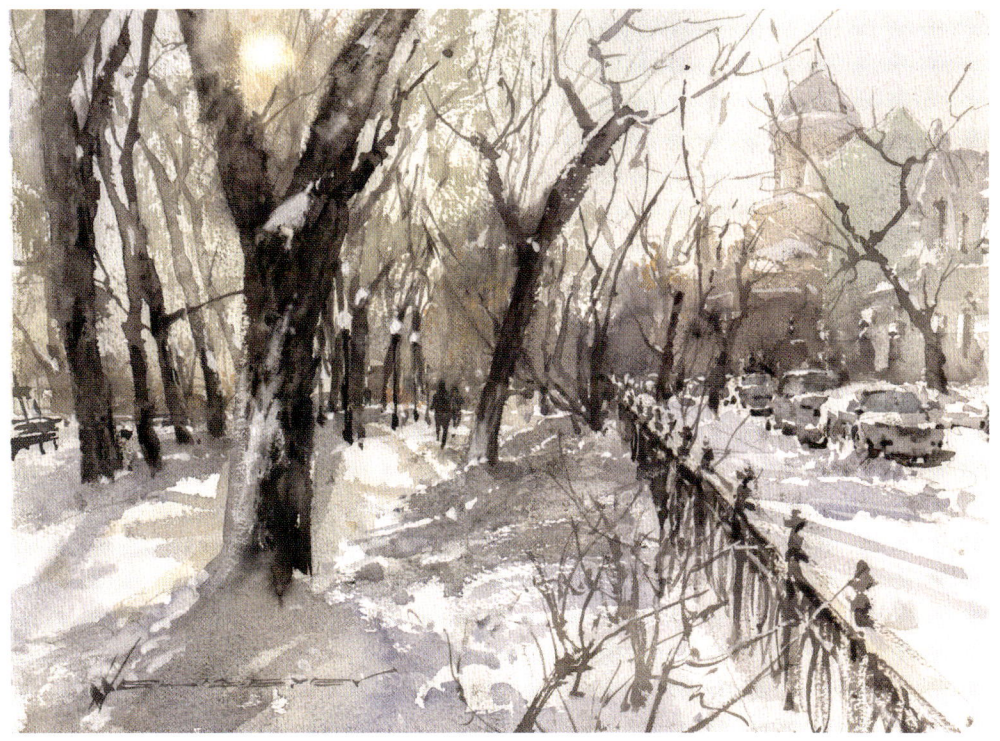

Winter Park, watercolor, 10" × 14½" | 26 × 36 cm

I've learned not to take these obvious decisions for granted and to question everything. Just a few minutes of contemplation can save hours of intensive work, preventing potential waste due to poor composition. I frequently use the camera on my smartphone as a tool to refine the composition even before starting the monochromatic sketch. The snapshots can also be used later, especially if the lighting changes or for making finishing touches in the studio.

Depending on the painting's size, envisioning the necessary level of detail becomes crucial. If that weren't challenging enough, considering the overall style of presentation is equally important. Taking a minute or two to gaze at the blank watercolor paper, mentally visualizing it already painted, can save an enormous amount of time during the actual painting process. This mental preparation provides a general idea that guides the painting in the desired direction.

After the imaginary final look, another critical step is mentally running through all the major painting steps, akin to painting it in one's mind. This brief mental walkthrough helps avoid mistakes that could lead to a loss of control over the painting.

While I've emphasized in my classes that total control looks unfavorable in watercolor, as it diminishes the role of happy accidents, maintaining general control over major steps is imperative.

SEQUENCE OF WASHES

The following steps demonstrate the envisioned general approach of painting everything with warm and light wash, followed by immediate detailing of the main building with cast shadows.

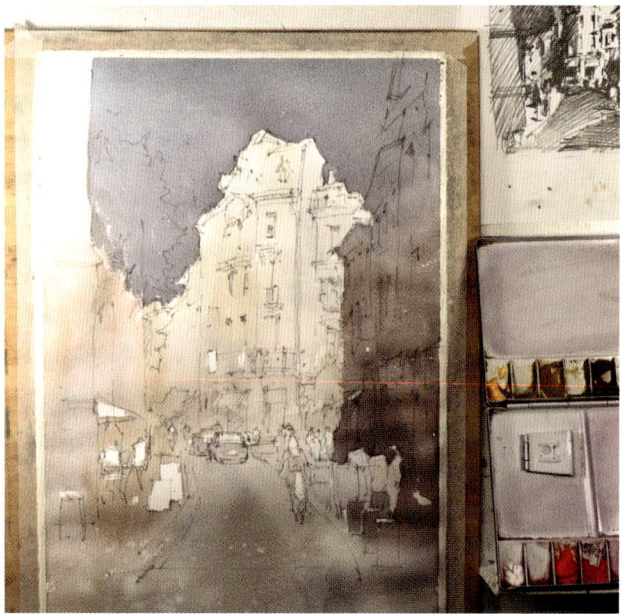

Avignon, first stage.

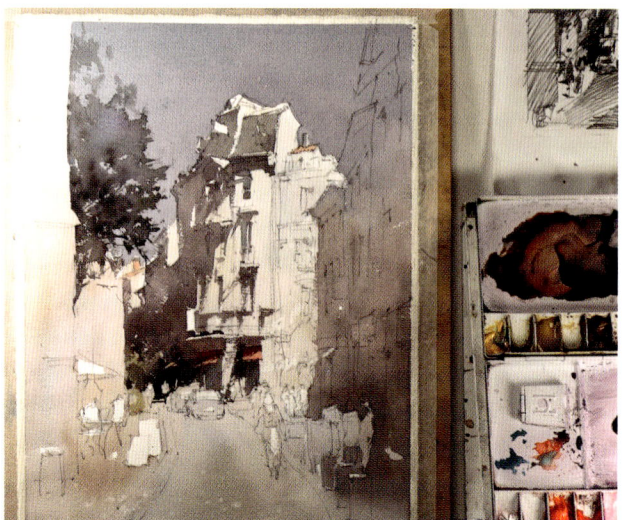

Avignon, dark stage.

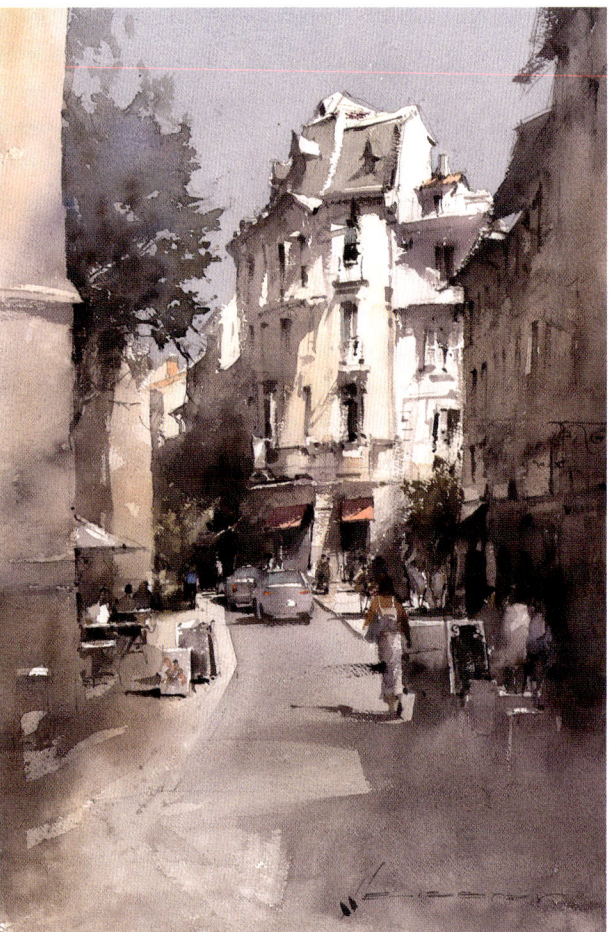

Avignon, watercolor, 22" × 15" | 56 × 37 cm

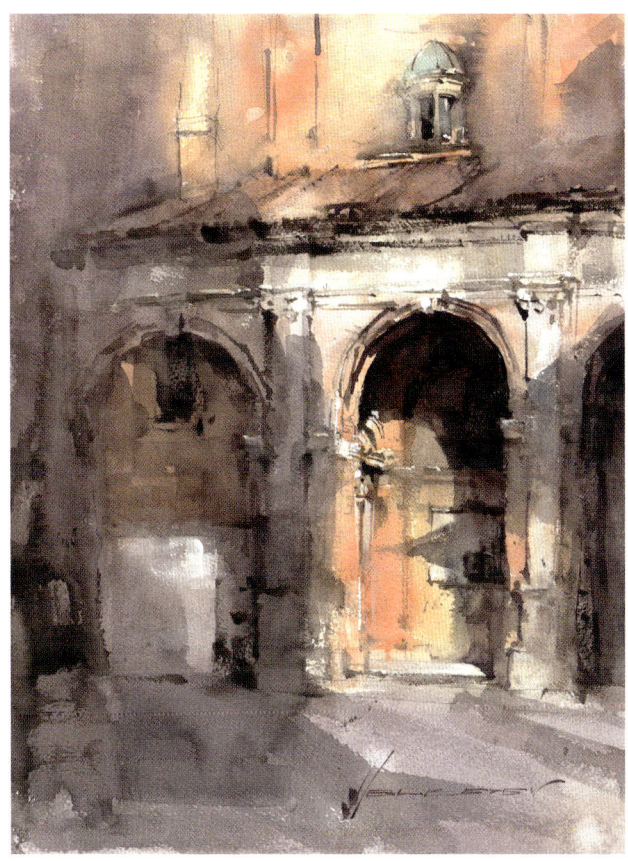

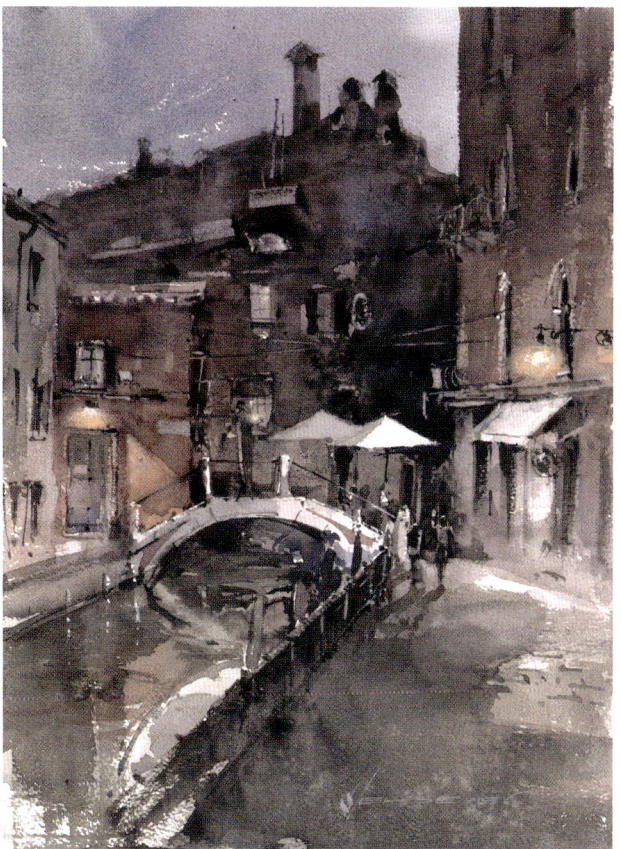

Bologna Arches, watercolor, 16" × 12" | 42 × 31 cm

Night in Venice, watercolor, 16" × 12" | 42 × 31 cm

Another vital aspect during this imagining stage is making a mental note of the general color temperature of the overall presentation—whether it will be warm or cool. If, for instance, I decide on a warm brown and ochre palette, I usually note where smaller cool areas will occur to balance the overall presentation, as in *Bologna Arches* (above left).

An additional area to keep an eye on is the amount of detail in the peripheries of the painting, as it's easy to overdo them with unnecessary detail. For this, I often consult my monochromatic quickly done sketch and stick to the level of detailing there as a reference.

Finally, one of the last but crucial aspects to envision is the overall darkness of the painting: whether it will be a low-key or high-key composition. Low-key paintings often exude a more powerful atmosphere, while high-key paintings tend to convey a more uplifting overall mood. *Night in Venice* (above right) illustrates low-key painting because it's a night view.

ENHANCING THE CHARACTER OF OBJECTS

What sets a painting apart from a photograph is the personal human act of creating each element in the painting, a crucial aspect that's absent in the process of capturing a photo by simply pressing a button on the camera. This distinction holds true for any photo, even those that are staged. In real life, the deliberate deformation of an object solely to enhance a specific element within it is impossible. Digitally manipulated photos don't fit this narrative, as they transition from being photos to becoming digital art.

The exclusive prerogative of having total control over the image belongs to the artist, guiding the creation from inception to completion in one uninterrupted process. This journey begins with the artist's impression of the painting's idea and concludes with the final brushstroke, resulting in a distinctive, painterly form. Consequently, each painting of the same object, executed by a group of artists simultaneously and in the same location, will display dramatic differences.

The decision of how and to what degree to manipulate the objects of depiction or the atmosphere lies with each individual artist. It's important to note that the ability to manipulate presents challenges, as it's easy to overdo the input and lose connection with reality, creating an overly stylized painting. Certain

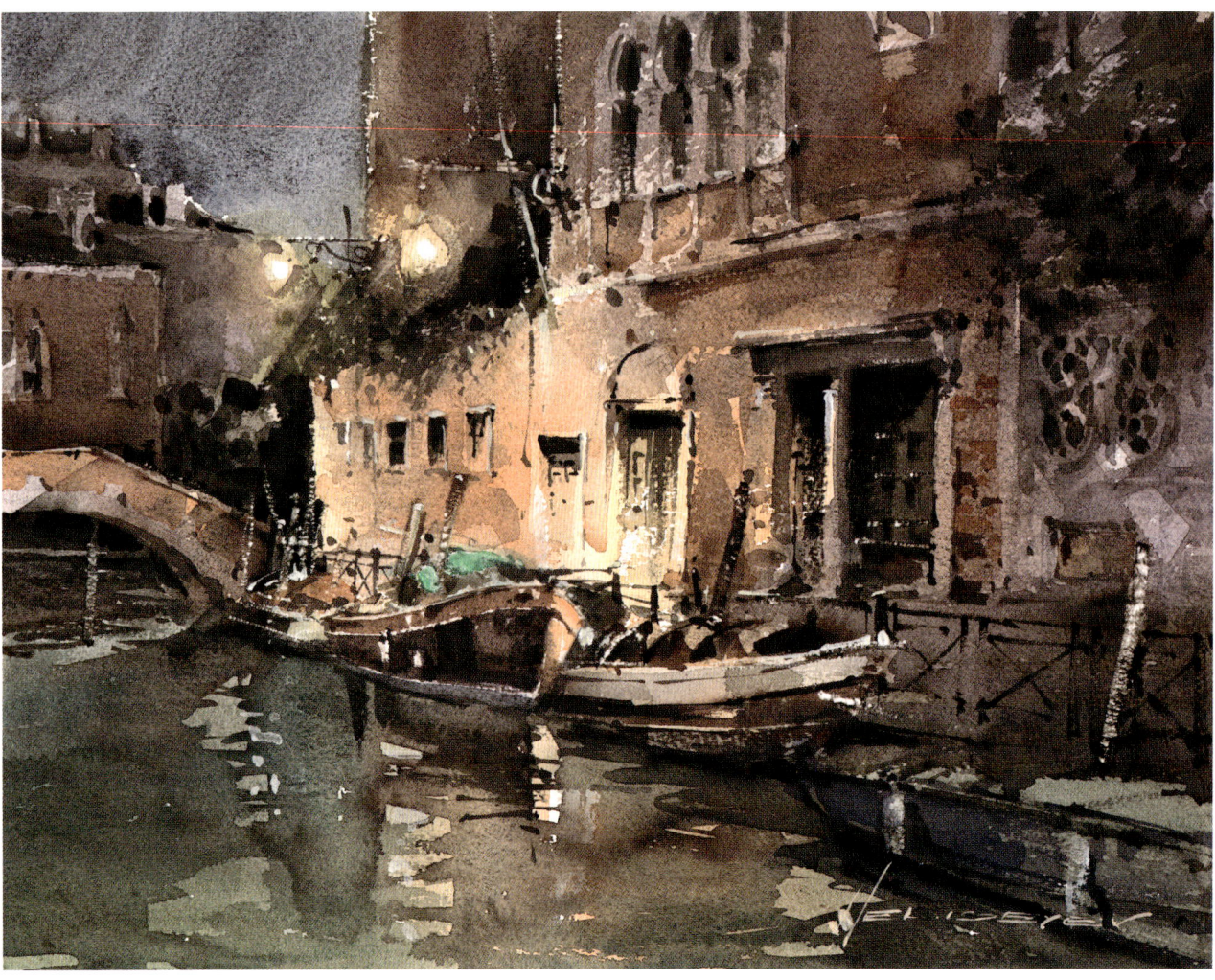

Venice Nights, watercolor, 11" × 14" | 27 × 36 cm

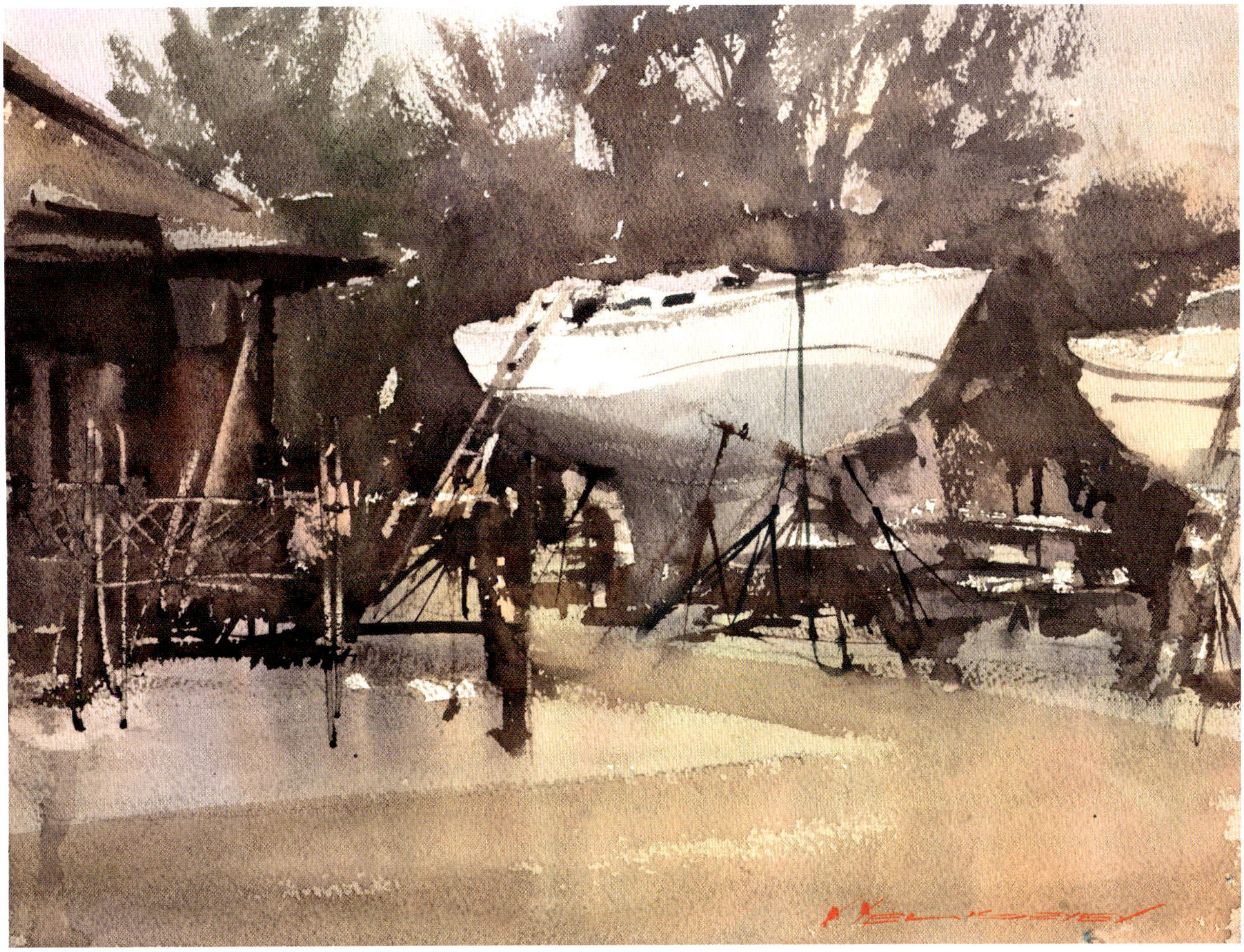

Boat Work, watercolor, 10½" × 14½" | 27 × 37 cm

areas in visual art are dedicated to deliberate deformations, and a separate exploration of this subject might be better suited for another book. Here, the focus is on fine art, which strives to represent the scenery in its unique state at any given moment.

Another crucial point to consider is that character enhancement should align with its intended purpose in the main area of depiction. Exaggerating every element in a complex composition might result in a competition among various elements within the same painting, each vying for attention. This can detract from the main narrative. It's often more effective to leave these elements as they are or, better yet, subtly subdued to merely support the intended story.

In *Boat Work* (above), the stark whiteness of the boat is set in contrast against the dark shack next to it, creating a striking contrast in the perception of these two objects.

Scan to view a
video tutorial

With that said, it's crucial for the painter to attain a subjective understanding of the scenery and emotionally engage with it. Before taking up the pencil or brush, I typically ensure clarity on why I chose to paint the scenery and identify its main character, object, or mood. This might range from a distressed and old surface with intriguing shapes to the mood enhancement of the scenery, encompassing sunny or subdued foggy states, among various possibilities.

Once the artist defines the idea for the future painting, it needs to be enhanced. For example, the aesthetically beautiful shape of the roof being depicted may be amplified to make a stronger statement. The winding country road can be drawn to appear a bit more winding, a moderately crowded city street can be made to look more crowded or intentionally empty, depending on the desired effect.

In *Rain Is Coming* (right), the markedly disparate sizes of the boats create the impression of the immense scale of one of them.

I often point my students to caricaturists, because they possess a unique ability to keenly observe specific features in a portrait or the posture of an object. They can skillfully enhance or dramatize these features to the point where the subject becomes instantly recognizable and well-represented through artistic means. It's important to note that while caricature represents an extreme form of enhancement, most painters don't need to adopt such an exaggerated presentation. Caricature itself is a distinct and specialized form of art.

If the artist lacks the ability to perceive the scenery through the eyes of a caricaturist or finds it challenging to discover anything distinctive about the subject, it likely indicates a lack of emotional involvement with the subject matter. In such cases, it's advisable to either postpone or reconsider the painting altogether.

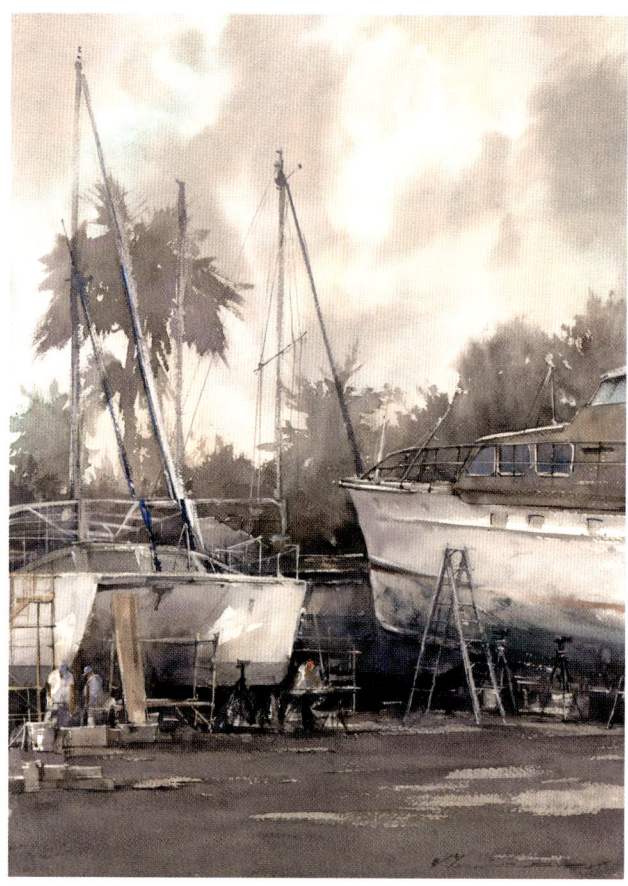

Rain Is Coming, watercolor, 30" × 22" | 54 × 74 cm

I would suggest not to force discoveries when scrutinizing a scene too intently, as they're supposed to reveal themselves clearly and loudly to the artist. Another observation from studying professional works is that each artist tends to be drawn to a specific aspect of the scenery, and one of the most significant aspects is the quality of light. While numerous unique and special objects surround us, it's the light upon these objects that can make or break their appearance.

Personally, I've found that light can dramatically alter the appearance and mood of a scene, prompting me to prefer viewing the subject at different times of the day in various lighting conditions. The works of Rembrandt, in particular, come to mind, showcasing powerful emotional character enhancement through strong side light without the need to depict every minute detail.

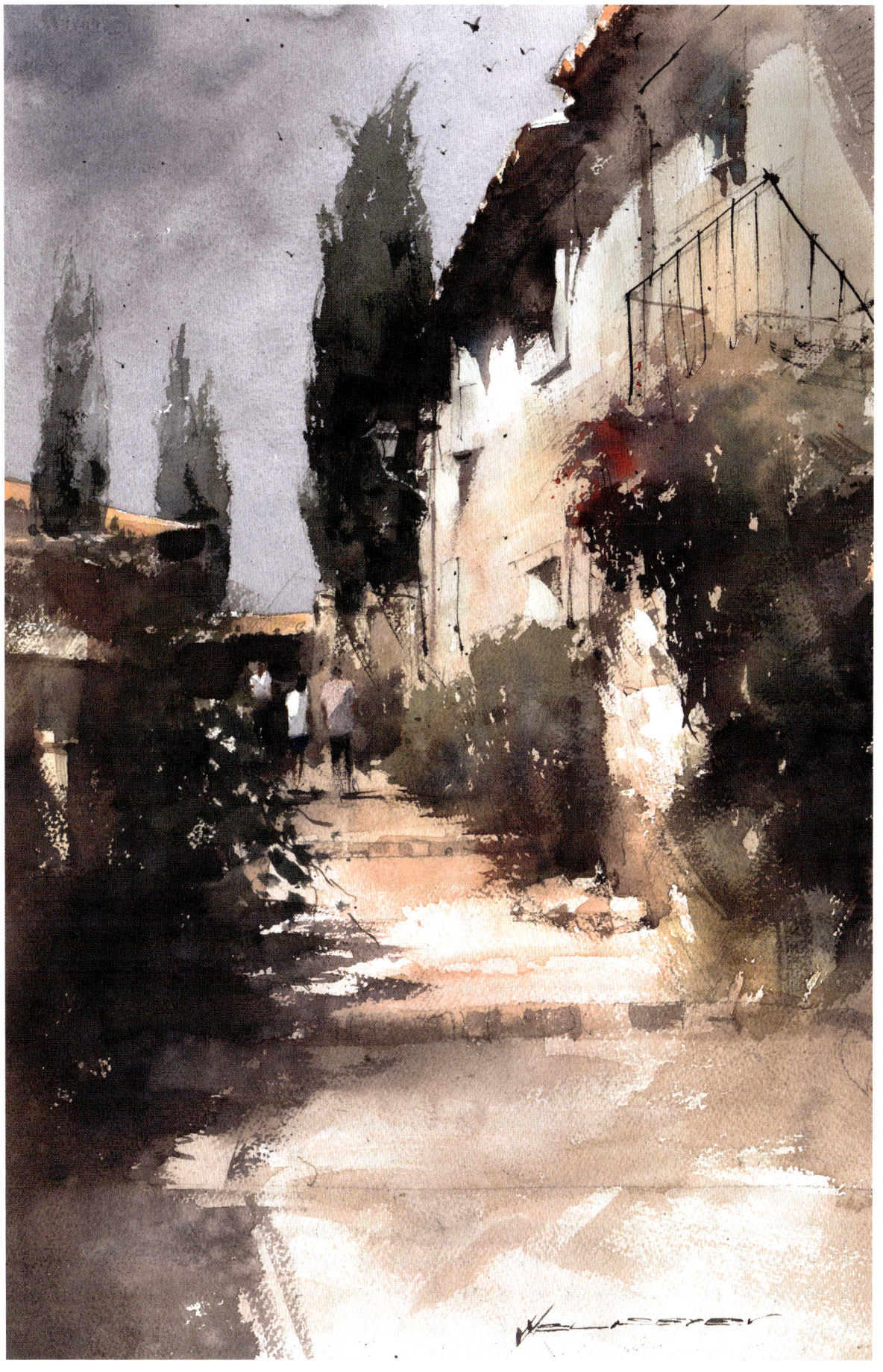

Joucas, watercolor, 22" × 15" | 56 × 37 cm

ACHIEVING REALISM IN WATERCOLOR

When we live our lives in this world, we process visual information in a very specific way. The human mind seems only to take note of information that is relevant at any given time. For instance, when walking in the countryside on the rural road (a common plein air landscape view), one usually cannot recall how many trees were just passed. Yet when we are ready to paint, we start counting everything and anything in order to faithfully reproduce it so it looks true to life. But as just noted, that isn't what we experience in reality. The results of painstaking copying the "real" objects does not reflect what we experience in real life. Maybe that explains the pretty boring and uninvolving nature of camera snapshots that we encounter most of the time. There is one important aspect of the photograph: It is objective, meaning that it's void of any emotional involvement, which is good in detective work but does not offer any insightful benefits to the painter.

Without stating the obvious needless details, the painter might get to capturing them suggestively, which enhances the artistic quality of work.

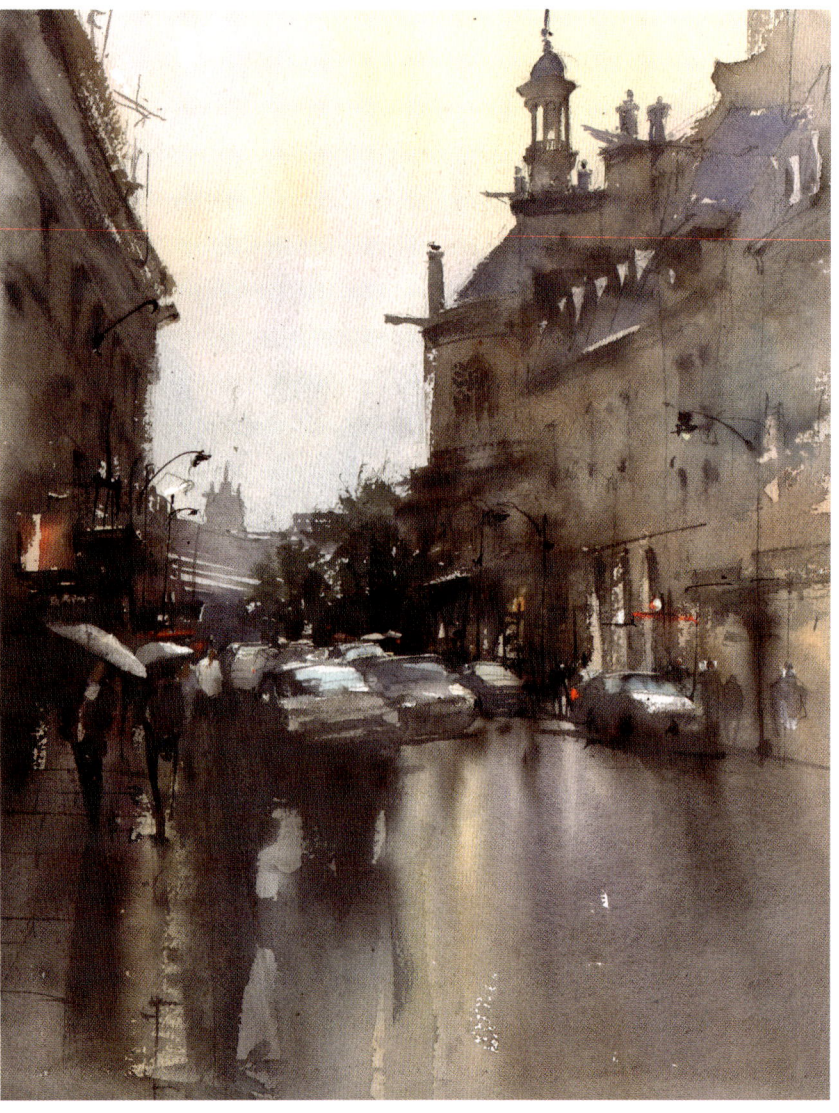

Rainy Paris, watercolor, 19" × 15" | 48 × 38 cm

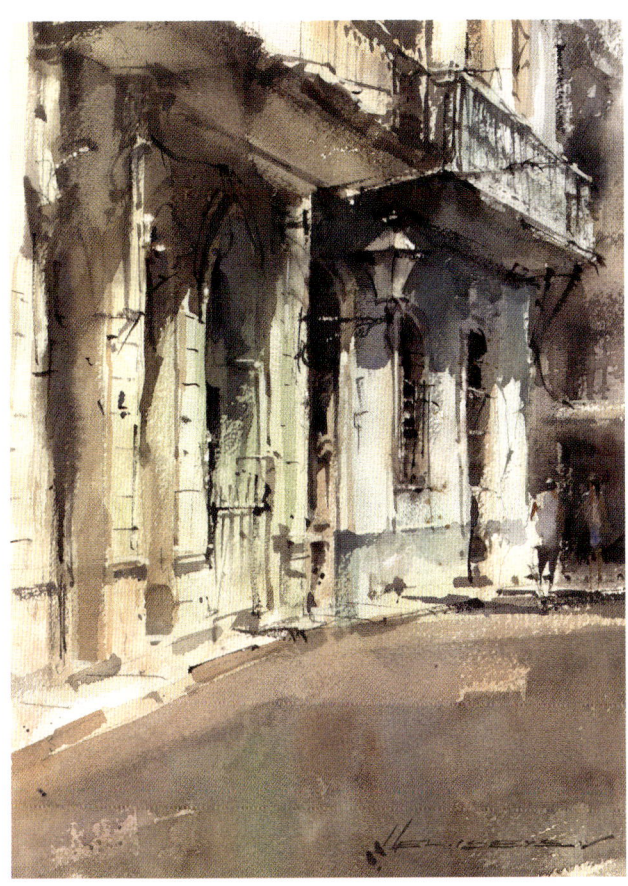

Havana Doors, watercolor, 14½" × 10½" | 36 × 27 cm

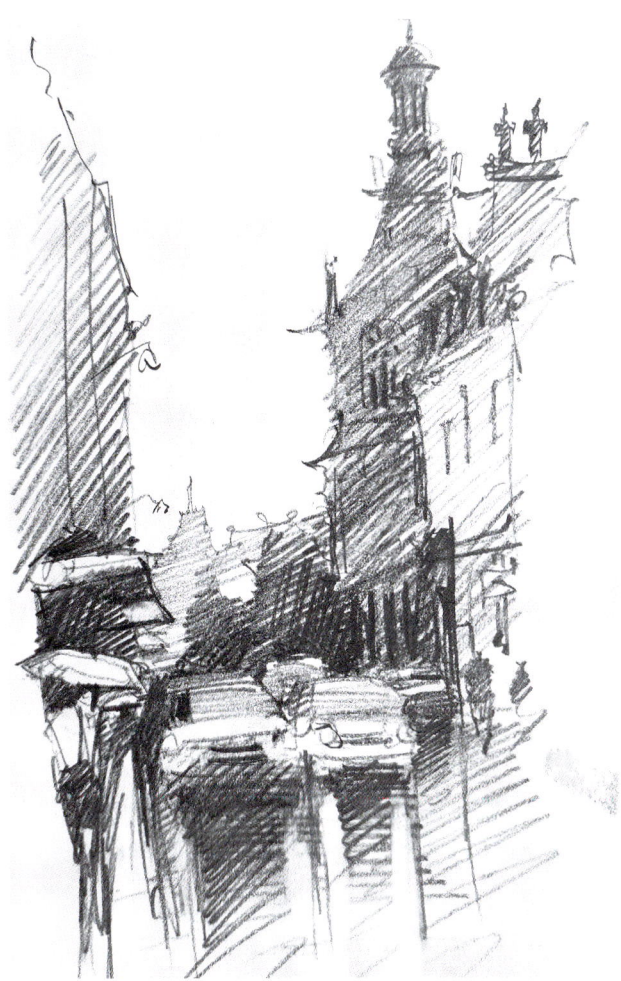

Rainy Paris, graphite sketch, 11" × 7" | 27 × 18 cm

So, in practical terms, it all boils down to reinterpreting the elements of the painting on the subconscious level, reflecting our real-life experience in the place we choose to paint. Maybe that is why loose, painterly, and suggestive paintings have such a very strong impact on viewers? Slightly unfinished in areas of no importance, paintings usually catch the viewer's eye, inviting the viewer to mentally complete those areas, involving them in the act of emotional co-creation with the artist. In practical terms, it all means that the better way of starting painting is to actually get involved with the scenery on an emotional level before picking up the brush.

A first step to capturing fleeting emotions is to create a quick sketch reflecting all of that, and keeping it as a reference in front of me throughout the whole painting process. My outdoor easel setup is equipped with a special shelf devoted to holding the sketch and the palette, so my eye constantly references not only composition and tonal balances but also the mood of the scenery and looseness of presentation.

INFUSING A STORY INTO YOUR ART

When they say, "every picture tells a story," the saying doesn't explicitly mention the type of story.

Now, the question arises: What kind of story should the artist aim to tell before picking up the brush, or is there a need for a story at all? This is a fundamental question when we discuss different genres within the visual arts. To move forward, we need to draw a clear distinction between decorative art and fine art.

Decorative art, by definition, seeks to adorn something. When we admire decor, we're not typically seeking a profound story; rather, we appreciate the pleasing colors, elegant lines, and shapes. The responsibility of a story falls squarely on the shoulders of fine art. Now, we come to the question of what constitutes a meaningful story. If the subject doesn't involve human activity, then what is the story?

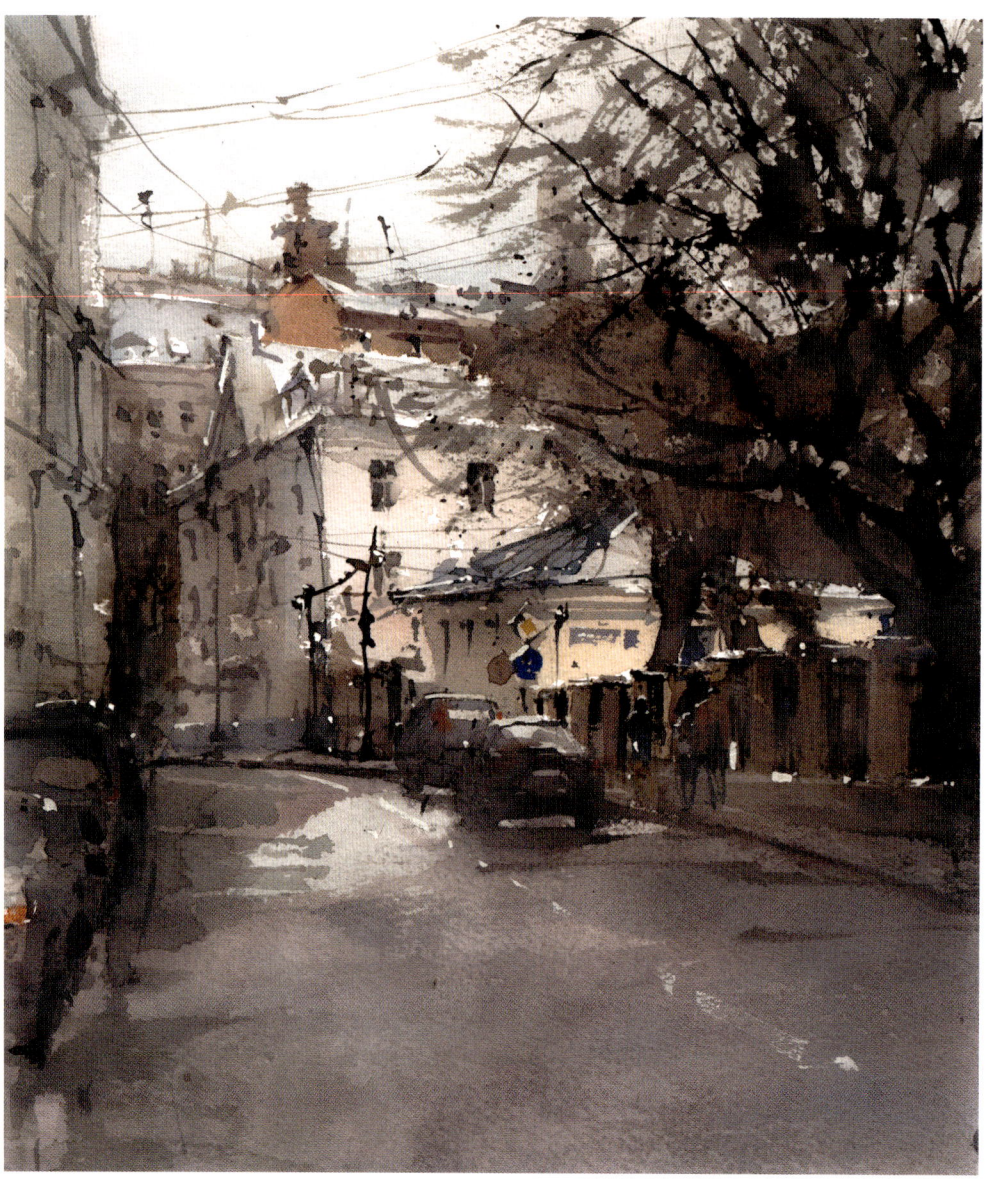

Moscow Street, watercolor, 10" × 9" | 26 × 22 cm

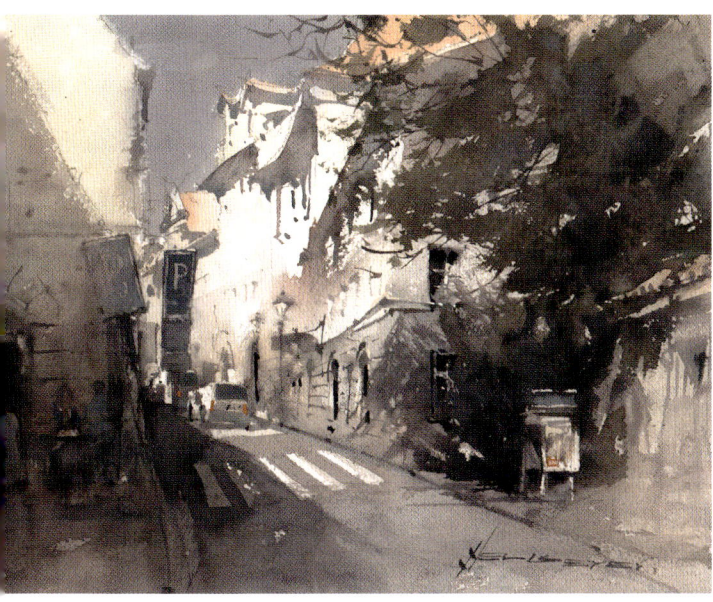

Prague, watercolor, 10" × 14" | 26 × 36 cm

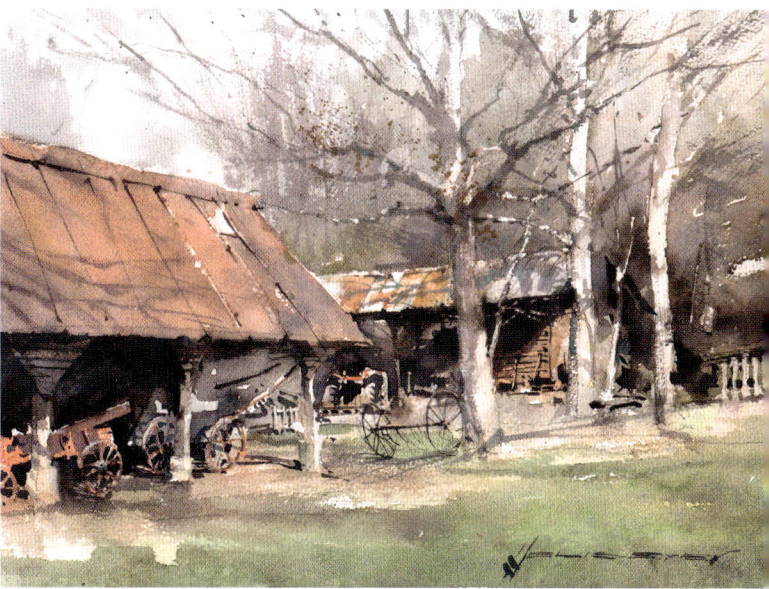

Georgia Spring, watercolor, 10½" × 14" | 26 × 36 cm

In a nutshell, it's a hidden story that uncovers profound insights within the familiar objects that surround us in everyday life. It offers a fresh perspective on the ordinary, a revelation that prompts viewers to contemplate the subjective viewpoint of the painter. This connection between the painting and the viewer initiates a deep conversation on a subconscious level. It's an intimate and deeply personal experience. If a work possesses profound insight, it can reveal different facets of the story to various viewers, evoking unique emotions on a very personal and intimate level.

It could be a foggy morning, a sunny day on a farm, or a freezing, smoky cityscape at dawn. In essence, it can be anything that captures the authentic ambiance of a particular place at a specific moment.

To effectively portray this in a painting, the artist must be able to feel and experience it personally. If the painter or writer lacks a connection, lacks a personal experience, or is unable to philosophically interpret the view, there will be no genuine story, and the output will fall short.

Fake narratives in art like the one showing the rainy day and lonely figure under the red umbrella exemplify the extreme commercialization of art. In fact, it goes beyond decorative art, which has its own merits, and ventures into the realm of clichéd storytelling through mood insinuation. Another pitfall is when storytelling falls victim to over-exploitation of a particular stylistic approach or theme. This could be an unusual play of light repeated over and over, an overused color combination, or a scenic motif that's been run into the ground. It's disheartening to see the same subject matter without a sense of individuality or a multitude of backlit scenes all exuding the same moody ambiance, whether it's farms or towns.

KNOWING WHEN TO STOP PAINTING

It's quite easy to overshoot the painting and risk ruining it by adding unnecessary details that contribute to a labored appearance without enhancing the narrative. In my experience, paintings that are intentionally left slightly unfinished possess a captivating allure. Such artworks extend an invitation to viewers, encouraging them to mentally engage with the piece and contribute to its completion, which was mentioned in the previous chapters. As individuals interpret and emotionally connect with the unfinished areas in the artwork, they unconsciously partake in a process of mental completion, filling in the gaps according to their own understanding and preferences. This collaborative engagement between the viewer and the artist adds a unique and enriching dimension to the creative experience.

At times, artists face the challenge of maintaining continuous awareness of the painting's evolving state, especially as it approaches completion amid the intricate details of nature. Juggling these considerations, it becomes crucial for the artist to maintain a steadfast grasp on the initial intended look of the work and adhere to it until the very end. This process inherently entails a nuanced form of generalization, requiring attention to both macro and micro levels of the artwork's components. This delicate balance ensures that the artist's original vision remains intact, guiding the painting through its intricate details while preserving the overall intended aesthetic.

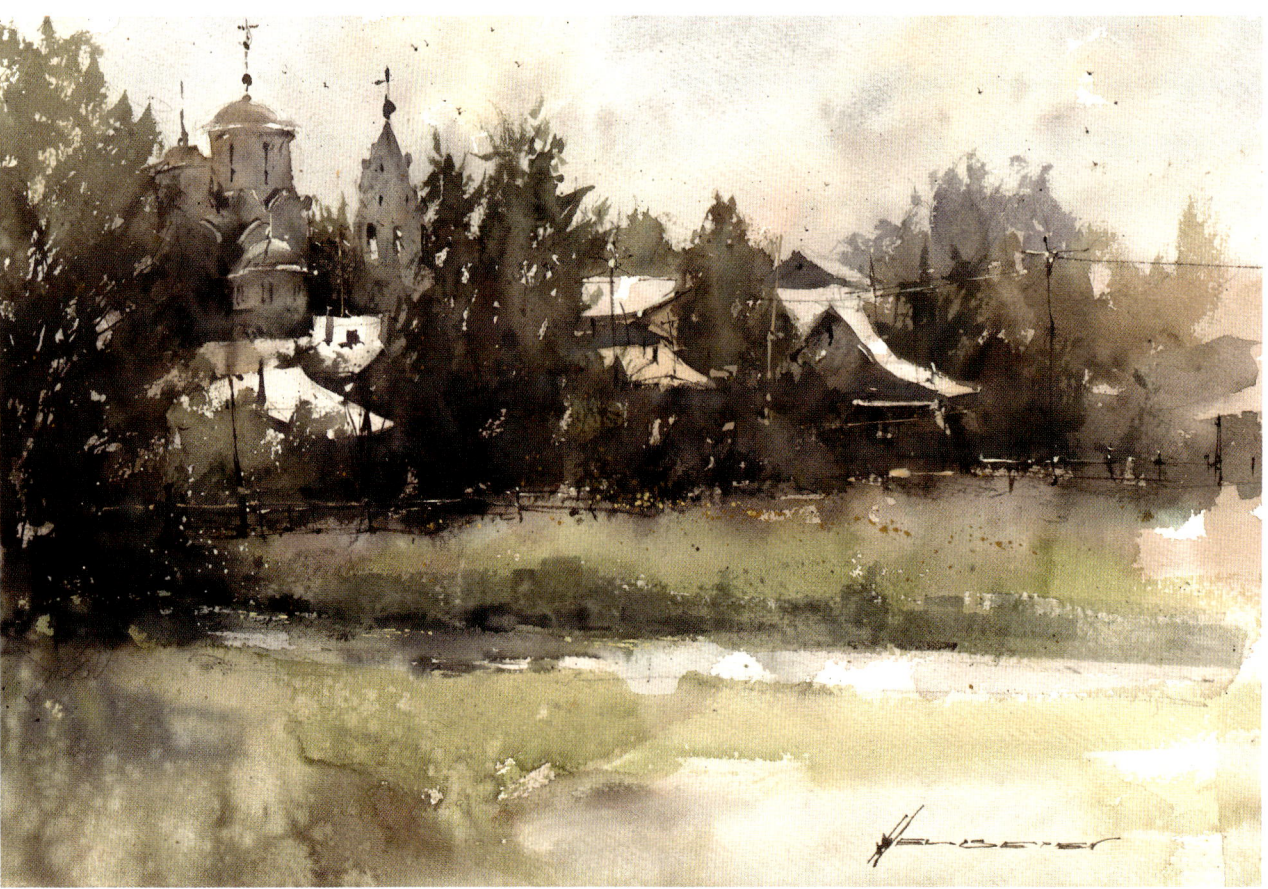

Suzdal Paysage, watercolor, 14" × 21" | 35 × 53 cm

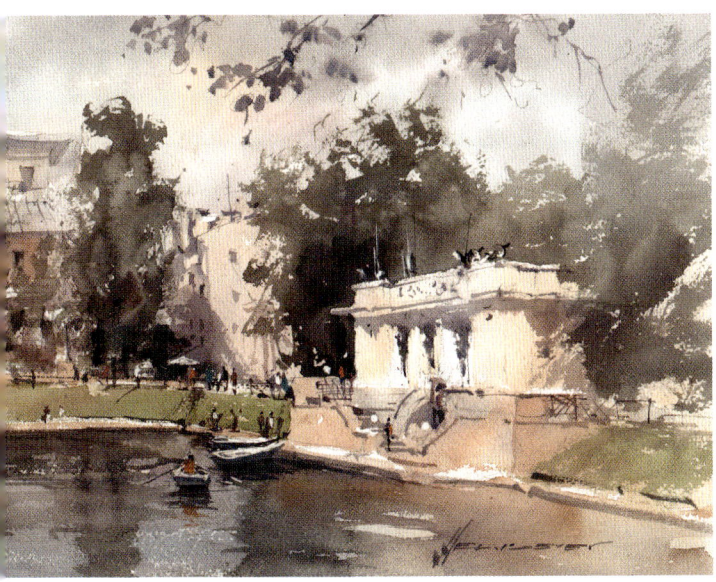

Patriarshiy Lakes, watercolor, 10" × 14" | 26 × 36 cm

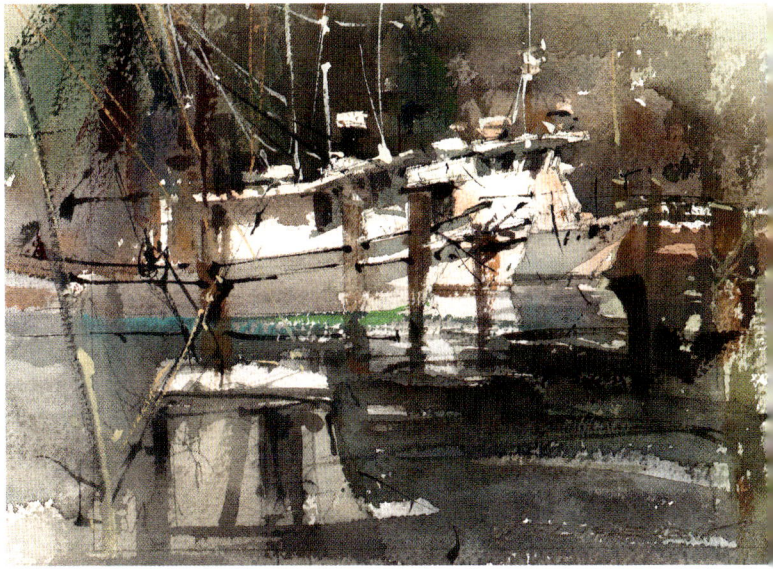

Three Boats, watercolor, 6" × 9" | 16 × 22 cm

A significant challenge often arises in the final stages of the painting process, particularly when artists may find themselves physically and emotionally drained. This can lead to difficulties in maintaining control over the implementation of finishing details, risking overdoing it and slipping into a mode of mindless replication. To mitigate this risk, I make a conscious effort to conclude a session with the painting left ever so slightly unfinished. This allows me to revisit it the next day or, preferably, the next week with a fresh perspective, making overdone or unfinished areas more noticeable.

Furthermore, conducting a rapid study before commencing the final painting often leads to discoveries regarding the optimal level of looseness to maintain. Interestingly, I've noticed that these preliminary sketches occasionally surpass the grand finished work in aesthetic appeal. This superiority may stem from the fact that every aspect of the sketch is approached in a suggestive manner, encompassing even the finishing touches.

Another valuable method I can recommend during the painting process involves engaging with the artwork and brushwork as if it were a quick sketch, regardless of the work's size. Stopping the process when focal areas are well defined, treating everything else as secondary, contributes to a synergistic unity within the entire piece. This approach encourages a dynamic balance, ensuring that the painting retains a sense of purpose while capturing the essence of the artist's vision.

PAINTING FROM PHOTOS: EN PLEIN AIR VS. INDOORS

One very important question often asked is whether it's acceptable to paint from photos in the studio. In my experience, painting en plein air versus in the studio does not differ significantly, except that the studio offers greater comfort and control, whereas painting outdoors provides a broader dynamic range of light (DRL).

Let's begin with a significant inconvenience: the sun's movement during the painting process. This can result in a subject that is completely different in lighting from when you initially started. Using a photograph in the studio completely eliminates this issue. Additionally, studio indoor lighting is well-controlled, providing an evenly and consistently lit workspace. Being in a temperature-controlled studio environment without distractions is crucial, not just for the artist's comfort but also for ensuring even drying times for watercolors. This becomes especially important during the years when an artist is learning the craft of watercolor.

In my studio, I typically employ a large color-calibrated monitor when working with photos to obtain information that is as close to reality as possible. Given the numerous advantages of working indoors, you might wonder why anyone would choose to paint outdoors, dealing with heat, wind, and distractions. The answer is simple: It's all about the dynamic range of light an artist works with outdoors, which is significantly wider. Although I'm not a scientist, it's safe to say that the DRL is perhaps hundreds of times greater outdoors than any photo can offer. DRL represents the extent of light and dark values available in a scene at both ends of the scale. This abundance of information about color and tonal values makes the process of judging and mixing colors much easier outdoors.

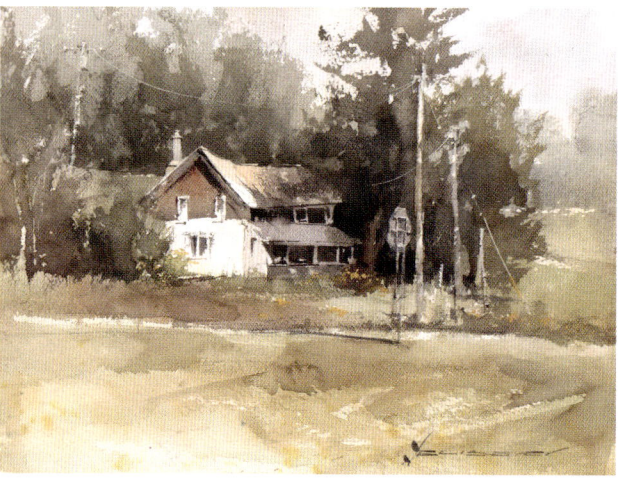

Early Light, watercolor, 11" × 15" | 28 × 38 cm

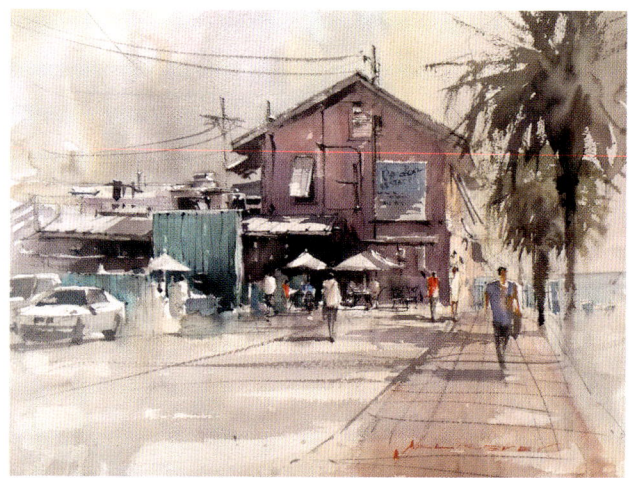

The Breakers Café, watercolor, 11" × 15" | 28 × 38 cm

Plein air work often appears more fluid and immediate. The abundance of color and tonal value information available outdoors speeds up the entire painting process, leaving less room for unnecessary contemplation of details and artificial painting effects. As a result, these paintings typically possess a more immediate appearance and embrace accidental imperfections, which are part of what gives watercolor its distinctive character.

Another aspect of working en plein air is that the artist deals with three-dimensional subject matter. Translating this information onto watercolor paper necessitates a process of improvisation and reinterpretation. Working with two-dimensional photographs primarily involves copying, which can diminish reinterpretation and force the artist into a copying mode, thereby robbing the artwork of its individuality and the true impression of the place as experienced in real life. This results in artwork that can sometimes resemble craft or illustration, rather than fine art.

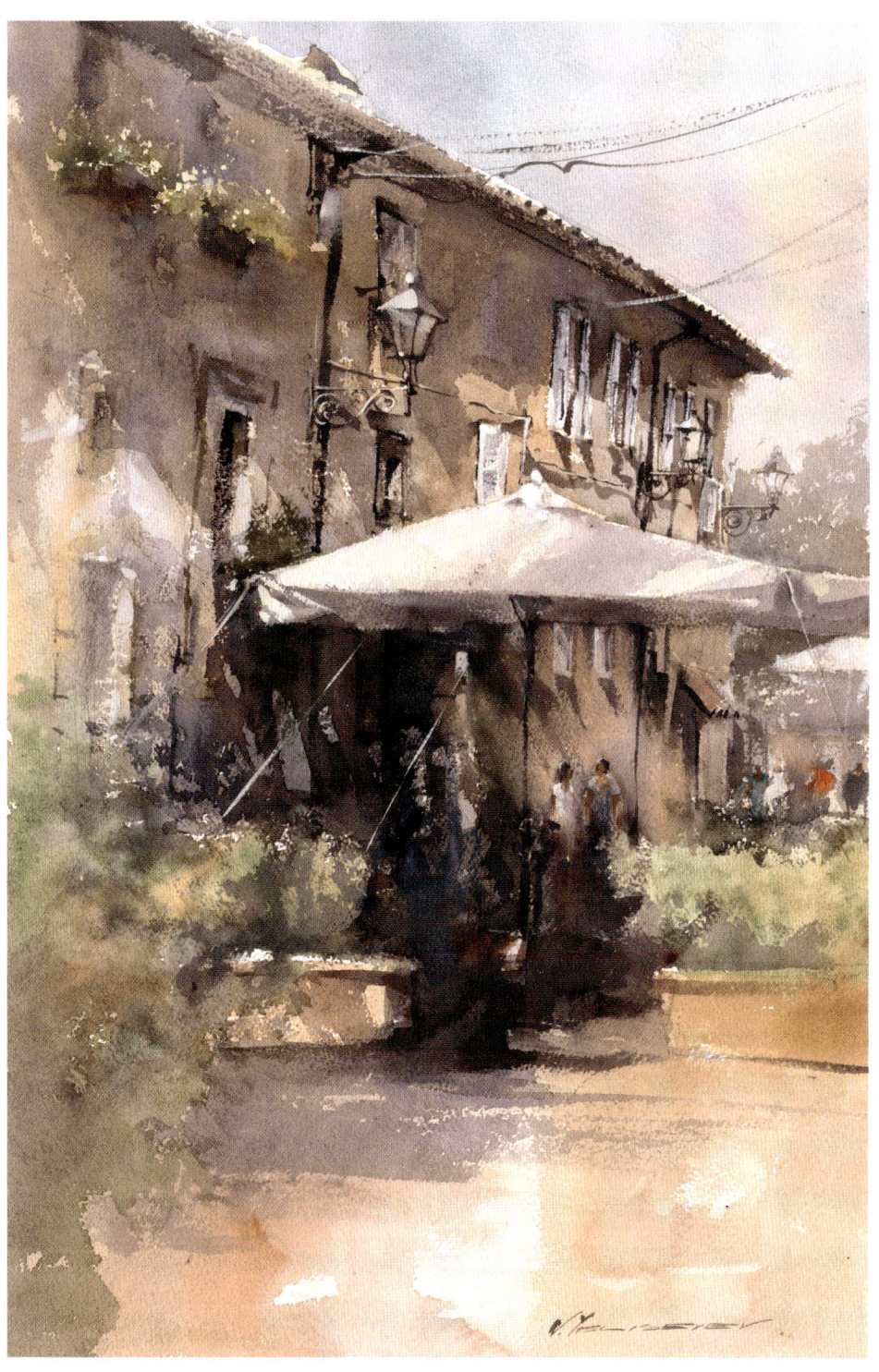

Orvieto Market, watercolor, 21½" × 14½" | 55 × 37 cm

THE IMPORTANCE OF DAILY PRACTICE

Another query I hear from my students: "Do I have to paint every day?"

The key takeaway is that there's no one-size-fits-all answer. While daily painting may not always lead to noticeable progress, taking breaks doesn't necessarily hinder improvement. Each artist's journey is unique, and the balance between consistent practice and periodic breaks varies from person to person. The important thing is to remain mindful of the enjoyment and fulfillment derived from the act of painting itself.

Given that, I've concluded that for artists in the learning stage, painting every single day can be highly beneficial. The accumulation of daily experiences contributes to meaningful progress, provided there's a crucial condition: each day's painting study must be dedicated to a task that is just beyond the artist's current skill level. To optimize this process, consulting with a knowledgeable individual, be it a teacher, instructor, or experienced peer, is essential. Further insights into the learning process can be explored in Mr. Lev Vygotsky's zone of proximal development (ZPD) and instructional scaffolding.

In my experience, working on one specific task should continue for several days until the painter feels comfortable executing it consistently throughout the process. Simply painting every day without a focused and deliberate approach will yield negligible results.

Despite not having a daily painting session planned in my routine, I've observed that when I'm focused on refining my skills or working on something of interest, I naturally end up painting every day. The key is not just about executing the task but reaching a point where implementing it becomes second nature.

This approach holds the potential for everyone to achieve incredible results. Students should be open to new ideas and avoid sticking to old habits, especially those acquired during workshops that may teach nothing beyond the instructor's style of painting. It's crucial to start with fundamental

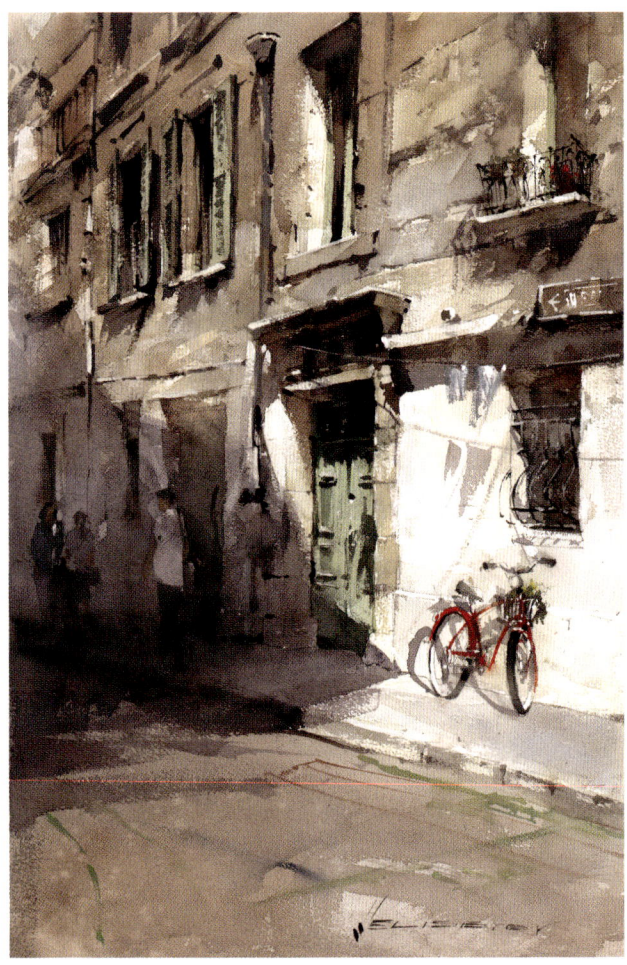

Avignon Street, watercolor, 21½" × 14½" | 55 × 37 cm

tasks and gradually progress to more complex ones, acknowledging that the journey of improvement has no definitive endpoint.

The issue of talent is undeniable—it exists, and we often encounter individuals who excel in various aspects of life, whether it's art, music, science, or sports. When observing the outcomes of their activities, everything appears effortless and easy. Under equal conditions, these talented individuals suddenly surpass everyone else, and the mysterious nature of this phenomenon remains unknown.

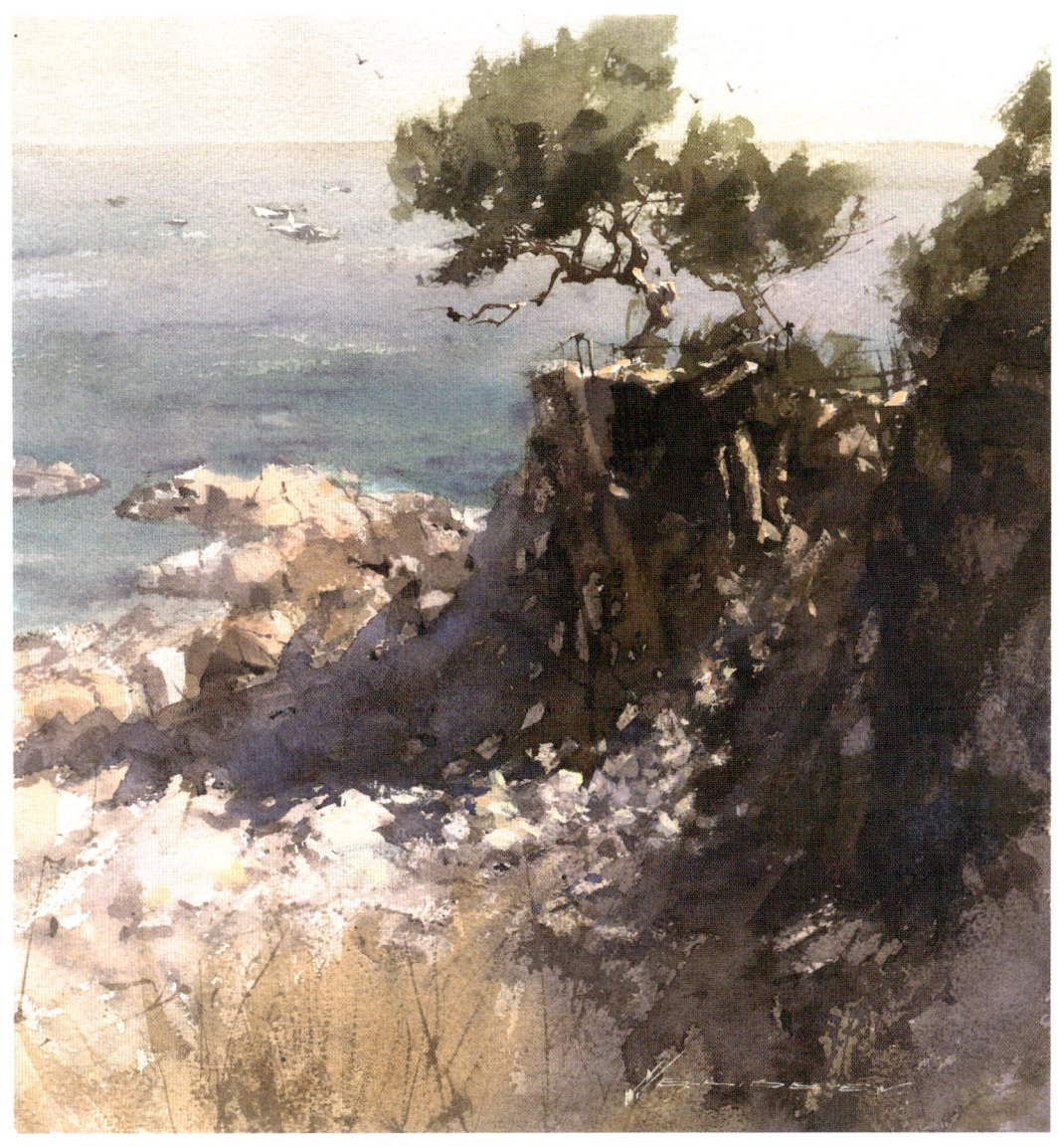

Stones of Palafrugell, watercolor, 15" × 14" | 38 × 36 cm

Providing advice to such naturally gifted individuals to paint every day may be counterproductive, as the dynamics of their talent are not fully understood. However, I firmly believe that if they engage in focused work on specific tasks, their progress will likely be accelerated.

Let's acknowledge the reality that mastering the art of painting is no easy feat, and simply dedicating time to the craft is not sufficient. I advocate for a systematic, step-by-step approach to learning, progressing from simple to more complex tasks. With well-structured tasks and consistent painting sessions, artists of any level will undoubtedly experience significant benefits.

The specter of burnout looms in the realm of excessive painting, a daunting legend that I have yet to confront personally. At times, I've sensed a forced quality in my work, a waning interest in the process. I firmly believe that persisting under such conditions may lead to burnout. The symptoms would likely manifest in the form of flat, low-quality pieces, resembling the output of a mechanical process rather than the skilled hands of an experienced painter.

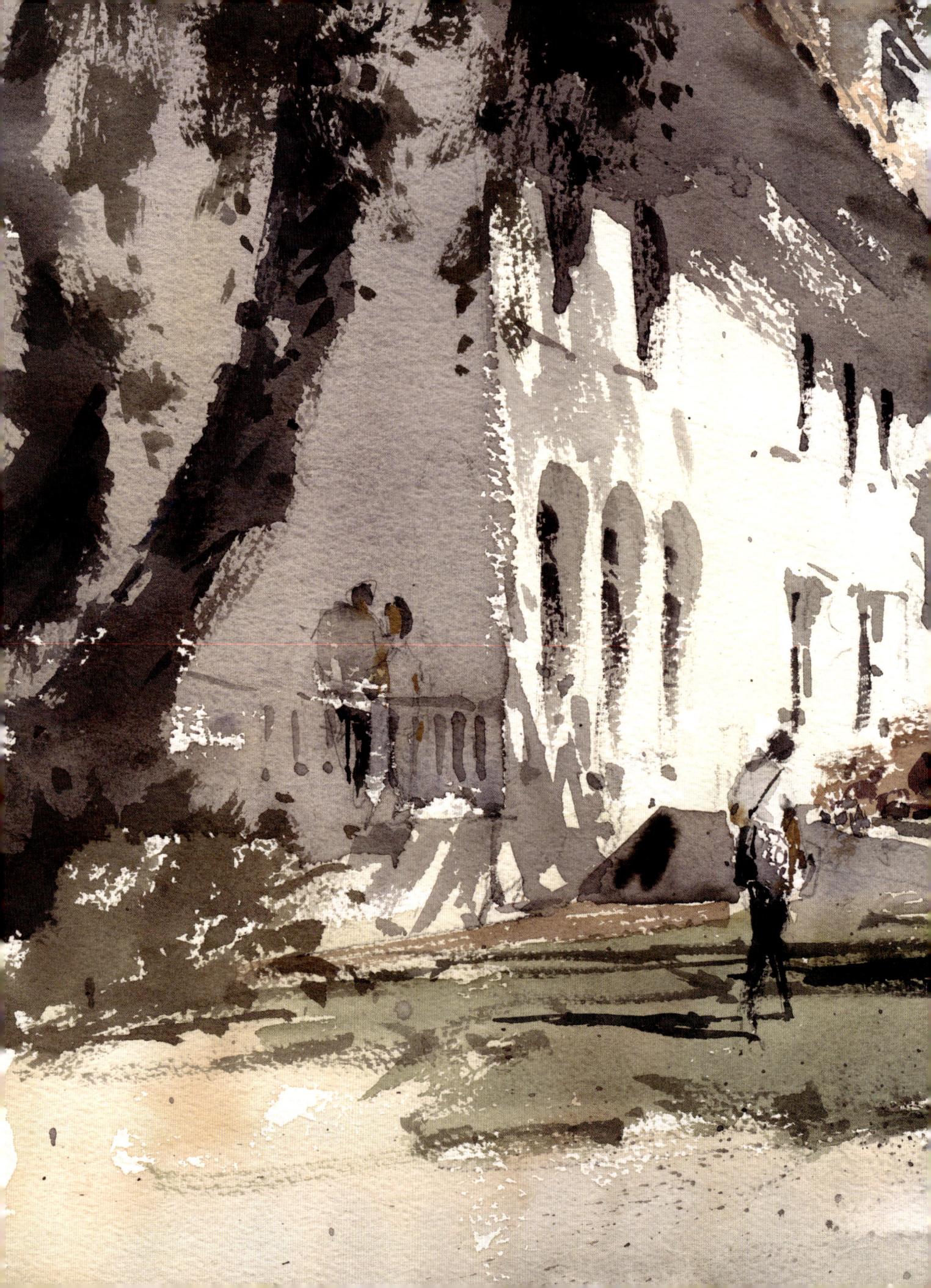

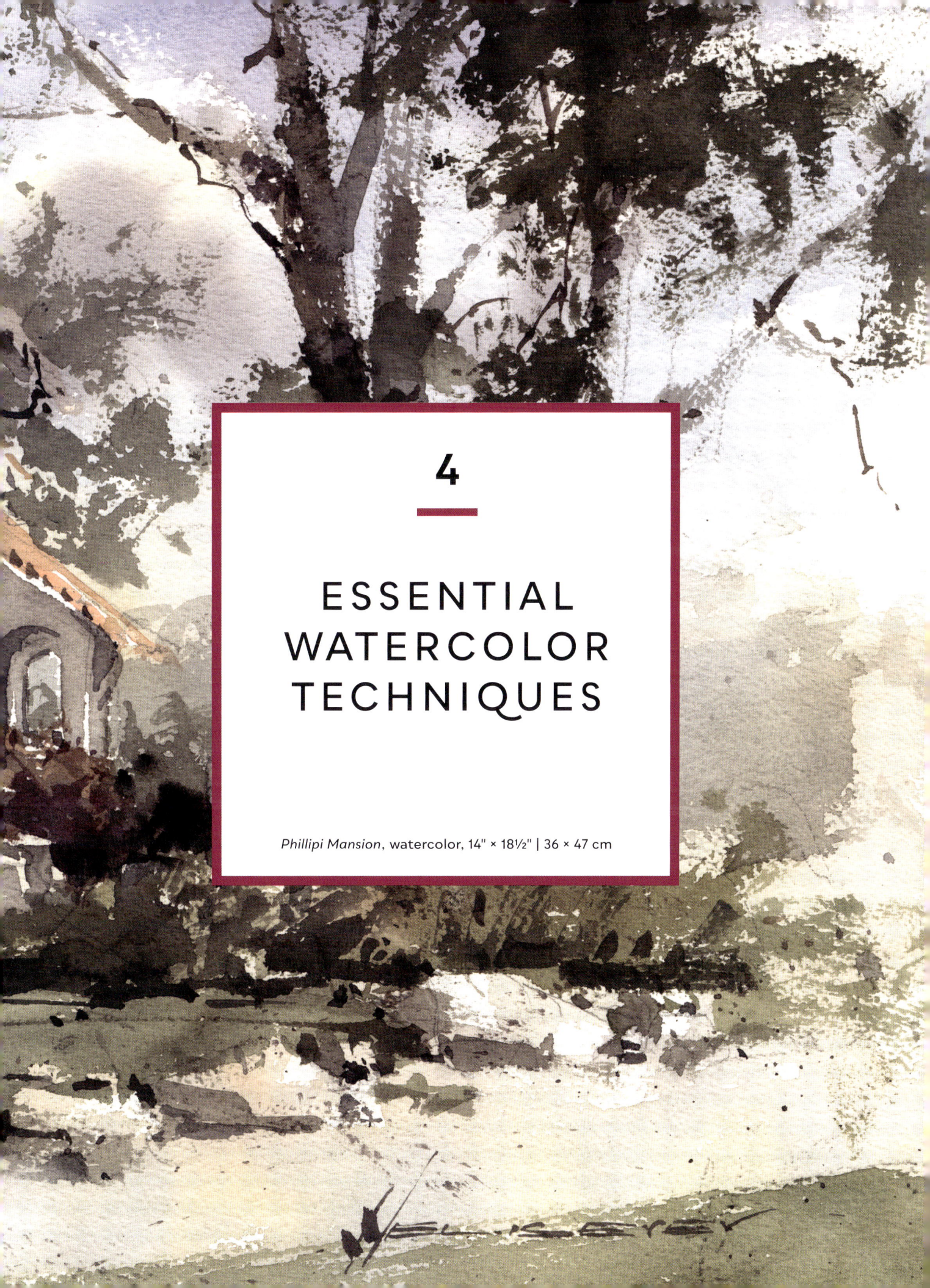

4

ESSENTIAL
WATERCOLOR
TECHNIQUES

Phillipi Mansion, watercolor, 14" × 18½" | 36 × 47 cm

LAYERING VS. WET-ON-WET TECHNIQUES

Various application methods are available when painting with watercolor, each tailored to the specific characteristics of the medium. One common and relatively straightforward technique is the layering method, where darker tones are achieved by applying multiple washes over dried layers. The number of layers can vary depending on the desired depth of color and tone.

Typically, the first layer covers the entire surface of the watercolor paper, focusing on the lighter areas. Subsequent layers are then used to build up midtones and cast shadows.

This technique requires patience, as each layer must be allowed to dry completely before applying the next. However, it offers the artist a high level of control over the entire painting. With careful planning, it can be easier to execute than the wet-on-wet method, allowing for more precise progress according to the artist's vision.

The wet-on-wet method of watercolor application presents a greater challenge, as it yields more unpredictable results compared to the layering technique. In this method, watercolor is applied onto a wet surface without waiting for the previous wash to dry. Mastery of this technique demands extensive practice, particularly in controlling the timing of paint application.

However, despite its difficulties, the wet-on-wet method offers distinct advantages. When executed expertly, it imparts a fresher and more natural appearance to the final result, aligning closely with the inherent qualities of the medium.

I often find it advantageous to combine both the layering and wet-on-wet methods in my paintings, leveraging the strengths of each to achieve nuanced effects. This approach allows me to add different color mixes to already painted areas without waiting for them to dry, enabling precise manipulation of isolated areas or adjustments to the overall color temperature.

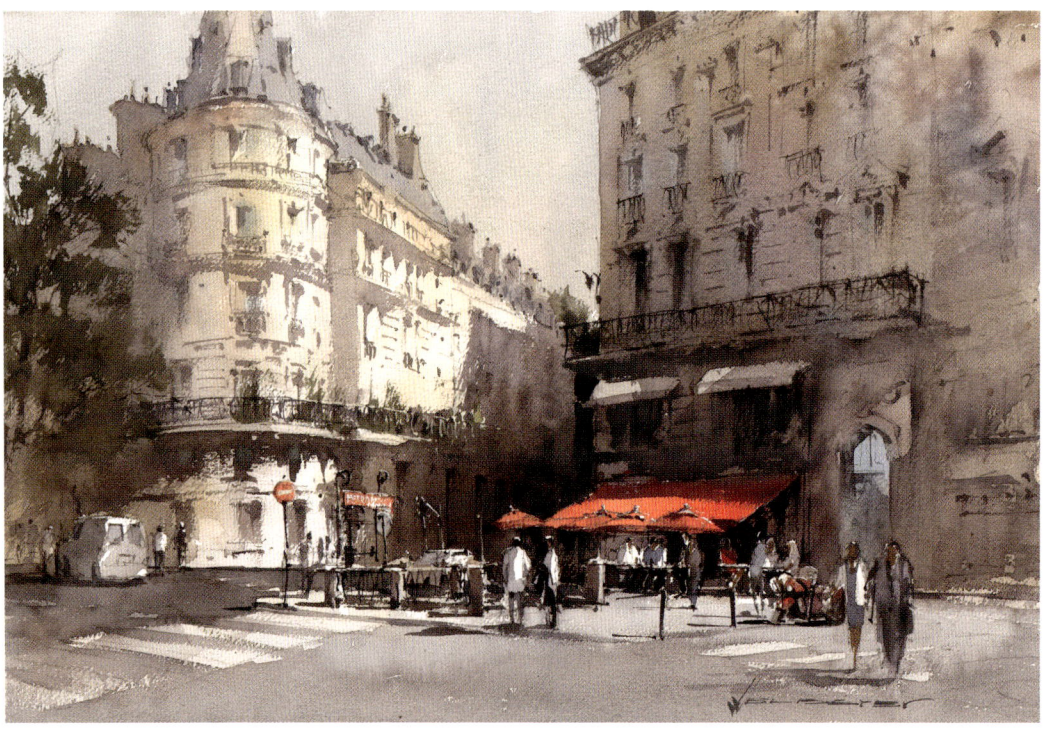

Paris Café, watercolor, 15" × 22" | 56 × 37 cm

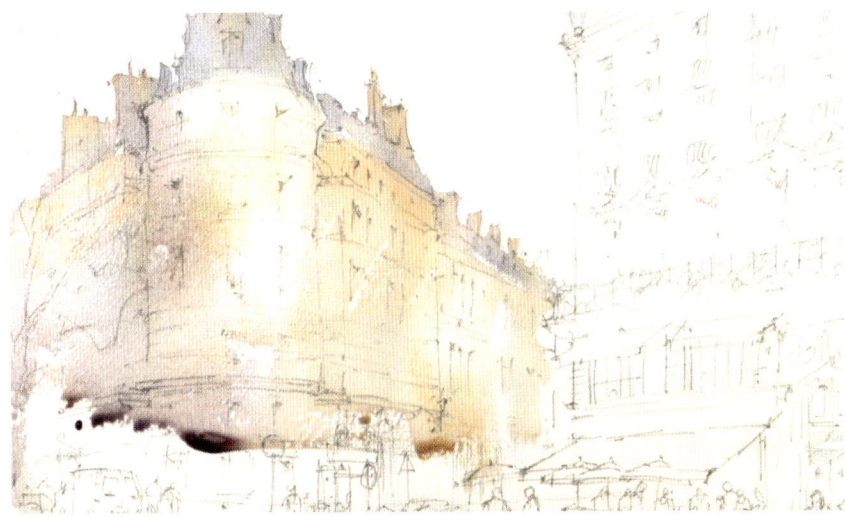

Paris Café, first layer: wash.

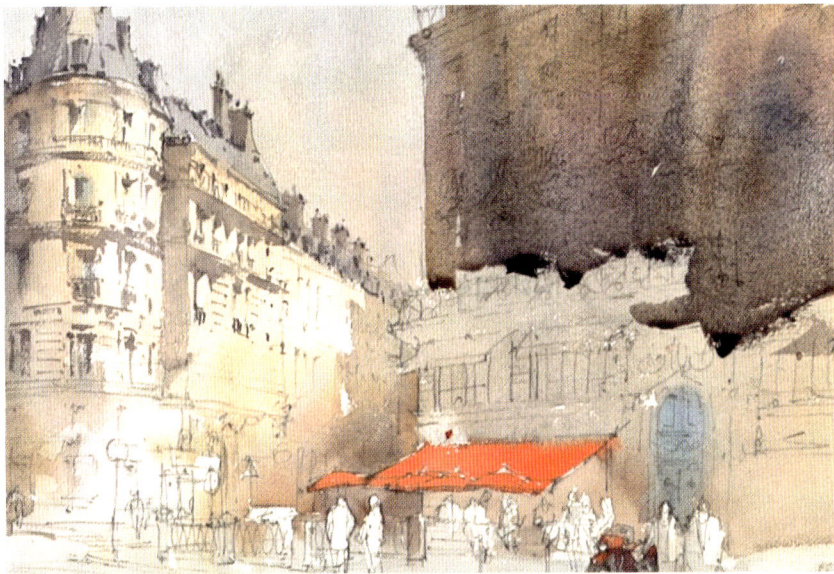

Paris Café, second layer: wash.

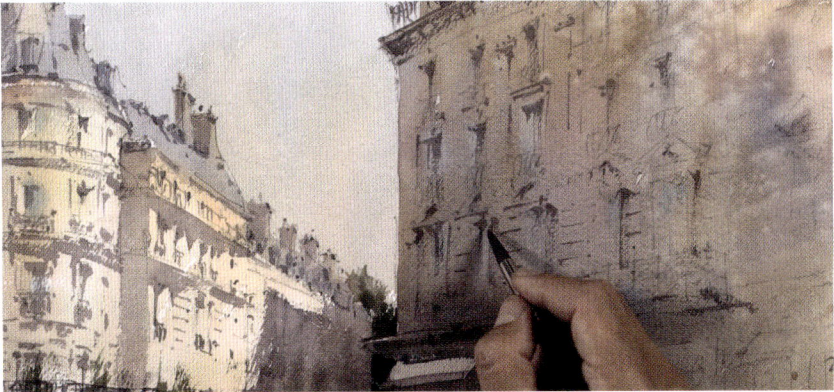

Paris Café, third layer: paint.

In reality, surfaces rarely exhibit uniform color and tone, making watercolor an ideal medium for expressing these subtle gradations with minimal effort. This technique is particularly effective when applied while the surface is still wet, as it facilitates seamless blending and transitions.

To mitigate the risk of premature drying, especially when painting outdoors where humidity levels can vary, I prefer to prepare my color mixes on the palette before beginning the watercolor application. This ensures that I can work efficiently and maintain control over the painting process.

Scan to view a video tutorial

ENVISIONING THE OUTCOME

In every painting scenario, it's essential for each artist to envision the desired outcome and determine which watercolor application method best suits the character of the scene they aim to portray.

For instance, when capturing the weathered charm of an old town streetscape with distressed walls, the wet-on-wet technique may pose challenges in depicting these textures. In such cases, employing a combination of layering and drybrush techniques can be more effective in conveying the desired effect, allowing for greater control over the depiction of surface details and aging.

At the same time, when painting expansive vistas with vast open spaces and deep perspective, the wet-on-wet technique is often the preferred choice. The same applies to paintings depicting rainy days or foggy mornings.

Ultimately, the choice of technique depends on the artistic vision and the specific characteristics of the subject matter being depicted. Experimentation and familiarity with different methods will empower artists to select the most suitable approach for each painting, allowing them to effectively capture the essence and mood of their chosen scenery.

I am often asked about wetting the watercolor paper before applying paint, but I have found that this technique does not benefit my painting style. Instead, I prefer to wet the paper with some pigment already added before proceeding with darker areas.

One of the most challenging aspects of painting with watercolor is the significant change in color intensity and tone value after drying. Wetting the paper beforehand can exacerbate this uncertainty, potentially necessitating additional layers of paint toward the end of the painting process. However, adding too many layers can compromise the transparency and vibrancy of the final watercolor.

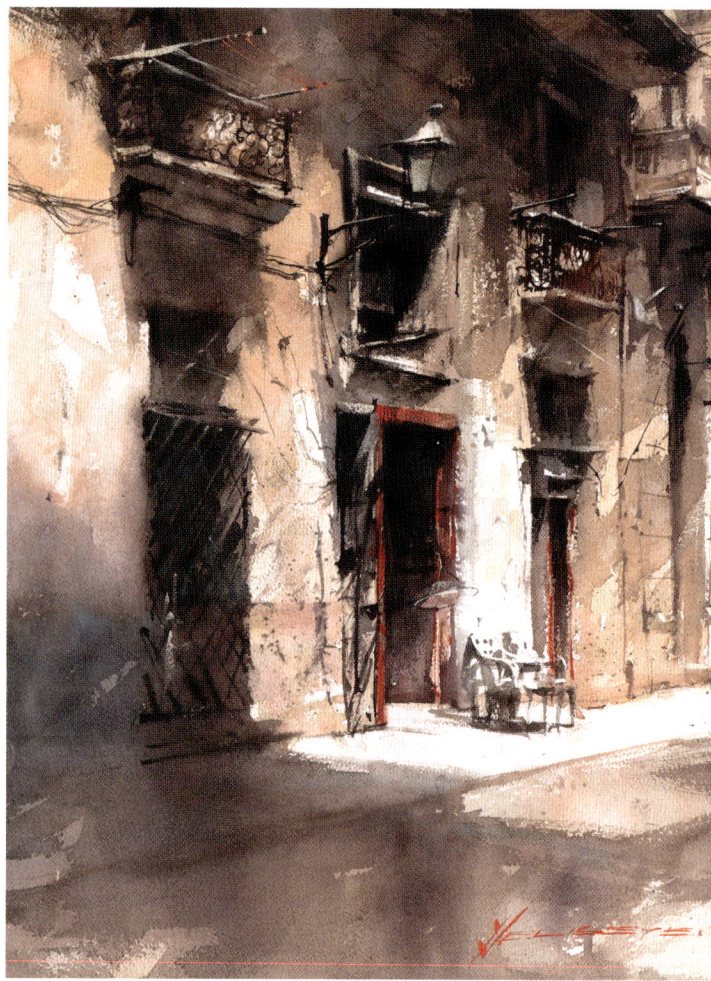

Two Chairs, watercolor, 21½ " × 17½ " | 55 × 45 cm

I would recommend beginner artists start learning watercolor techniques with the layering method and then progress to more advanced techniques such as mixing colors directly on paper and using wet-on-wet techniques.

COVERING LARGE AREAS
IN WATERCOLOR

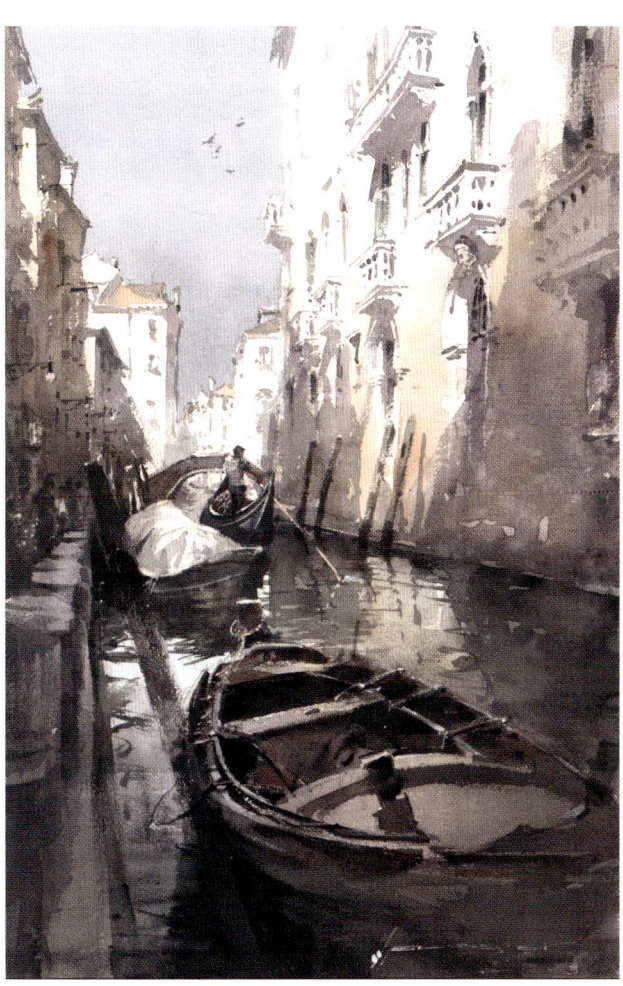

Venice Watercolor, watercolor, 21½" × 14½" | 55 × 37 cm

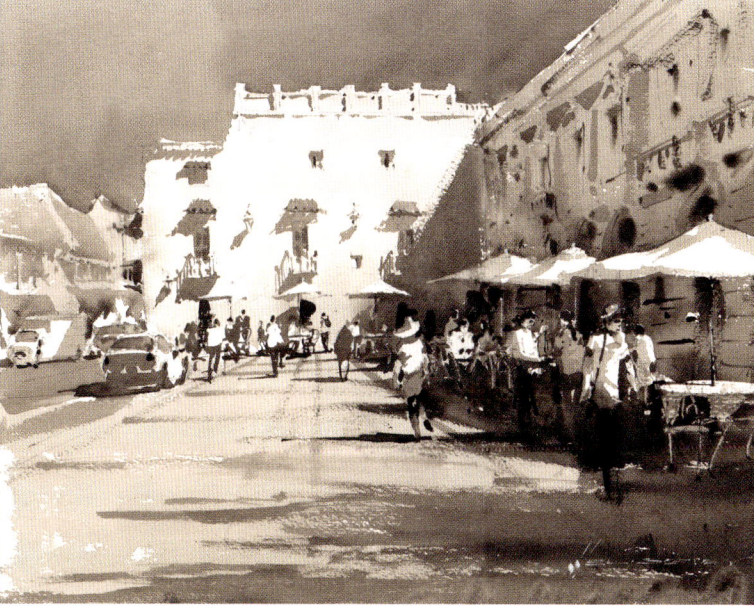

Cartagena Plaza, watercolor, 14" × 18½" | 35 × 47 cm

In the art of painting, whether it's the vast expanse of the sky or the intricate details of the landscape, the choice of brush size plays a crucial role.

When it comes to determining the appropriate brush size, the rule is straightforward yet essential: Use the largest brush that allows you to work comfortably and effectively, until the brush's size becomes too big and switch to smaller one.

When using the same mix of color in the painting, it's essential to mix enough of the color on your palette to cover the desired surface area without interruption. This ensures a consistent tone throughout your work, as remixing the exact shade can be challenging. It's advisable to err on the side of excess rather than risk running out mid-process.

ESSENTIAL WATERCOLOR TECHNIQUES

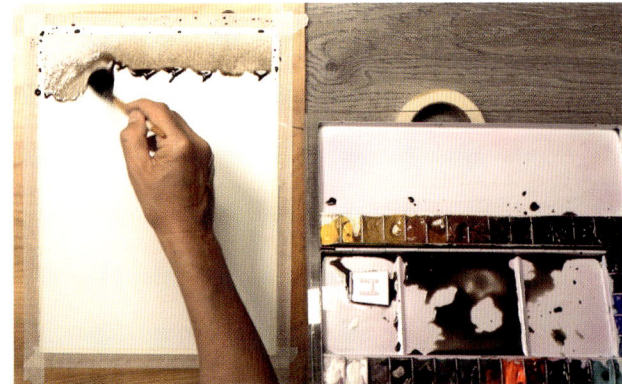

1. Start of wash technique.

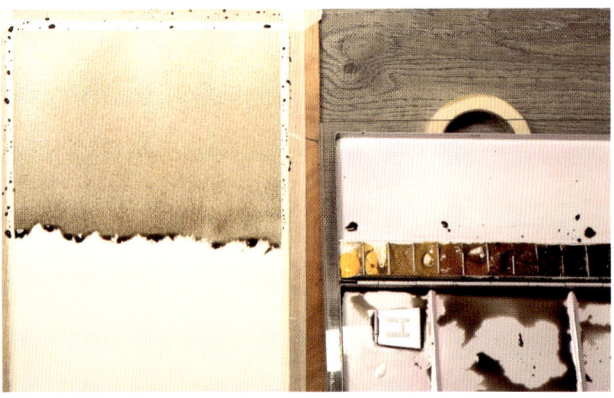

2. Wash application, mid-process.

3. Completed sepia wash.

DEMONSTRATION: BASIC WASH

It's crucial to remember that this method of watercolor application involves working on a slightly inclined board with your watercolor paper securely attached. Make sure to tape the paper around all edges using masking tape to prevent warping which might interfere with watercolor application.

I begin at the top of the paper and use a zigzagging motion in a horizontal direction to apply a wide wash of watercolor, using the full width of your brush. Allow the paint to settle and flow naturally across the paper. After a few seconds, you'll notice beads of paint forming at the lower edges of the wash.

The size of these beads is critical for achieving smooth results. Larger beads generally result in smoother transitions and more even color distribution. The key is to maintain a balance between bead size and the angle of the inclined board so they don't run down.

For the next application, I begin just below the painted edge of the previous wash, ensuring that the new wash engages with the beads of paint left by the previous application. It's important to maintain a continuous flow to avoid visible horizontal bands of slightly darker color, which can occur with prolonged delays between washes.

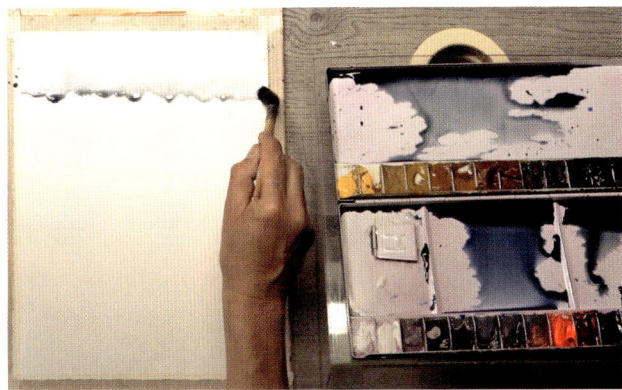

1. Start of tonal gradation wash.

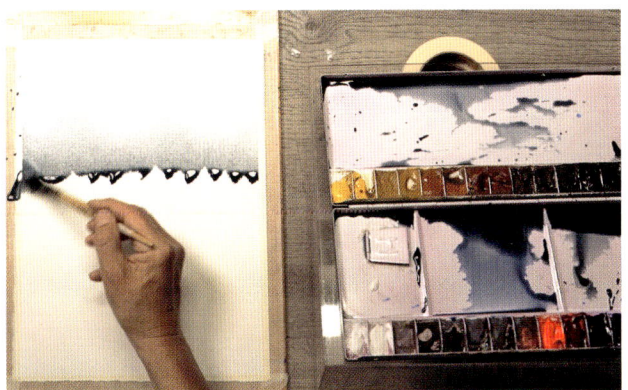

2. Tonal gradation wash, mid-process.

3. Completed tonal gradation wash.

DEMONSTRATION:
TONAL GRADATION WASH

The same principle of painting technique applies when creating any tonal gradation with paint. It's preferable to begin with a lighter wash and gradually darken it by adding pigment in the palette area first. Each consecutive horizontal band applied should interact with the beads from the previous band, but not with the area above it, ensuring smoother transitions in tone or color. Each consecutive band of wash should contain extra pigment added to the mix in the palette area.

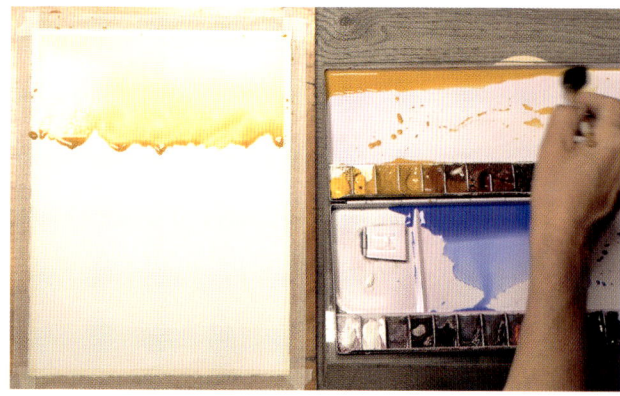

1. Start of color shift wash.

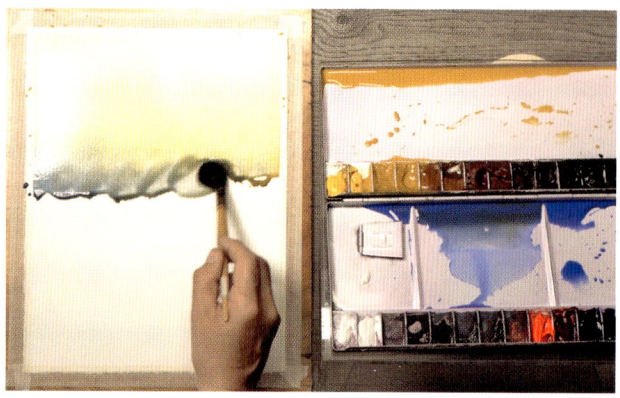

2. Color shift wash, stage two.

3. Completed color shift wash.

DEMONSTRATION: COLOR SHIFT WASH

Again, it's important to prepare all basic mixes beforehand on the palette. Keep in mind that intermediate tones of paint will be achieved through interaction with the lighter beads from the previous horizontal wash band. Keeping these beads as large as possible will aid in achieving smooth transitions from light to dark tones. The board low incline angle is important in this exercise.

ACHIEVING TEXTURE FOR REALISM

DRYBRUSH TECHNIQUE

Nothing can quite replace the drybrush technique when I aim to convey the distressed look of old walls in historic towns. This method is particularly effective when painting on rough-surfaced paper over a previously painted area.

I use a synthetic fiber brush to achieve the desired effect, especially when covering relatively small areas. While a natural brush is also suitable, the stiffer synthetic fibers leave more defined marks on a rough watercolor surface. The key is to paint only the bumps on the surface of the watercolor paper, avoiding the valleys. To achieve this, I hold my brush in a mostly horizontal position so that the brush tip does not engage in the painting process. While painting, it's easy to overdo the effect, resulting in an excessively busy look. I remind myself that achieving overall realism requires covering only a portion of the surface to give the impression of distress on the wall's surface.

I carefully analyze the direction of light and overall light distribution in the scenery to define focal areas, implementing the drybrush technique strategically in these key areas. This technique is most effective in illuminated areas that are in halftone, as direct light tends to bleach out imperfections on surfaces like buildings and pavement. Skillful manipulation of distressed areas through measured application goes a long way in convincing the viewer of a realistic presentation without overwhelming the overall effect.

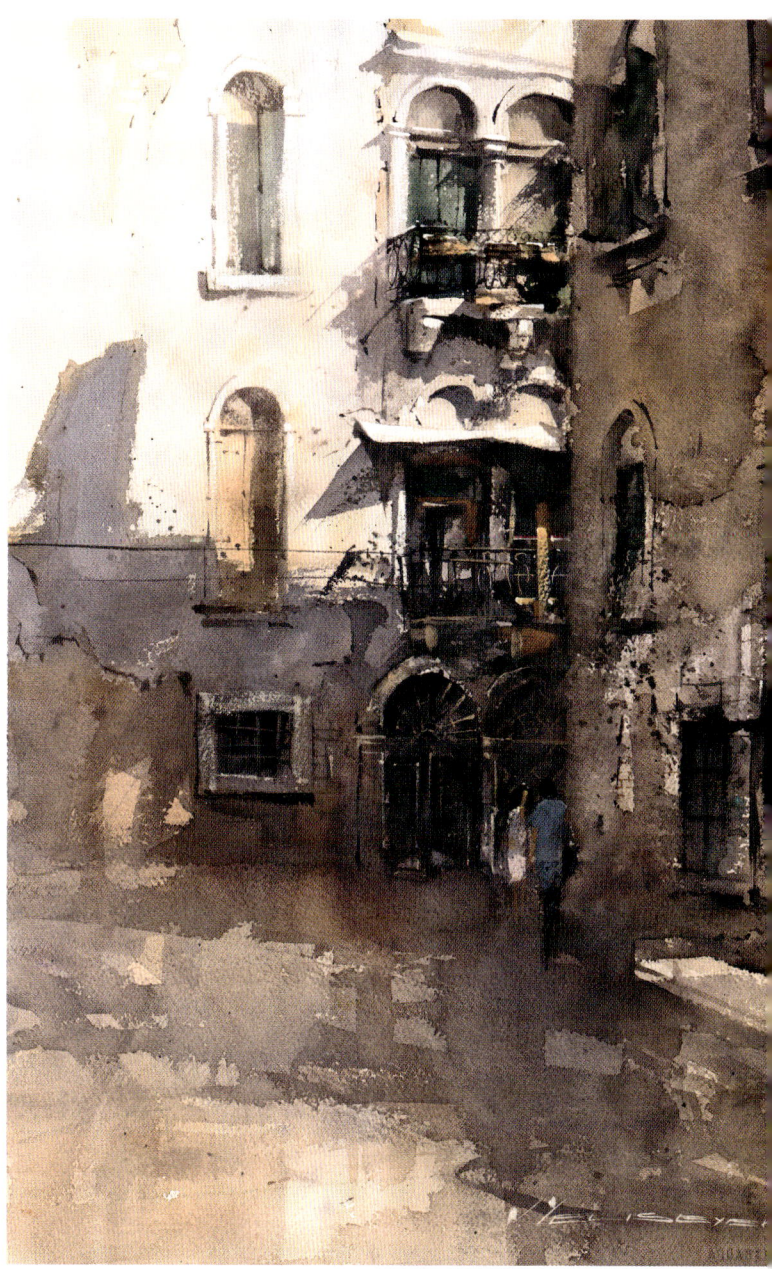

Shades of Venice, watercolor, 21½" × 14½" | 55 × 37 cm

SPLATTERING, APPLYING WHITE GOUACHE, SCRATCHING OUT

In addition to the drybrush technique, incorporating splattering and applying white gouache next to some splatters can create an almost illusory effect of indents on the surface. This application should also be executed with precision and restraint, using just enough to achieve the desired effect.

It's inevitable that color variations will occur when painting distressed walls, and they don't necessarily need to correspond to a realistic pattern on the wall. I often take advantage of these "imperfections" to indicate different layers of plaster accumulated over many years by adding shadow lines between these areas, which can have a great effect.

Scratching out light areas is another excellent method for adding texture, as the resulting scratch marks rarely have a uniform appearance, enhancing the sense of realism. To successfully implement these marks, it's crucial to add them when the paper is still wet to a satin finish degree. If done earlier, the scratch lines will appear dark, having an opposite effect.

I've developed a strategy: At the end of the painting process, I re-wet the area using a sprayer or moist brush and then scratch out the desired areas without any issues. Another advantage of this method is that if scratching is done earlier in the process, applying an even light wash on top of it will darken that area, even if the scratching was successful initially.

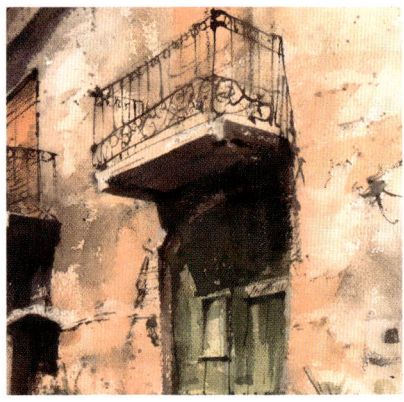

Green Door, detail.

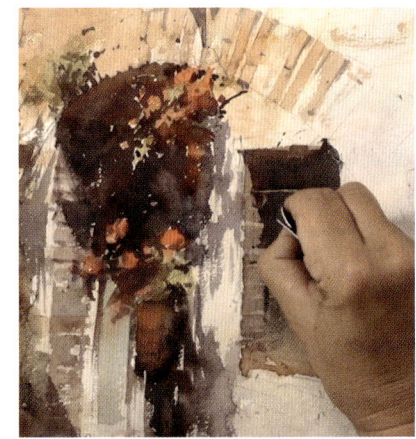

Scratching process.

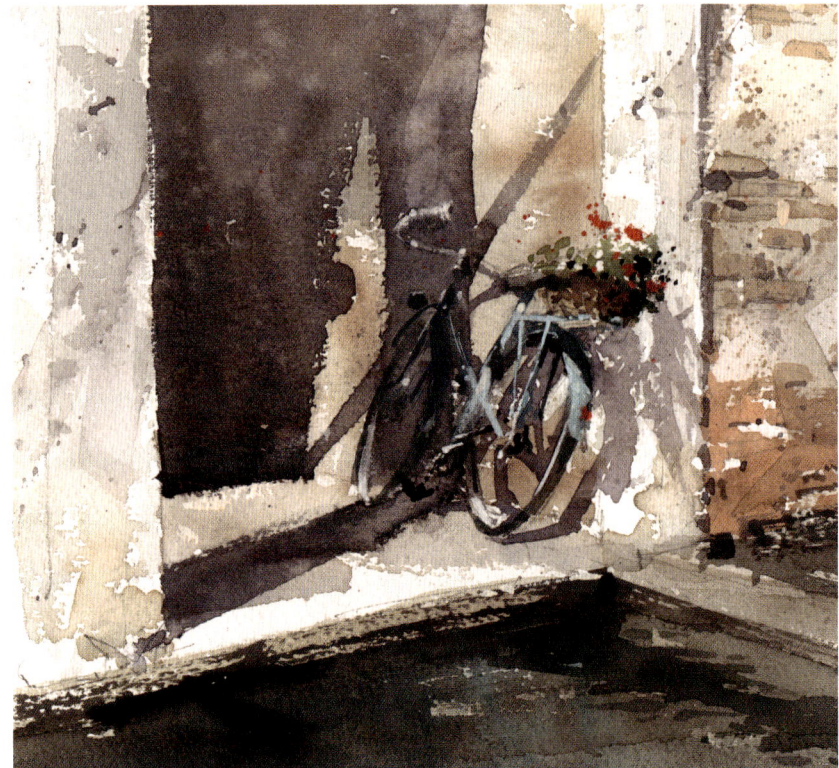

Venice Arches, detail.

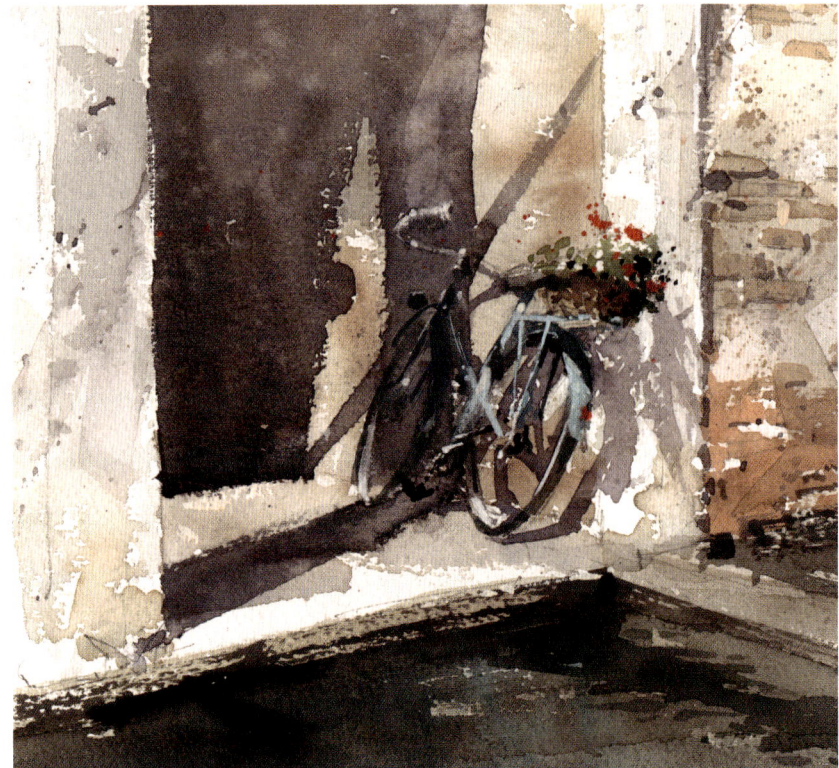

Assisi, window detail.

MASTERING DRYBRUSH TECHNIQUES

CHOOSING THE RIGHT TOOLS

I have already described how useful the drybrush technique can be when painting distressed walls in old towns. However, this technique can be beneficial in many other situations as well. Before I describe those, I would like to once more emphasize the importance of having the right tools. Using the correct tools makes it easy to implement the technique and saves a lot of frustration. Of course, before applying it to the final piece, I recommend practicing on scrap paper to get a good grasp of it.

The paper I use for this technique is rough paper. Even cold press watercolor paper does not fully exhibit the potential of this watercolor application method. Although any reasonably good quality brush can be used on this type of paper, I often prefer a synthetic fiber brush because of its stiffer fibers.

APPLYING PAINT

I hold my brush almost horizontally to the paper surface to avoid painting with the pointy tip of the brush. This horizontal movement allows the brush to cover only the bumps of the paper, creating the desired effect.

The size of the effect depends on the type of paper used, but I can vary the density of coverage by applying more or less pressure. The importance of the paper is evident here, as I prefer to work on an irregular, uneven surface that creates more natural results. I avoid papers with a machinelike, regular bumpy surface.

I use the drybrush technique in a variety of situations, not only when there is a need to show distressed textures on surfaces. One of the most common uses is when I paint the foliage of trees, tree bark, shimmering reflections on the water surface, or when I want to give a painting an unfinished look at the edges.

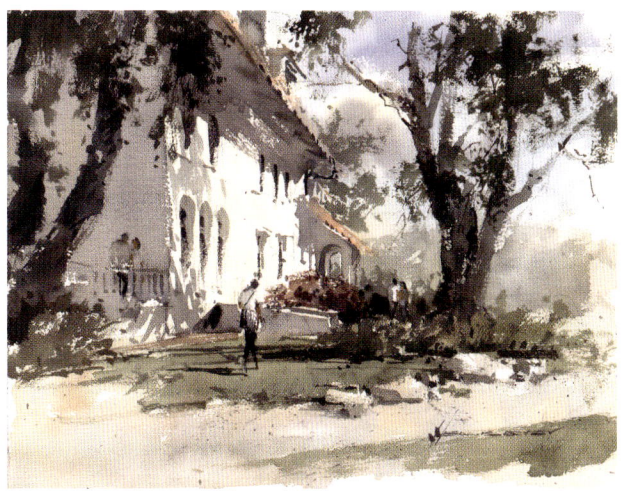

Phillippi Mansion, watercolor, 14" × 18½" | 36 x47 cm

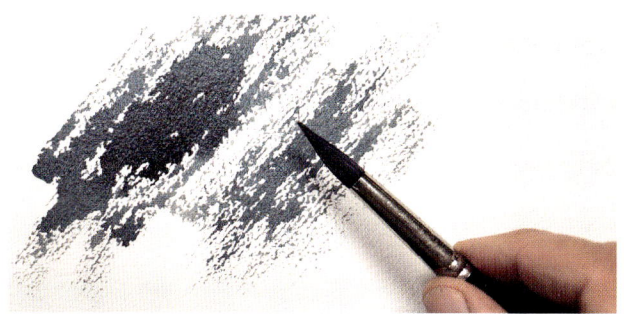

Horizontal brush hold.

Even-tooth rough surface.

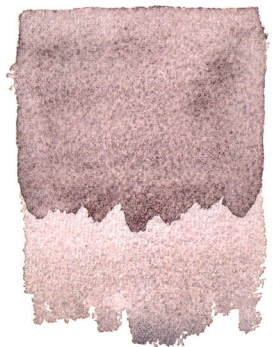

Darkening edges.

Drybrush, second layer.

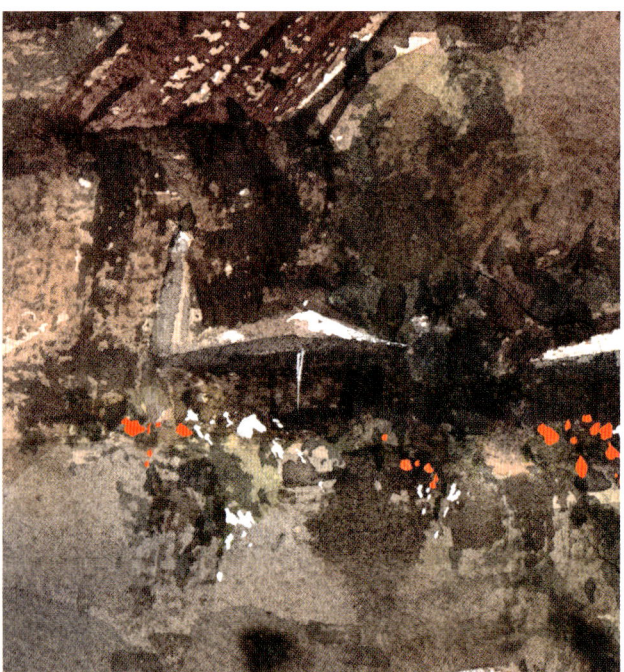

In Ghent, detail.

In addition to the uses mentioned above, one of the most significant applications of this technique arises when there is a need to darken a previously painted surface. Due to the transparent nature of watercolor, any subsequent layer of paint applied to darken the surface often fails to accurately repeat the shape of the already painted area. Even when done painstakingly, the resulting edge tends to look darker than the inner surface, creating a dark outline that appears quite artificial.

I have found that employing the drybrush technique over the previously painted surface not only successfully darkens it but also eliminates the need to precisely conform to the outline of the previously painted area. The loose nature of this watercolor application allows for a more natural and cohesive appearance.

Another advantage of using the drybrush technique is the effortless integration between layers, allowing the original paint to show through in some places and resulting in a more natural look. The overworked look of watercolor is hard to avoid when employing traditional layering methods, but the drybrush technique is an indispensable tool for achieving an effortless, natural appearance.

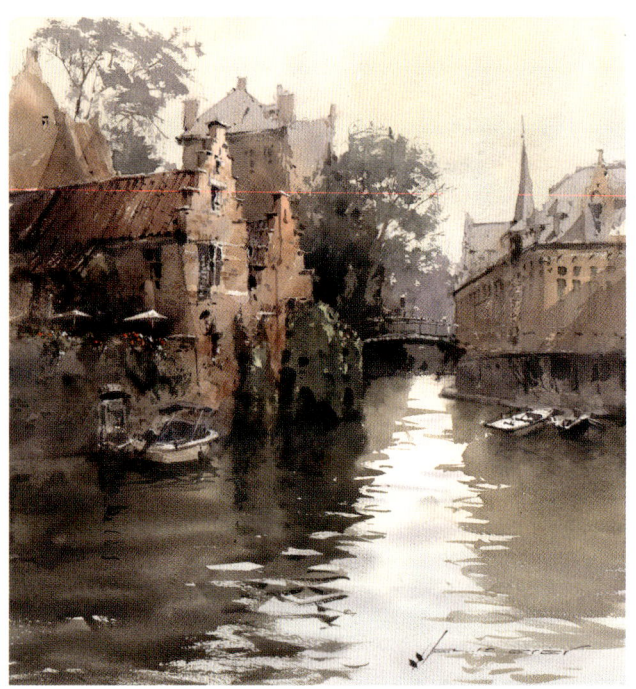

In Ghent, watercolor, 17" × 16" | 43 × 41 cm

Scan to view a video tutorial

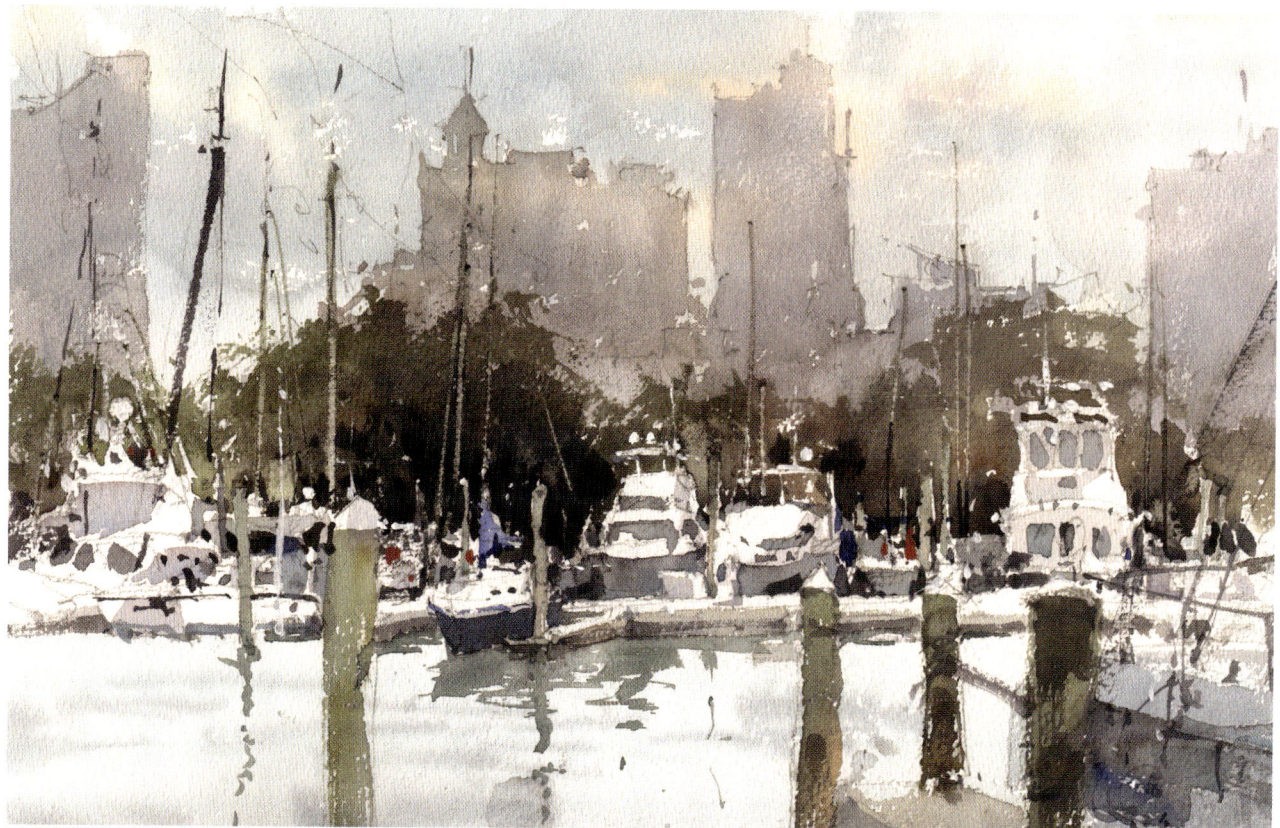

Marina Jack, watercolor, 9" × 14" | 23 × 36 cm

In "Navigating the Three Planes of Vision" (p. 114), I briefly touch on the subject of implementing the drybrush technique in the foremost plane—the foreground. In this plane, every subject is painted using the drybrush technique to avoid a precise and focused appearance. This approach reflects the fact that we rarely concentrate on the foreground in our day-to-day lives, providing a more natural depiction of reality.

I've previously highlighted the effectiveness of the drybrush technique in achieving a loose and painterly appearance in watercolors. When executed skillfully, this technique speaks volumes about the nature of the resulting artwork, conveying a sense of freedom and departing from stiffness and precise presentation. In the portrayal of light, the precision of brushstrokes becomes less significant compared to where they are applied. This observation underscores the idea that the viewer's mind already possesses sufficient information to mentally complete the work.

The drybrush technique serves as an indispensable tool for engaging the viewer in the creative process, a facet often overlooked. The mere involvement of the viewer, not only in the storytelling aspect but also in its technical execution, holds significant power and contributes to a heightened sense of satisfaction during the observation of the finished artwork.

It's crucial to remember a fundamental aspect of watercolor, or any other medium in representational art—it's a human act of improvisation and reinterpretation of reality. The masterstroke of the drybrush technique often embodies the human essence of painting, avoiding an attempt to replicate reality in a photorealistic manner. Instead, it tells the story of a subjective interpretation of the world around us, breaking away from strict realism and embracing the unique perspective of the artist.

THE IMPORTANCE OF TIMING IN WATERCOLOR

One of the crucial yet rarely discussed aspects of watercolor painting is the importance of timing. Unlike oil painters, who have the luxury of unlimited time between brushstrokes but often lament the slow drying process, watercolor artists face the opposite challenge. Watercolor dries quickly, forcing painters to work swiftly, make split-second decisions, and implement them immediately.

Throughout this book, I emphasize the necessity of thinking ahead and preparing paint mixes in advance. This forward planning is essential when working with watercolor. The painter must envision the final image, at least in general terms, to guide their artistic direction effectively.

Watercolor techniques require meticulous planning, especially since different colors can be added while the wash is still wet. This brief window of opportunity allows for smooth blending; however, once the wash begins to dry, these additions can cause unpredictable and undesirable effects such as blooming, which is difficult to control. In nineteenth-century Britain, artists used special frames with stretched moist fabric under watercolor paper to prolong the drying time of washes. While this technique can be beneficial for wet-on-wet watercolor, I often need the watercolor to dry faster, particularly after applying the first wash, so I can start layering my darks.

When I paint the sky, all colors and tones are premixed and ready on my palette. This preparation is essential because the sky must be painted in one continuous session, capturing clouds and subtle tonal variations as they occur. In this extreme case, the timing of watercolor application is of utmost importance.

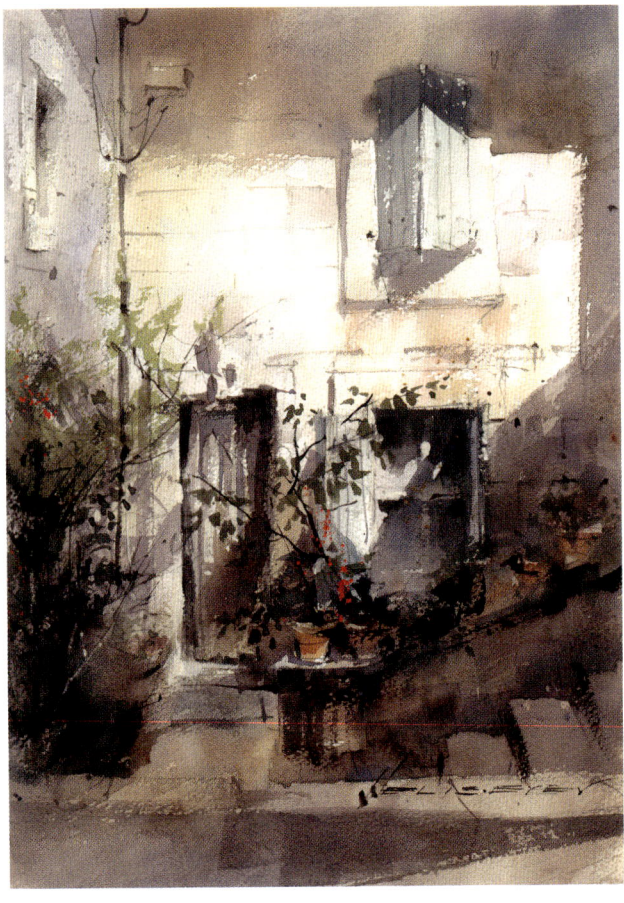

Italian Light, watercolor, 14½" × 10" | 37 × 26 cm

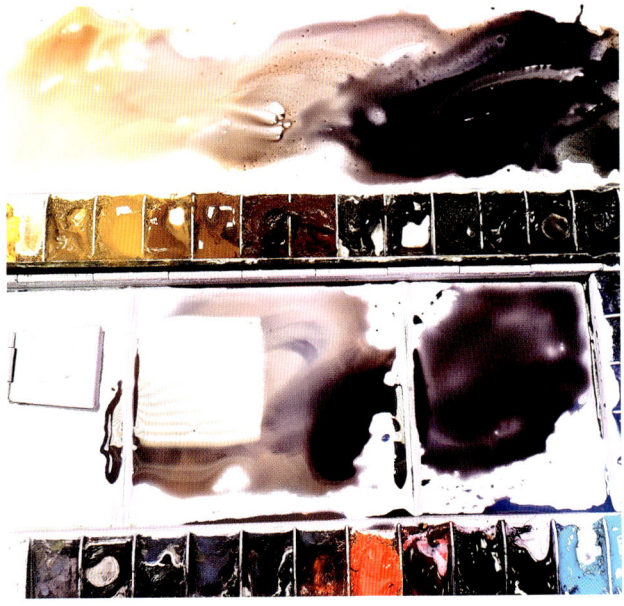

Palette tonal watercolor mixes.

Sphere, lit areas.

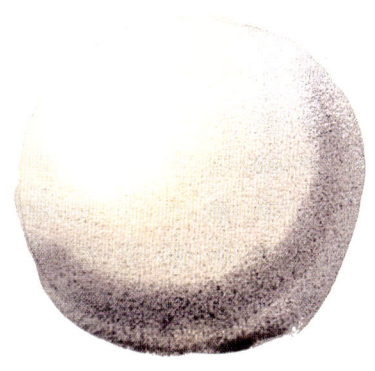

Sphere, completed wash.

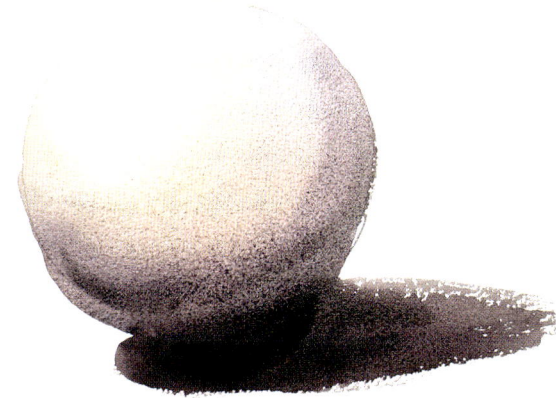

Sphere with cast shadow.

In some cases, it's necessary to change the value or temperature of an applied watercolor wash. This correction is still possible while the wash is wet, but it must be done almost immediately to avoid blooming effects. Soft gradations between different surfaces should also be painted at once to prevent the formation of a dark line of separation between them.

I often paint midtones and their resulting cast shadows simultaneously, without interruption. To achieve this, the darker tone of the cast shadow needs to be prepared on the palette at the same time as the midtone, but as a heavier mix. This prevents it from blending completely with the midtone, especially in larger application areas. This technique creates wonderful lost and found edges in the work, which are difficult to achieve otherwise.

The reflections of the boats in *Venice Bridge* (below) were painted in a single session to ensure seamless integration between the boats and the water below.

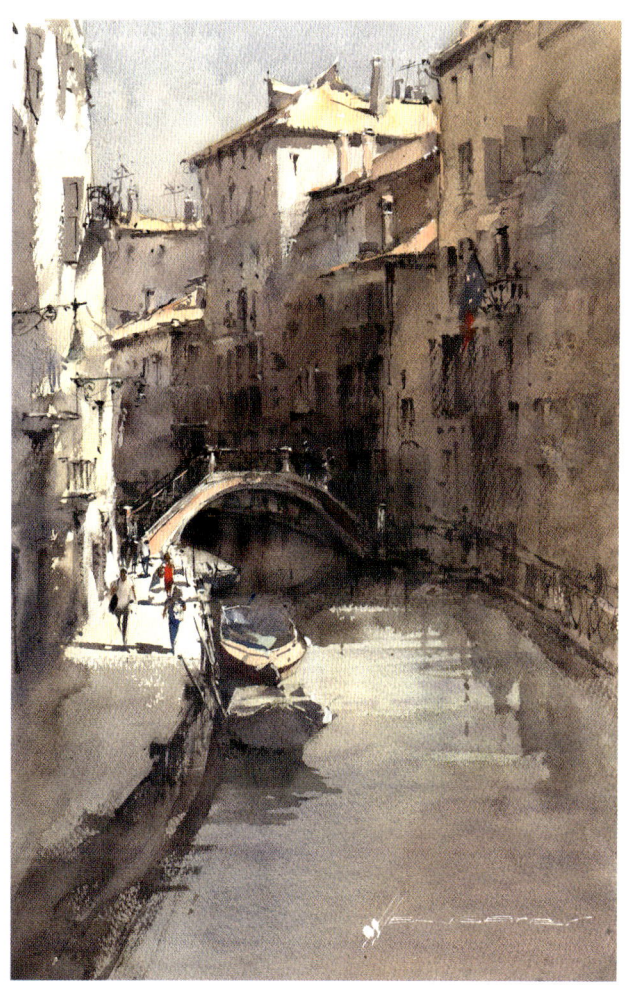

Venice Bridge, watercolor, 21½" × 14½" | 55 × 37 cm

SPLATTERING AND SCRATCHING EFFECTS

I use splattering and scratching techniques almost at the end of the painting process to enhance the appearance of watercolor. These methods are effective for expressing textures, flowers, leaves on trees, and bright lines on darker backgrounds. When traditional painting methods fall short, these techniques help me achieve the desired effects and significantly streamline and simplify the painting process.

The splattering method of watercolor application is particularly effective for showing textures on surfaces, especially when used in conjunction with other techniques such as drybrush. It excels at creating smooth transitions between different painted areas when the paint is still wet. I often use splattering to depict flowers in a landscape or areas of foliage. This technique is far superior to applying dots one by one, as it creates a more natural look. To enhance the composition, additional dots can be painted after splattering to create a more dynamic grouping or to increase the size of some flowers.

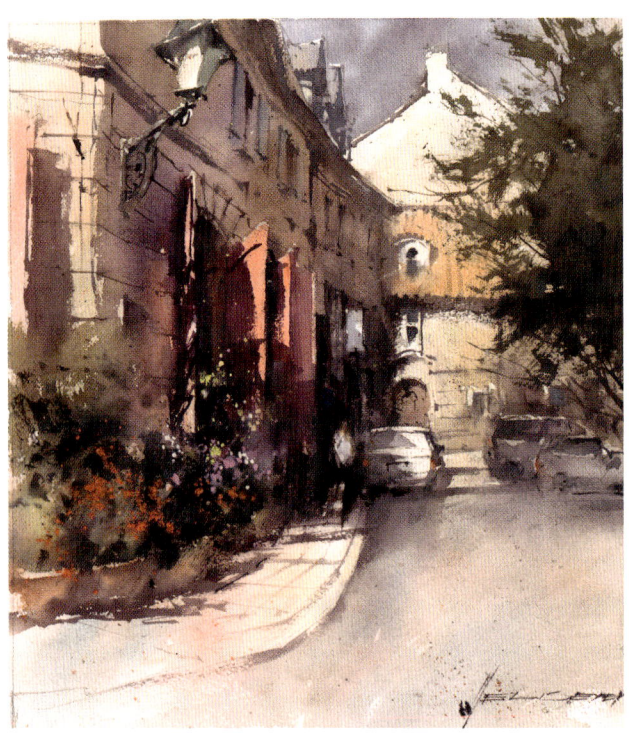

Flower Shop, watercolor, 16" × 14½" | 41 × 37 cm

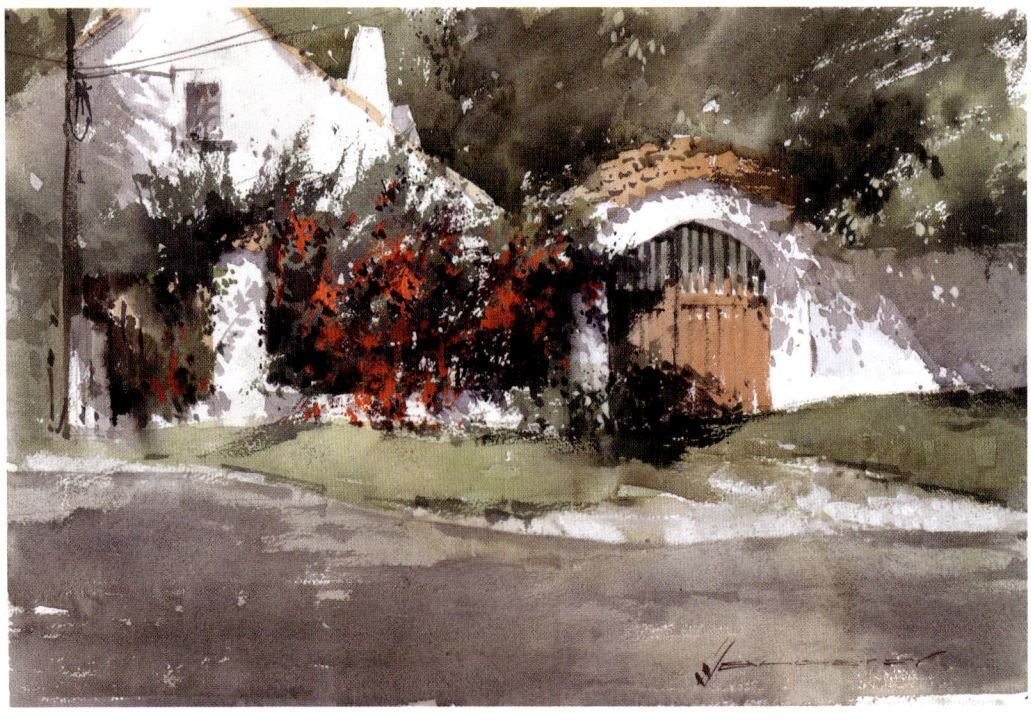

The Gates, watercolor, 21½" x14½" | 55 × 37 cm

Because I mix flower splatters with gouache, I use the splattering method at the end of the painting process. This prevents any consecutive washes from smearing their crisp appearance. For a softer effect, such as background elements, it's better to apply splattering on a slightly wet surface.

When painting the foreground, splattering water on the corner of the painting can create light dots that resemble pebbles or small stones against a darker background. This technique often provides a sufficient finishing touch to the foreground.

For the best scratching effect, a palette knife with slightly rounded tips is suitable, provided it's applied gently to avoid excessive damage to the paper. The goal is to remove only the top layer of paint without creating holes in the paper. In the absence of specific tools, any reasonably hard scraper, including fingernails, can be used for scratching.

The most important aspect of successful scratching is timing. While it's hard to specify the exact number of minutes after water application due to varying humidity, the best time to scratch is when the wash takes on a satin finish. If done too early, the scratch will appear as a dark line, which is the opposite of the desired effect. Because the drying times of washes are not exact, if a line appears dark, I let it be, as trying to fix it is nearly impossible. As a remedy, I can add a lighter line on the lit side to enhance it, but more often, I let it slide and I wait before continuing to scratch in that area.

Whenever possible, I prefer the scratching method to painting white lines with gouache. The scratched appearance is less vibrant but better integrated with the surrounding area, drawing less attention to itself. This subtle integration is beneficial since the scratched lines are rarely meant to be the centerpiece of the painting.

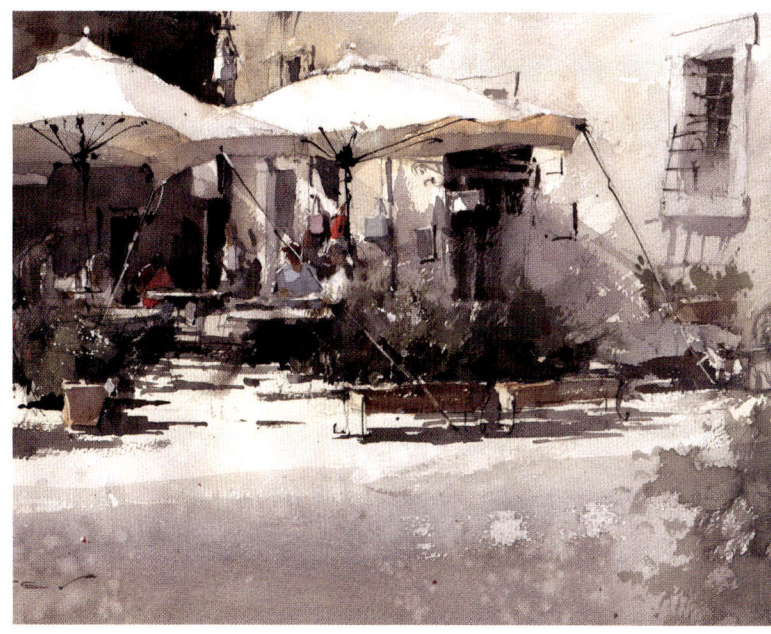

Orvieto Café, detail.

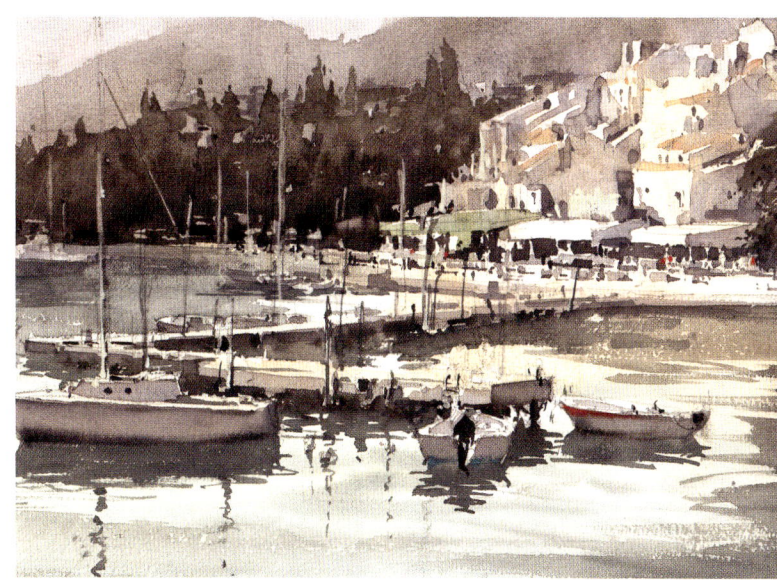

Cavtat Marina, detail.

Scan to view a video tutorial

INCORPORATING GOUACHE INTO WATERCOLOR

The question of why artists use gouache has a few straightforward answers. One reason is that opaque colors or pure white gouache can cover the layer of paint underneath, similar to oil paint. This capability allows artists to streamline the painting process when adding highlights, reflections, and finishing touches, such as wires, against a dark background.

In "Splattering and Scratching Effects" (p. 84), I explain that while I sometimes prefer to scratch out lines and highlights, using gouache is very acceptable from my point of view. This is because gouache can be mixed with watercolors to match the color of the paper and can be used as a drybrush technique to avoid razor-sharp edges. Many painters successfully use masking fluid to preserve highlights. However, after numerous attempts, I decided to give up on masking fluid because achieving a seamless synergy between the painting and the white paper proved difficult. On the other hand, painting with gouache on top of watercolor feels more natural, as it maintains the integrity of the painting process.

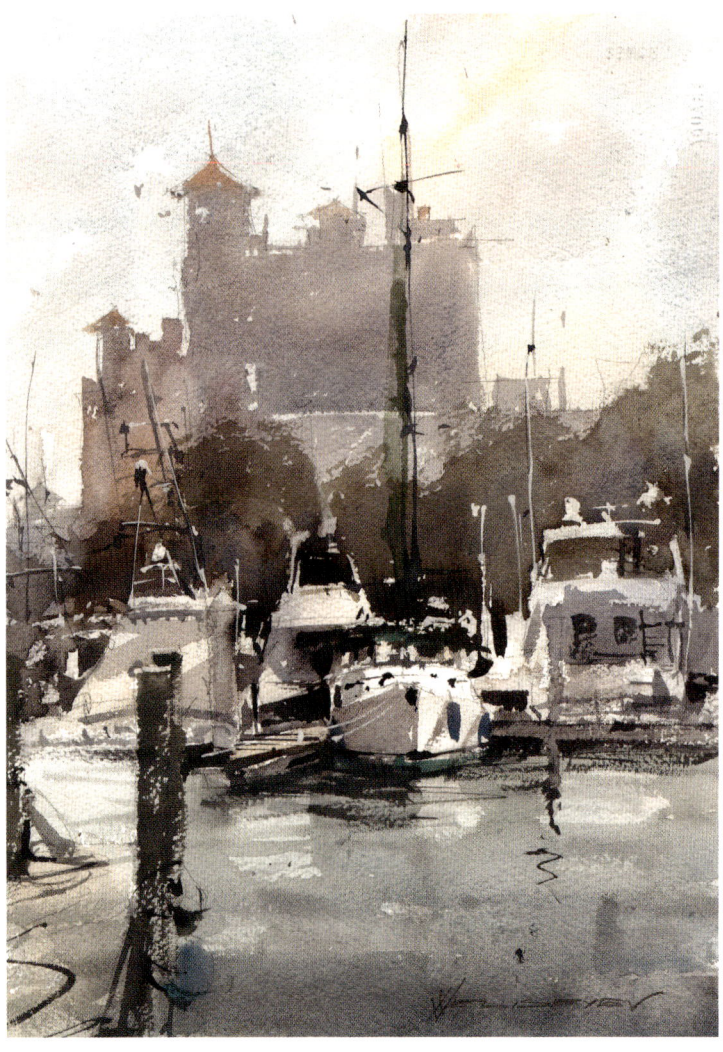

Sarasota Harbor, watercolor, 14" × 10" | 36 × 36 cm

When observing artwork, I prefer to focus on the overall impression, including its transparent quality, rather than scrutinizing tiny opaque areas. That said, I have noticed that the greater the skills of the painter, the less gouache intervention is required. Often, it's better to leave small imperfections alone, as they are typically natural to the watercolor medium and can enhance its allure.

To unify the look of gouache with watercolor, it's better to use drybrush techniques. This minimizes the opaque quality of gouache and helps it integrate more seamlessly with the underlying watercolor layer. The same approach applies when painting thin light lines; the drybrush technique will help achieve a more cohesive and integrated appearance with the surrounding watercolor washes.

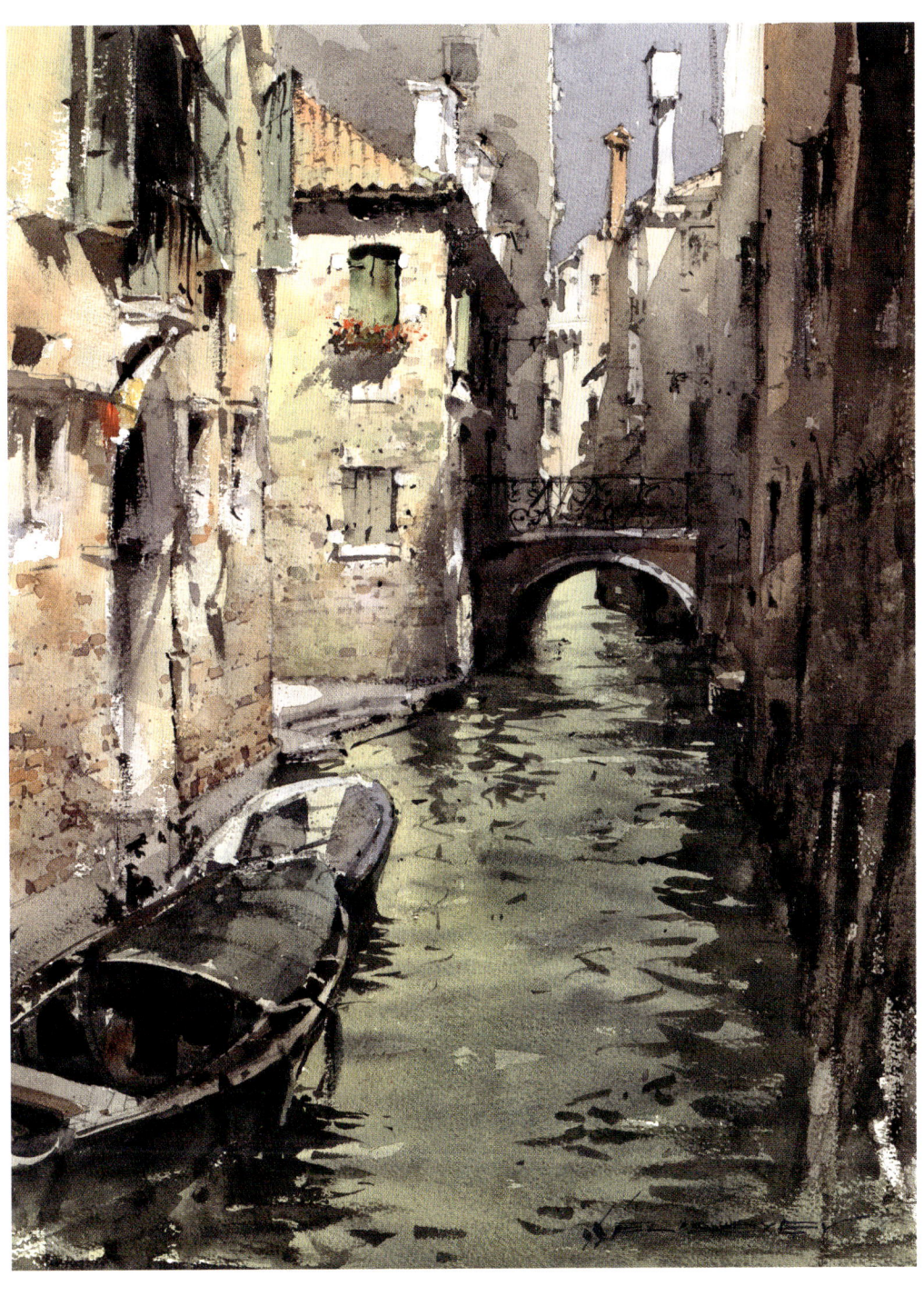

Venice, watercolor, 19" × 14" | 48 × 36 cm

CAPTURING THE SKY IN WATERCOLOR

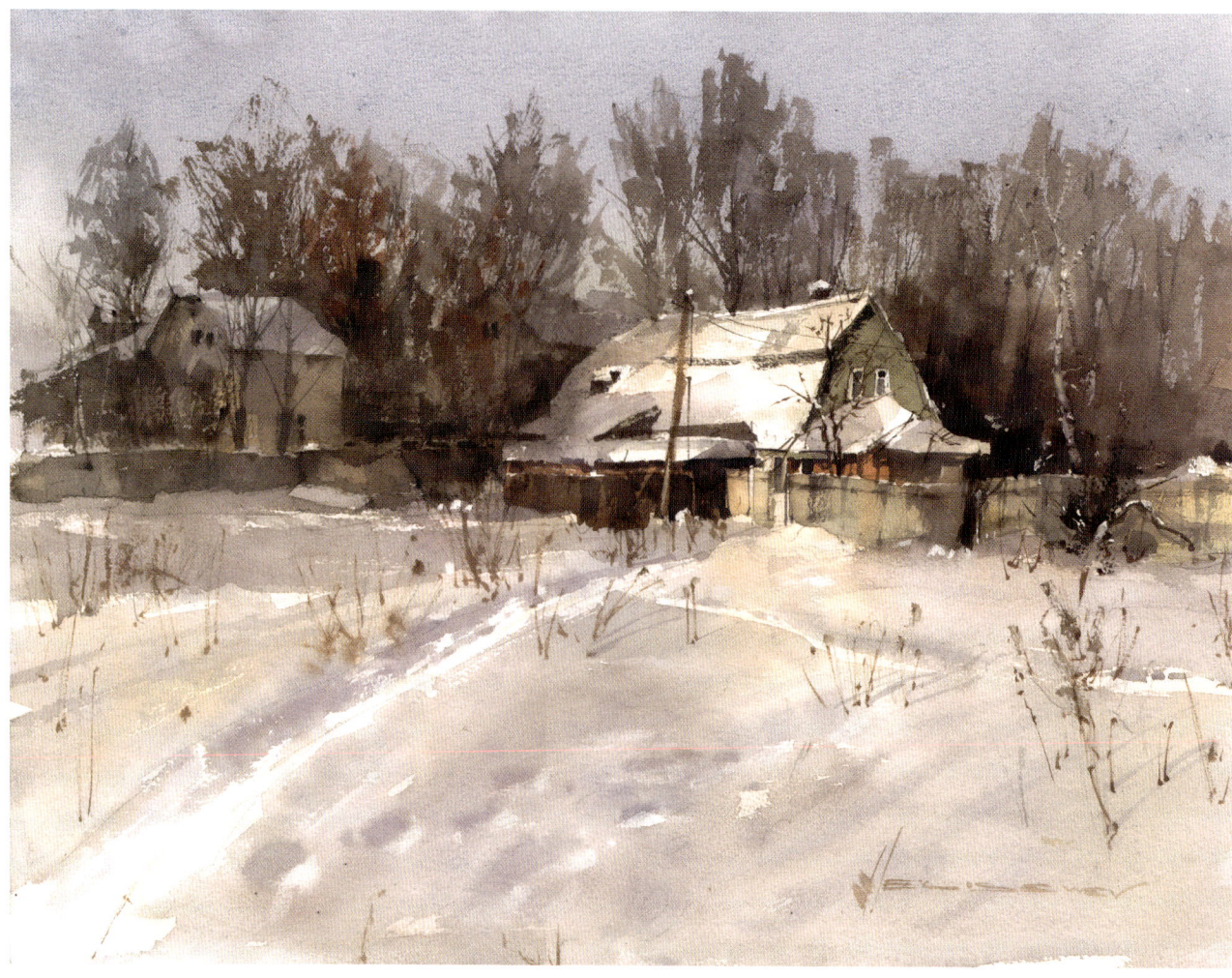

Golitsyno Winter, watercolor, 14" × 18½" | 36 × 47 cm

It's nearly impossible to avoid capturing the sky in any scenic watercolor paintings. The sky is a constant presence in nearly every artwork I create, and it's not an exaggeration to say that its depiction is always unique. When painting the sky, I explore two possibilities: one with clouds and the other without. When working en plein air, I deliberately observe the sky conditions at the beginning of the painting process and strive to reflect them in my artwork, irrespective of the current state of the sky. Recognizing the fleeting nature of the sky's appearance, attempting to chase its changes becomes a futile endeavor.

I recall that the final decision to paint a particular scenery crystallizes at a specific moment in time. I strive to adhere to the observed sky conditions from the beginning, preserving its state at that precise moment. Another crucial choice I make is intentionally simplifying the sky's appearance, especially when the subject matter is visually intricate. In such cases, the addition of clouds under the sky might overly complicate the composition, prompting me to paint the sky as a uniform shade of blue or any color that harmonizes with the overall visual narrative.

DEMONSTRATION: BLENDING TO REDUCE INTENSITY

Considering the visual characteristics of the sky, it's crucial to remember that focal areas are seldom found there. This implies that the intense blue color prevalent in the sky could potentially play a disruptive role in the overall impression of the painting. Therefore, more often than not, I strive to mitigate this intensity by blending my selected blue base color with other pigments, aiming to maintain a more subdued and balanced appearance.

It's challenging to pinpoint the exact colors I use each time, as it depends on the specific view. However, I've observed that incorporating various shades of gray proves effective in reducing intensity. Nevertheless, I make a conscious effort to stay true to the overall color temperature of the sky, influencing its tone and value accordingly.

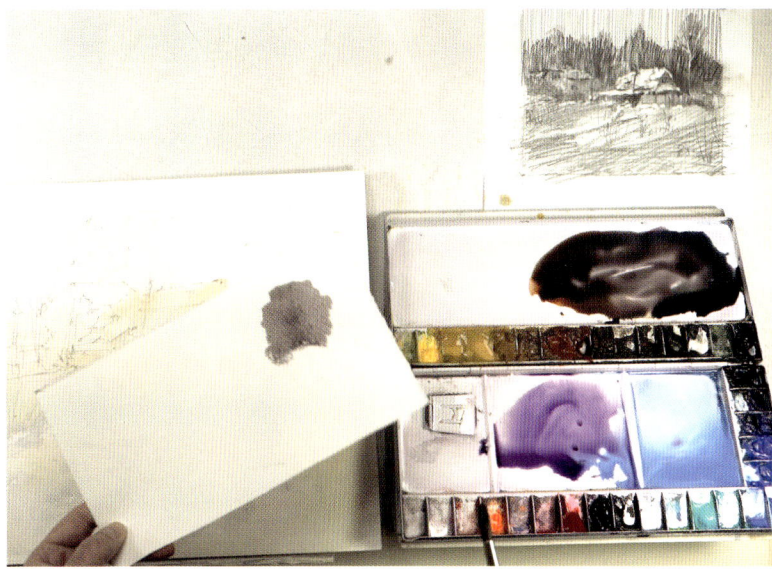

Sky color mixes.

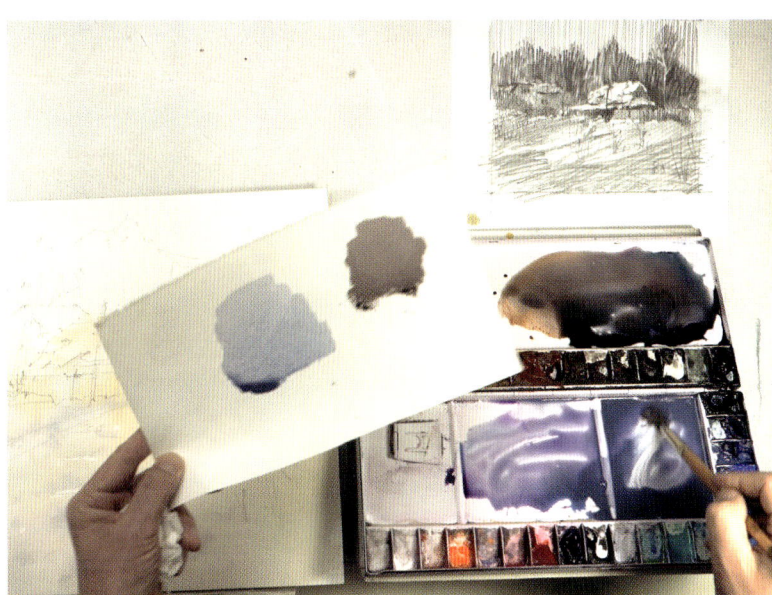

Dark sky color mix.

DEMONSTRATION: APPLYING A SKY WASH

The ability to expertly paint uniform sky wash requires some expertise especially if the area of watercolor coverage is somewhat large.

When considering the method of application, it's crucial to tilt the painting surface to some extent, allowing for a certain level of control in guiding the wash in the desired direction. I paint the sky using horizontal zigzag bands, which gather the beads of paint at the lowest points. I attentively monitor the size of the beads to prevent them from breaking while running down, ensuring they remain present. A surface inclined at about 5 to 10 degrees is beneficial, and if the beads fail to appear, it indicates that I haven't used enough water in the pigment mix. It's very important to use these beads for the second row of wash without engaging the first row of paint.

DEMONSTRATION: PAINTING CLOUDS

When deciding to paint clouds, I recall that they are rarely purely white and often possess a subtle warm hue due to being illuminated by a hot object like the sun. Therefore, I frequently begin by using yellow ochre in a very light wash with ample water, shaping it as desired. Subsequently, I apply the base blue color for the surrounding sky. Carefully working around the yellow ochre wash, I leave small specks of unpainted paper at the top of the ochre wash. I intentionally maintain inconsistency in the outline at the top, creating the impression of accidentally left unpainted areas.

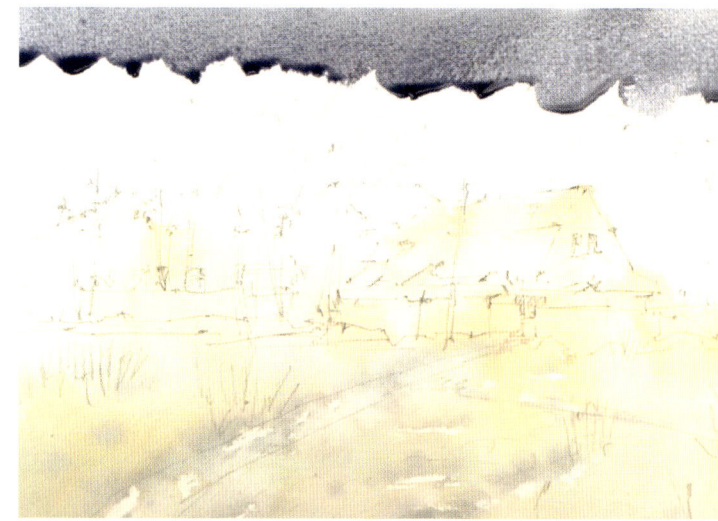

Zigzag watercolor application.

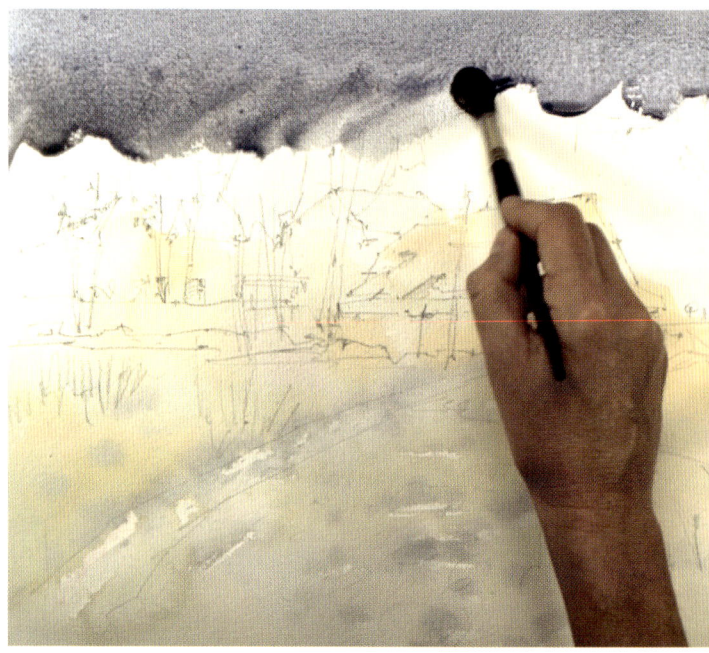

Working with beads.

Scan to view a video tutorial

The residual mix of gray proves useful in the subsequent step. Adding this midtone under the cloud, which is tonally darker than the base blue, completes the sky painting area. During this process, I find it unnecessary to precisely adhere to the outline of the light wash of the cloud, allowing for artistic license and interpretation.

All the steps described above must be executed while all elements in the sky area are still wet. This creates a synergy between the clouds, the base blue sky, and the midtone under the clouds, ensuring a harmonious integration of these components.

Natural atmospheric phenomena on this planet occasionally necessitate lightening the base blue color tone toward the horizon. To achieve this effect, I may add water to the blue mix used in that area or use a slightly warmer blue temperature. Ultimately, this decision is made to complement the overall composition, and I often find that lightening the sky toward the bottom can enhance the composition according to my preferences. In the picture below, the decision was made to paint the ground without interruption, which is always advisable when possible.

A completely different approach is adopted during sunsets, with the sky illuminated in bright orange colors. If you take on the challenge of painting the sky during these hours, it's important to remember to introduce warm colors into surrounding objects and reflections since they will receive some warm light. I keep the cast shadows cool to stay true to realistic atmospheric conditions.

Throughout the process of painting the sky, I keep in mind the overall desired final look of the watercolor, recognizing that the sky is just one element that must harmonize with everything else in the painting. The capacity to alter the sky's appearance to suit my preferences is a valuable asset in my artistic toolbox, and I approach it with intention rather than mindlessly.

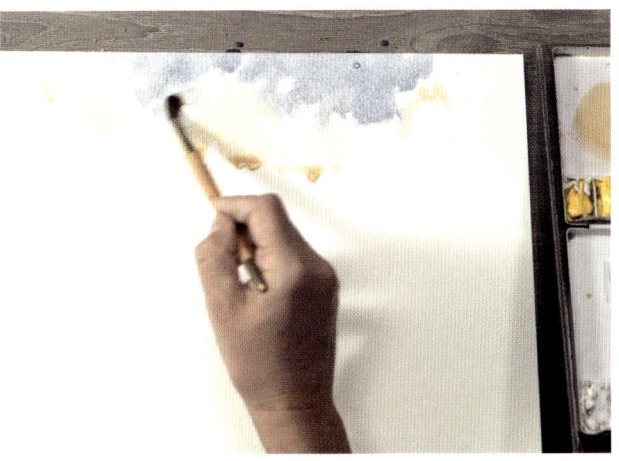

Applying blue around clouds.

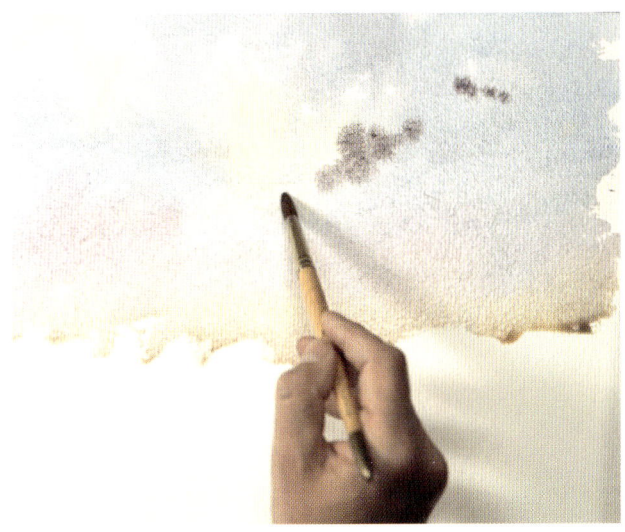

Applying midtones beneath the area of the clouds.

Completed sky wash.

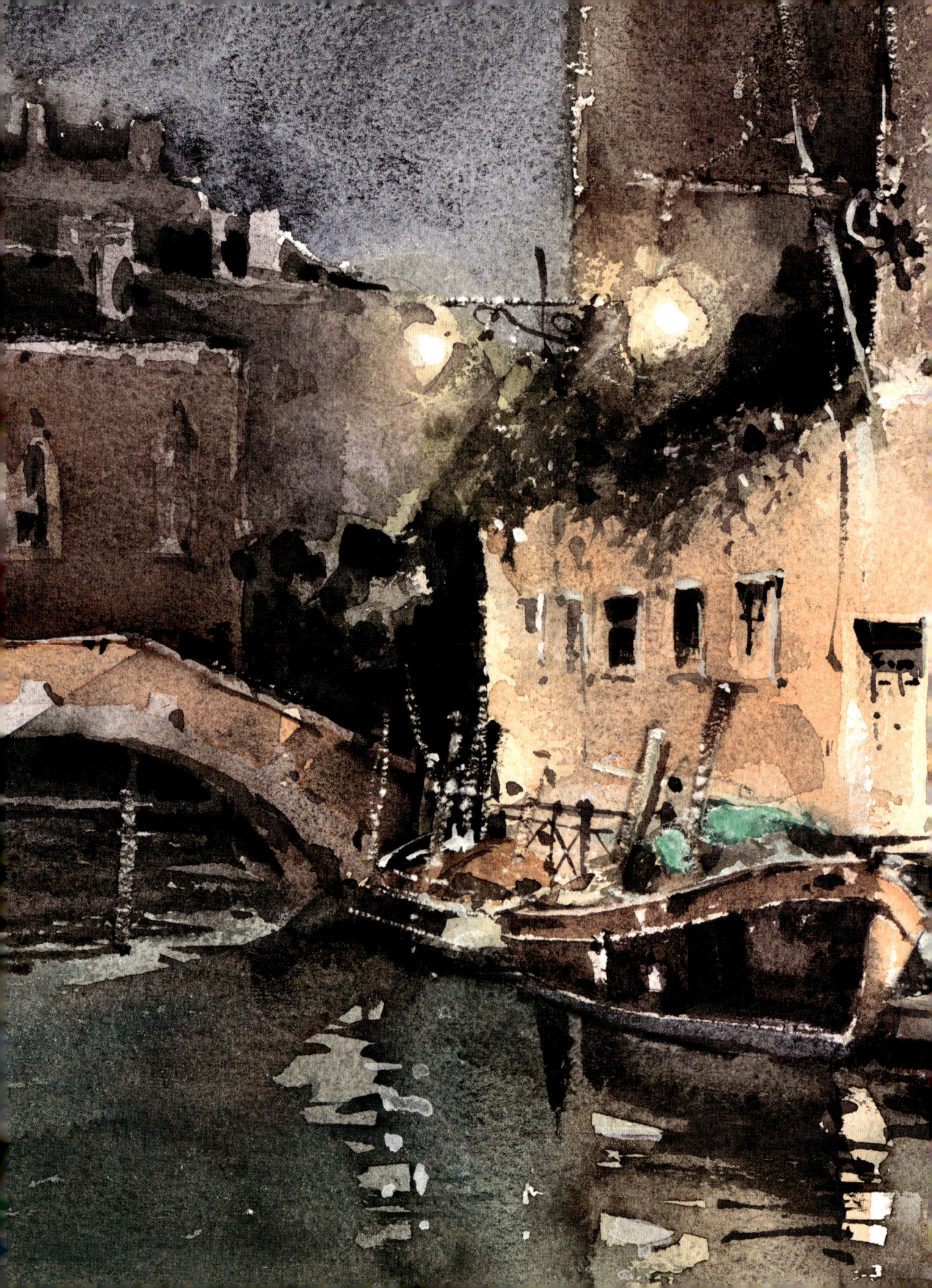

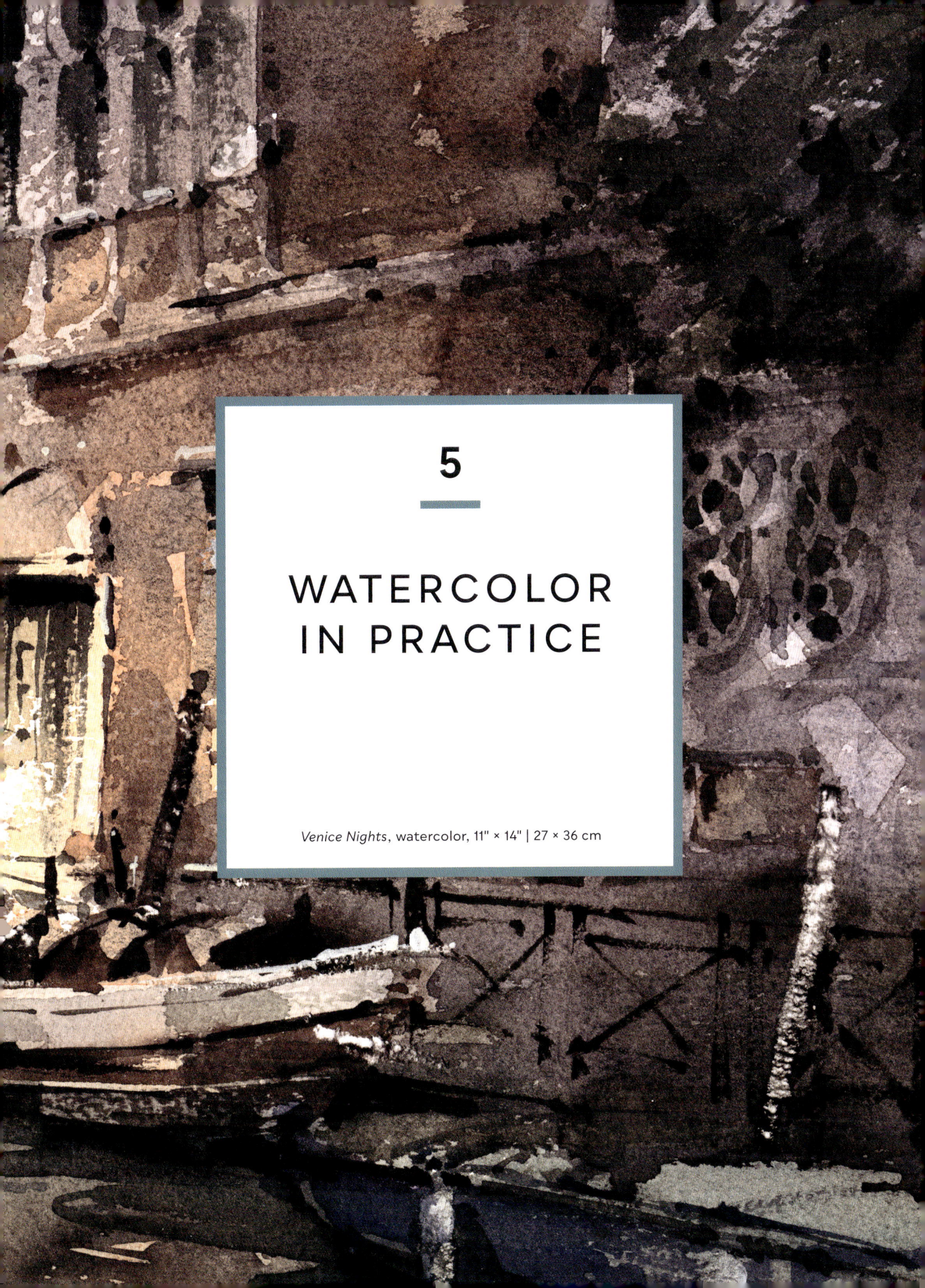

5

WATERCOLOR IN PRACTICE

Venice Nights, watercolor, 11" × 14" | 27 × 36 cm

UNDERSTANDING LIGHTNESS AND INTENSITY IN WATERCOLOR

It's essential to grasp the distinction between the values and intensity of colors, as they describe entirely different aspects. Beginner painters often overlook this crucial difference.

LIGHTNESS

In watercolor painting, value, or lightness, are essentially determined by the quantity of water in the pigment mix, creating a heightened perception of light. Unlike oil painters who rely on titanium white, watercolor artists achieve transparency by using a higher water content, allowing the underlying white paper to show through.

This technique is universally applicable, emphasizing that the luminosity resulting from water content surpasses the impact of using vibrant pigments like cadmium yellow without water. A common observation is that beginners often employ excessive amounts of pigment, either straight from the tube or with minimal water, resulting in areas that lack the radiant quality of a well-lit area, resembling undiluted watercolor paint rather than effectively conveying the brilliance of a sunlit surface.

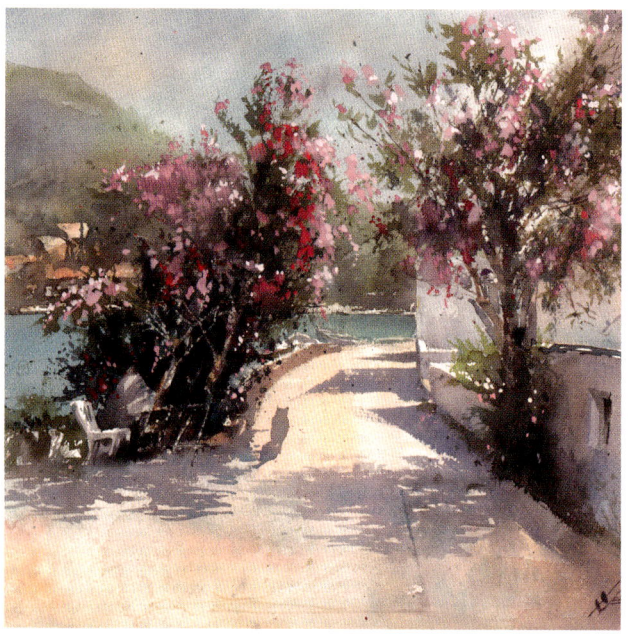

Bougainvillea Road, watercolor, 14" × 14½" | 36 × 37 cm

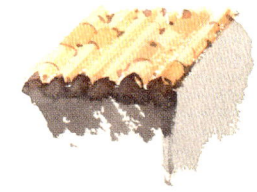 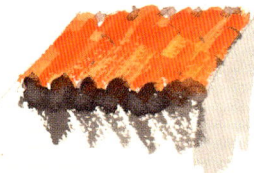

Roof tiles in two values.

Value range.

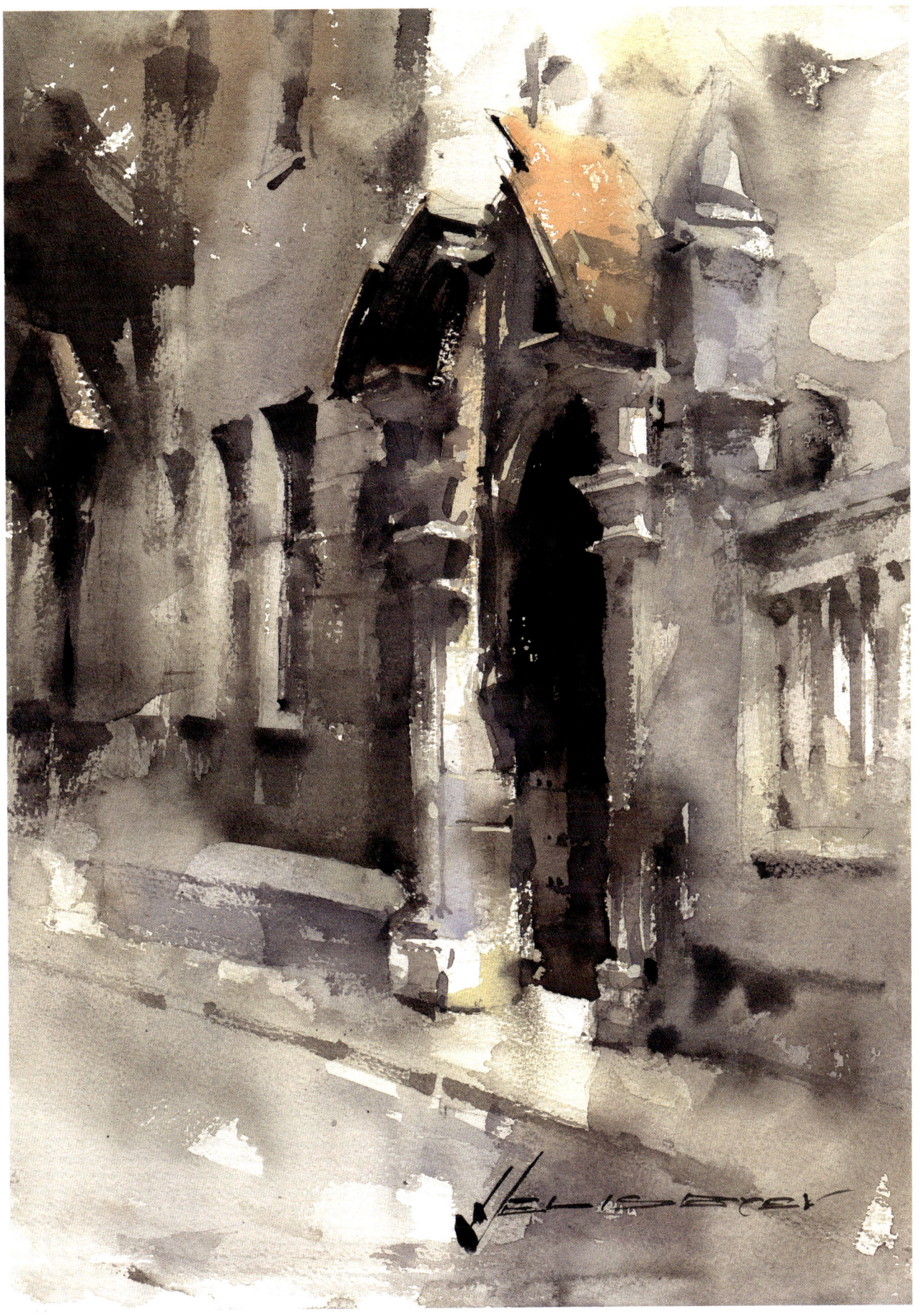

The Gate, watercolor, 16" × 12" | 41 × 30 cm

COLOR INTENSITY

The intensity of color, in contrast, is unrelated to lightness; instead, it straightforwardly reflects the quantity of pigment primarily used in the mix with other pigments. For example, when an excess of red is introduced into a blend of blue and ochre, the resultant area becomes red-dominant, or can be described as red intense. This understanding holds significant importance when engaging in color mixing, a fundamental aspect of fine art essential for conveying the colors in our surroundings on watercolor paper or canvas.

In **A**, three samples of gray with red, yellow, and blue were mixed using the same primary colors.

In practical terms, it's simply impractical to acquire ready-made colors for every subject we aim to depict, making color mixing the only viable solution to use colors that are both suitable and aligned with our artistic vision. In "Exploring Primary Colors in Watercolor" (p. 106), I elaborate on the notion that employing three colors for each consecutive dark area is sufficient to mix a comprehensive range. The proportions of each color in the mix then determine the desired color temperature.

To illustrate this concept further, let's consider the mixing of greens. Combining two colors, specifically yellow and blue, typically in equal amounts, will achieve a green hue with a neutral temperature situated between the warm and cold spectra on the color wheel. Observing the color wheel, we notice green flanked by warm and cold colors on either side. To shift the green toward the warmer end of the spectrum, adding more yellow to the mix creates a warm green or an intense yellow green. Conversely, an excess of blue in the mix produces the opposite effect.

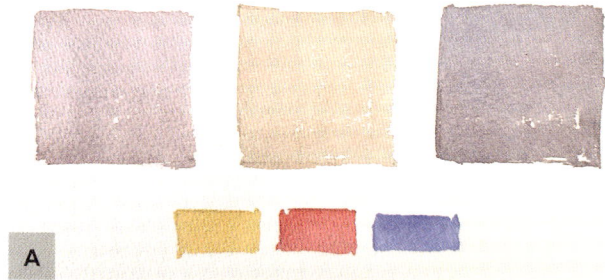

Color intensity.

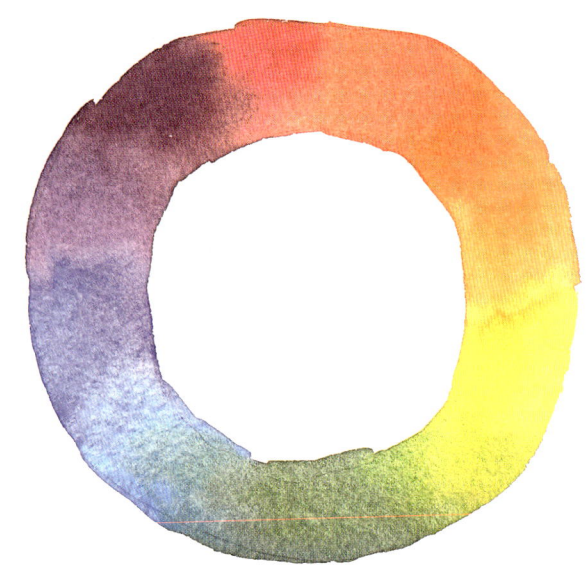

Color wheel.

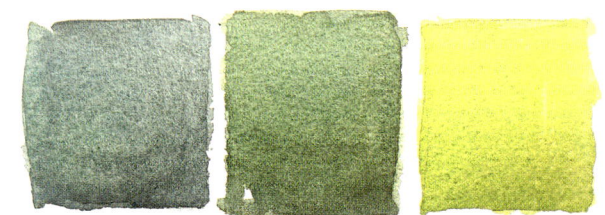

Green color range.

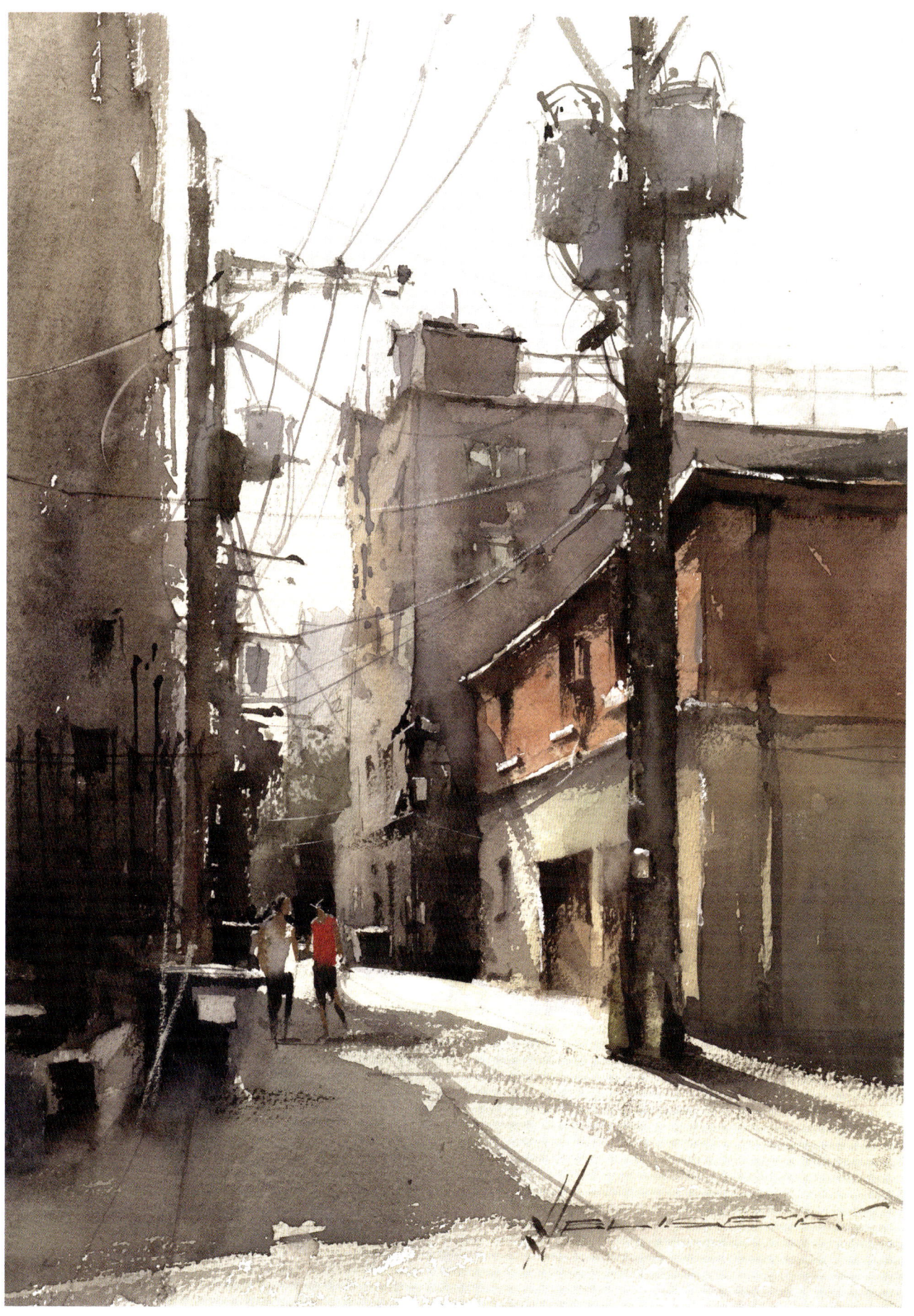

Chicago Back Alleys, watercolor, 14" × 10½" | 36 × 27 cm

THE THREE STAGES OF THE WATERCOLOR PROCESS

It's no secret that mastering control over watercolor painting becomes significantly easier when commencing with illuminated areas and progressively transitioning to darker tonal values until completion. This method aligns seamlessly with the technique of layering, where each successive layer overlaps the previous one and lighter layers are gradually covered by darker washes. However, executing this approach demands meticulous planning, as beginners typically perceive scenes as patches of light and dark rather than discerning them into layered tonal values.

Learning to break down a scene in terms of tonal values and adopting a professional approach to the painting process poses a challenging task. One notable challenge lies in the fact that, unlike oil painting, the watercolor process is somewhat counterintuitive. In our everyday observations, we tend to first notice intricate details, such as the delicate features of a building facade.

This natural sequence of observation, however, needs to be reversed when undertaking watercolor painting to avoid the risk of significant errors.

STEP 1: INITIAL STAGE

In the initial stage of my painting process, I focus on covering the entire or nearly the entire surface of the watercolor paper with light washes, emphasizing illuminated areas while deliberately disregarding darker tones. During this stage, the watercolor wash fluidly transitions from warm to cool colors, loosely adhering to the boundaries of objects. The principle of "paint through the lines" takes precedence at this point. I may introduce a second layer of light washes, incorporating defined half tones and surface distress if deemed necessary.

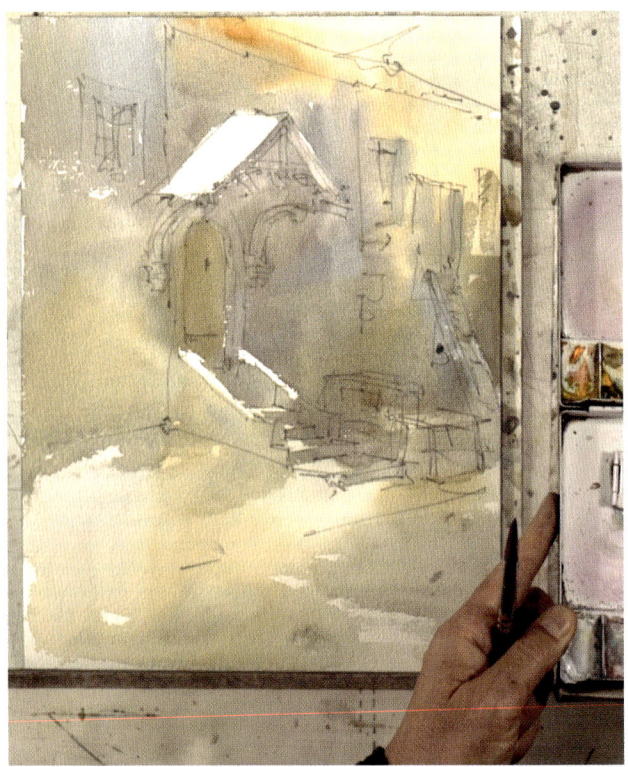

1. Initial stage.

A crucial rule during this stage is to consider the lit areas of the elements as complete and untouched until the final stages of the painting. It's only at the very end that I deliberate on which lit areas to retain and which ones to tone down, allowing for a more strategic and considered approach to the overall composition.

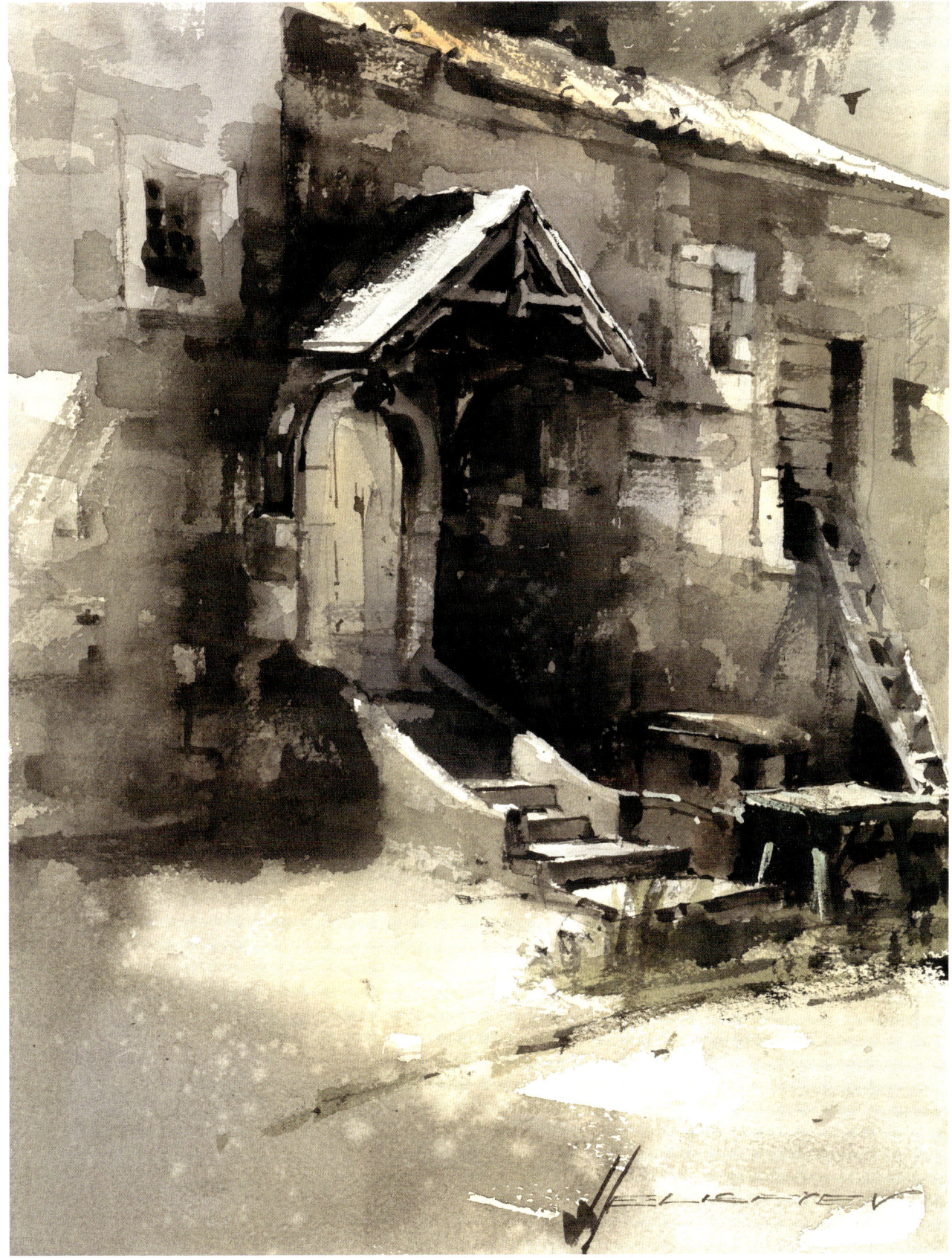

The Steps, watercolor, 22" × 14½" | 55 × 37 cm

STEP 2: MIDTONES AND CAST SHADOWS

In the second stage of my watercolor painting process, I turn my attention to addressing the dark areas. In this phase, I consolidate midtones and cast shadows into a single stage, emphasizing soft and subtle borders between them. Our natural inclination is to focus on the contrasting areas between illuminated and dark regions in a scene, often neglecting the details within the shadows.

Given that beginners tend to replicate information from the scenery or photographs with the same diligence as they do in well-lit areas, their paintings may end up resembling illustrations, lacking emotional impact. To counteract this tendency, I make a conscious effort to avoid mindlessly copying reality. Squinting becomes a valuable tool during this stage, helping me filter out unnecessary details, especially prominent in the darker areas where excessive information is prone to accumulate.

Throughout this phase, I also find it essential to differentiate midtones from cast shadows by carefully considering tone values, gradations, and changes in color within the corresponding areas. Upon completing the second stage, the painting often takes on an appearance of near-completion on a global scale, featuring clearly identifiable focal and secondary areas that contribute to the overall composition.

Success in this stage is contingent on a gradual, thoughtful approach to intensifying the areas of darkness. The key is to lead the painting methodically, allowing the expanses of dark tones to evolve incrementally. It's important to emphasize that the preliminary sketch, completed earlier in the process, proves invaluable at this juncture, serving as a reliable reference to maintain the desired tonal relationships. This reference ensures that the interplay between darks, midtones, and lights is harmonious, contributing to the overall success and impact of the artwork.

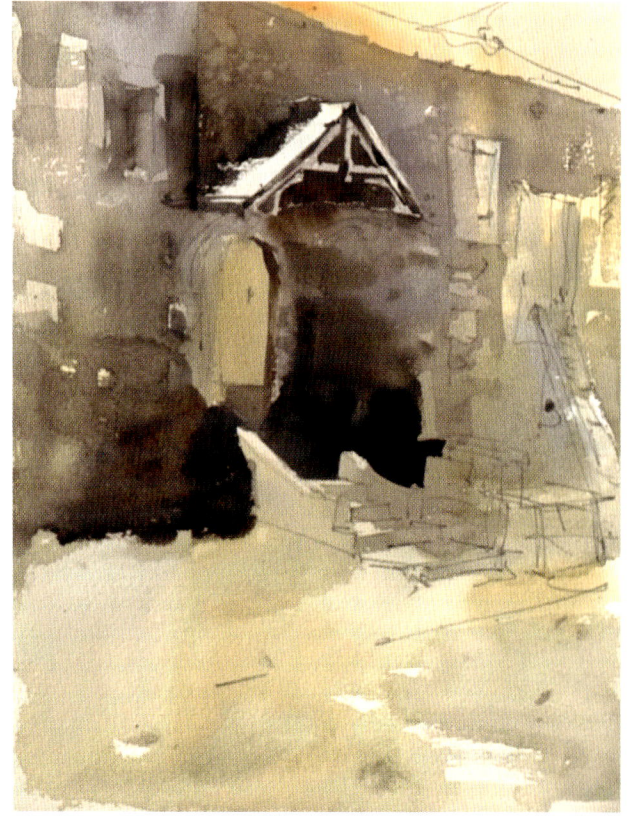

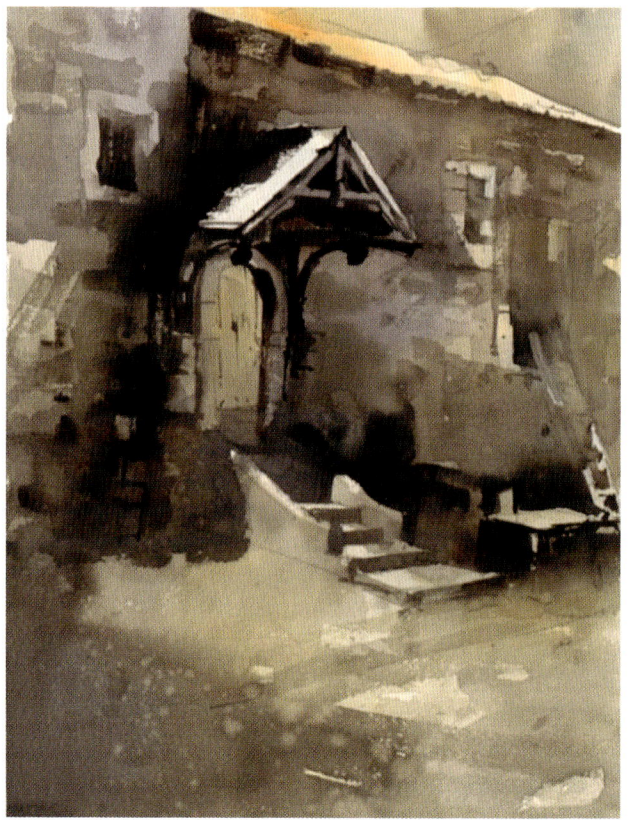

2a. Midtones stage.

2b. Cast shadows stage.

STEP 3: FINISHING TOUCHES

The third stage involves adding intricate details to enhance its overall aesthetic appeal. This step allows for the inclusion of smaller elements in the painting. The selection and quantity of these elements are subjective, as they depend on the artist's vision. However, a crucial guideline is to maintain a minimalistic approach, ensuring that only essential details are included to convey the scenery's character.

Furthermore, the third stage encompasses the application of unifying washes, a technique elaborated upon in the corresponding chapter. This method serves multiple purposes, acting not only as a remedy for potentially overdone calligraphy work but also as a tool to establish a sense of order within the artwork. The primary objective is to structure the hierarchy of lights and darks, ultimately crafting a compelling and focused image.

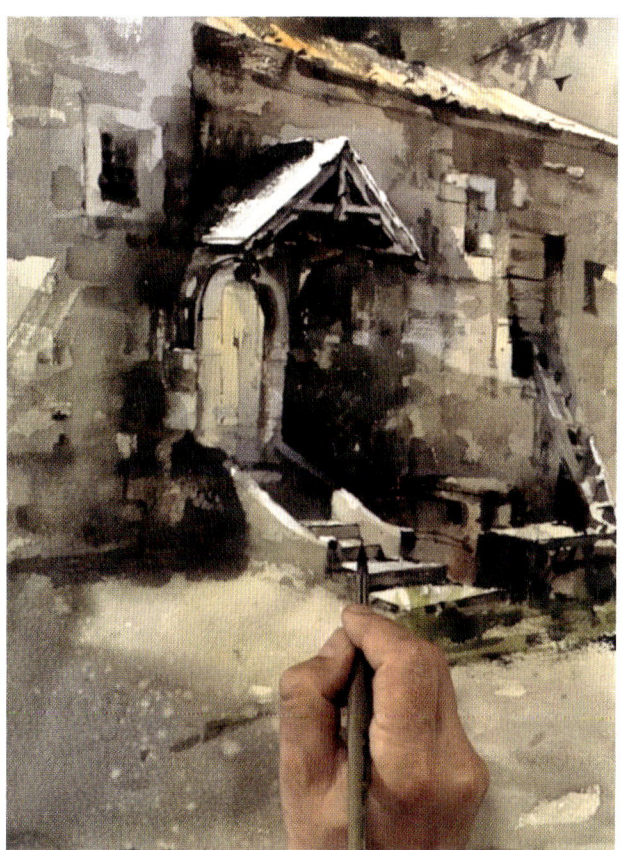

3. Finishing touches.

Scan to view a video tutorial

MASTERING THE LIGHT-TO-DARK WATERCOLOR TECHNIQUE

The uniqueness of the watercolor technique, which uses white watercolor paper to capture light instead of white paint, dictates a specific sequence of watercolor application that differs remarkably from oil and other media. The watercolorist is compelled to paint the lit and radiant areas first, allowing for the subsequent application of darker tones on top of the previously painted areas.

Since each painting consists of a combination of adjacent tonal values, it's much easier to maintain control over this crucial aspect of the painting process by starting with the lightest light and gradually increasing darkness until completion. This approach minimizes the risk of over-darkening the lit areas.

Another aspect of layered watercolor application is that when a light wash is applied on top of a dark one, there is a significant risk of smudging the edge of the dark layer, potentially leading to an excessively soft presentation. For beginner watercolor painters, especially those transitioning from oils, it's a serious challenge to abandon the practice of painting the image as a series of separate light and dark areas and instead start thinking in terms of layers.

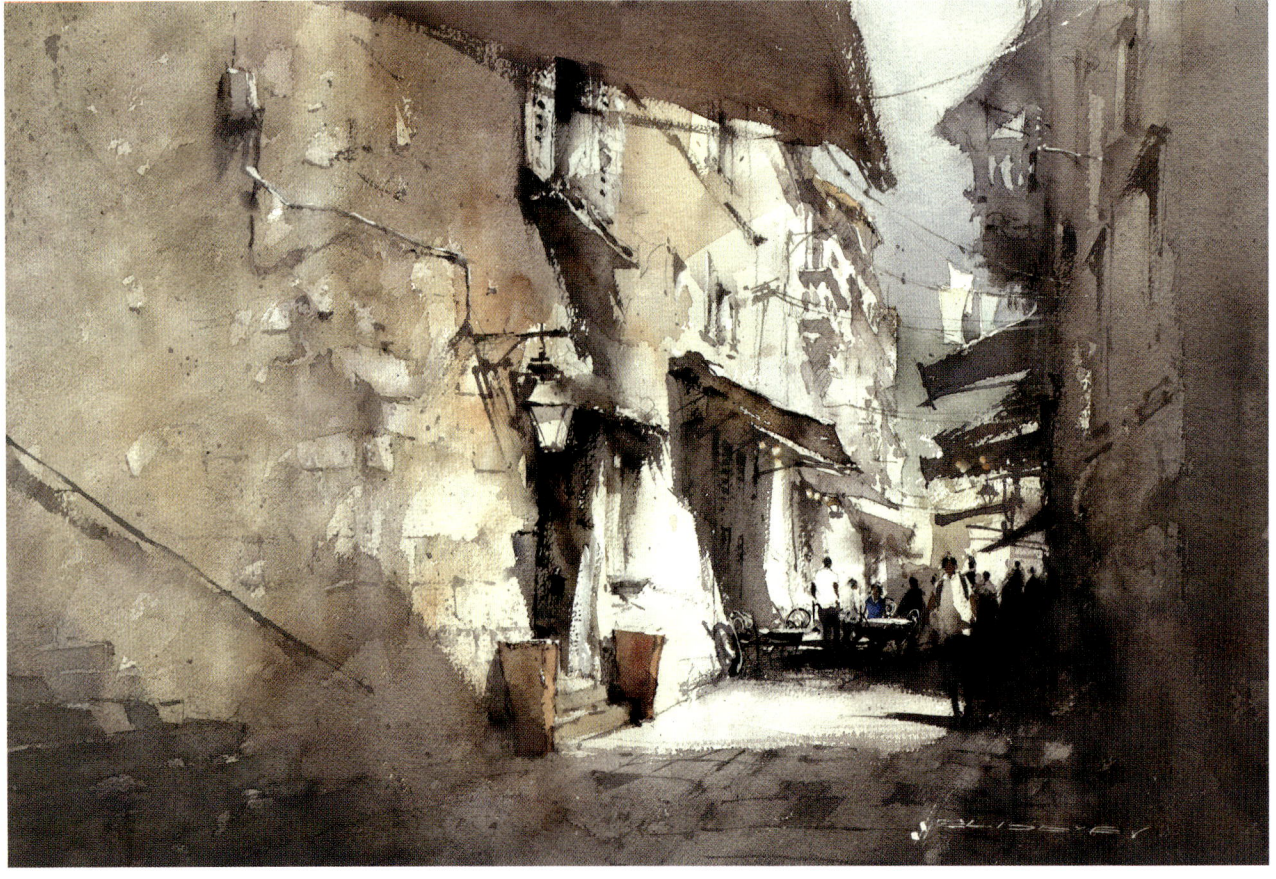

Dubrovnik, watercolor, 14½" × 21½" | 36 × 55 cm

Additionally, it's relatively easy to finish an oil painting with a series of bold and loose dry-edged brushstrokes filled with the brightest paint, a technique that is simply not possible in watercolor. Therefore, the idea is to approach watercolor painting as a series of bold and immediate brushstrokes filled with dark pigment mixes, aiming to achieve a similar immediate-looking work of art by the end of the process.

Achieving edge-to-edge certain area coverage in watercolor poses significant technical challenges. I've observed three potential outcomes in this endeavor. In the first scenario, each edge remains distinct, not touching its adjacent counterpart. In the second, edges slightly overlap, resulting in excessively dark outlines around the painted objects. The third scenario combines both, creating a painting that appears overworked.

This method becomes particularly challenging when filling gaps in densely painted drybrush areas, such as foliage and shrubs. However, when painting watercolor correctly from light to dark, these issues become nonexistent, as demonstrated in (A).

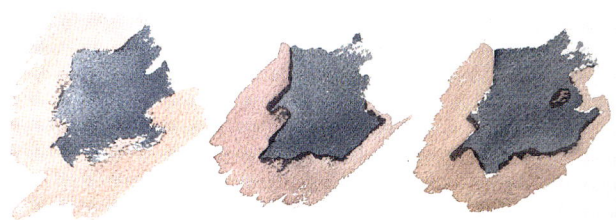

Three mistakes of edge-to-edge paintings.

Correct painting as layered process.

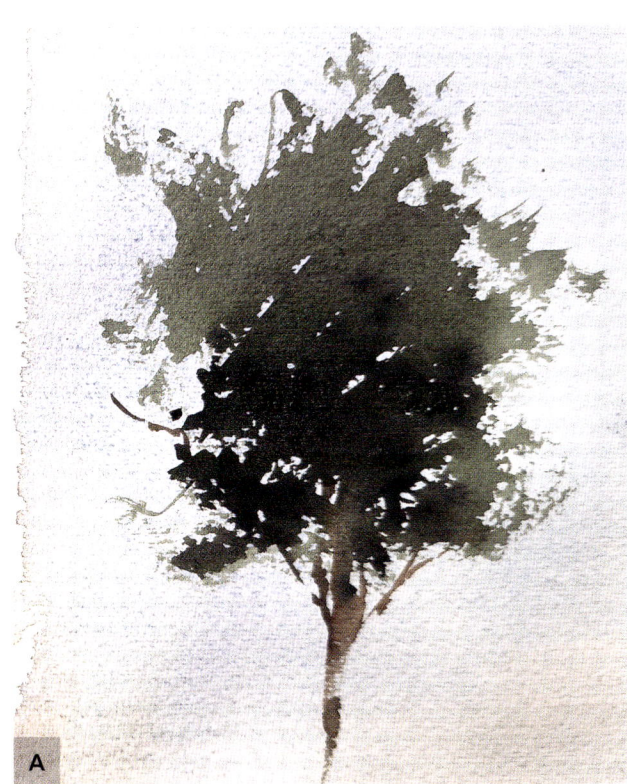

A

Layering method.

B

Mistake of painting tree foliage before the lighter background.

LIGHT-TO-DARK PROCESS

Each time I embark on a watercolor painting, my initial step involves applying a light wash of paint to represent illuminated areas. As mentioned previously, this light wash covers the entire surface of the watercolor paper, encompassing even the dark areas. I am aware that this initial light wash will not impact the subsequent layers of darker hues. In the rare instances where the influence of the previous layer carries over to the next, the interference is minimal, fostering a subtle and harmonious color unity between the layers.

In the next step, I apply the darker tone. I paint these halftones only when the initial layer has completely dried to prevent blooming. This layer often shows subtle distress on the surfaces, and all nuanced details within the illuminated areas.

Next, it's time to address the midtones, understanding that they are generally lighter than the cast shadows. I carefully select these midtones from various elements I aim to depict. More often than not, I paint them directly, seamlessly attaching the darker cast shadows to eliminate any discernible edges between them.

I've often been questioned about the placement of the sky in the sequence of events, with the common belief that the sky should be painted first. In my experience, I find it more effective to paint the sky when it's its turn in the progression of darkness among other elements. This ensures a continuous and uninterrupted sequence of dark tones.

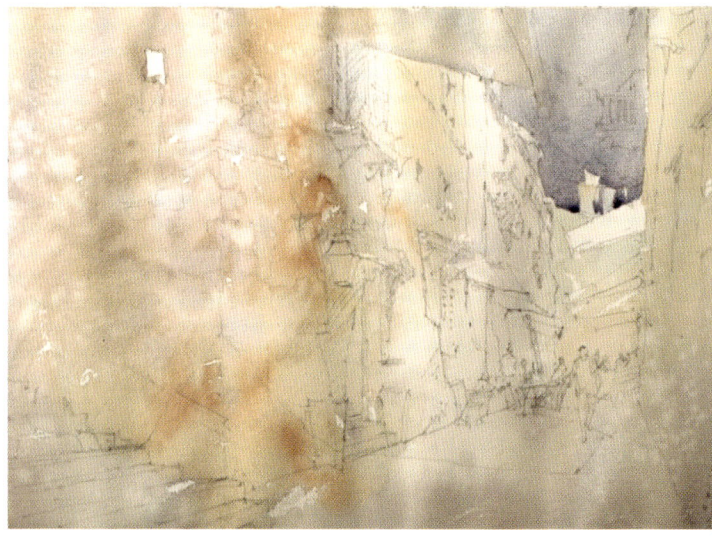

1. Light areas.

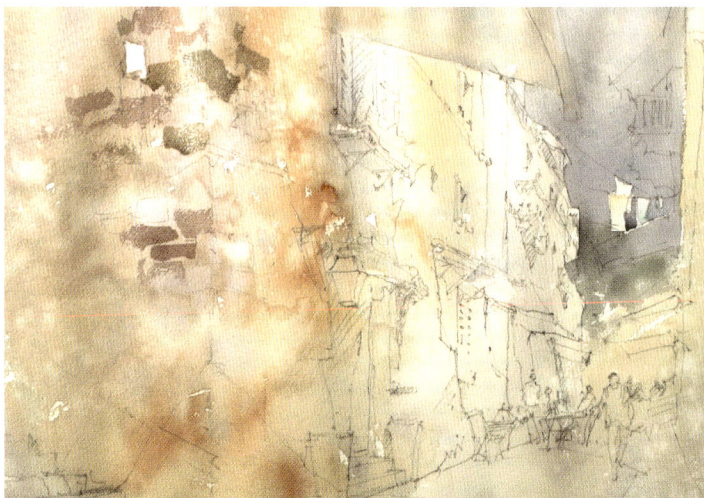

2a. Darker tones (painting wall distress).

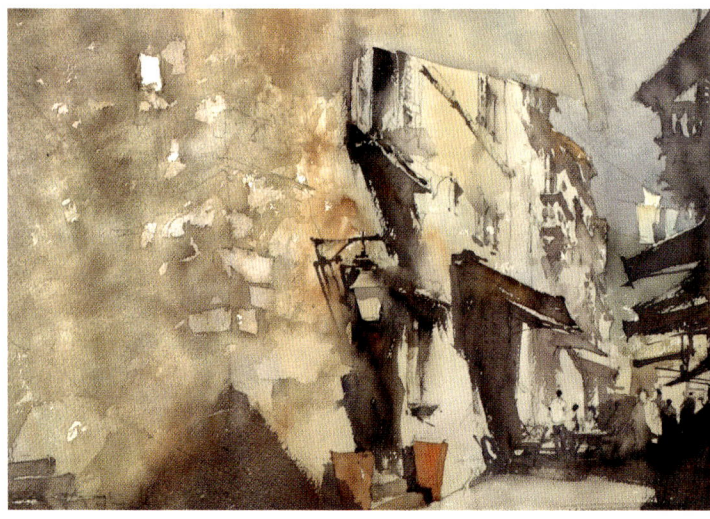

2b. Darker tones (midtones and cast shadows).

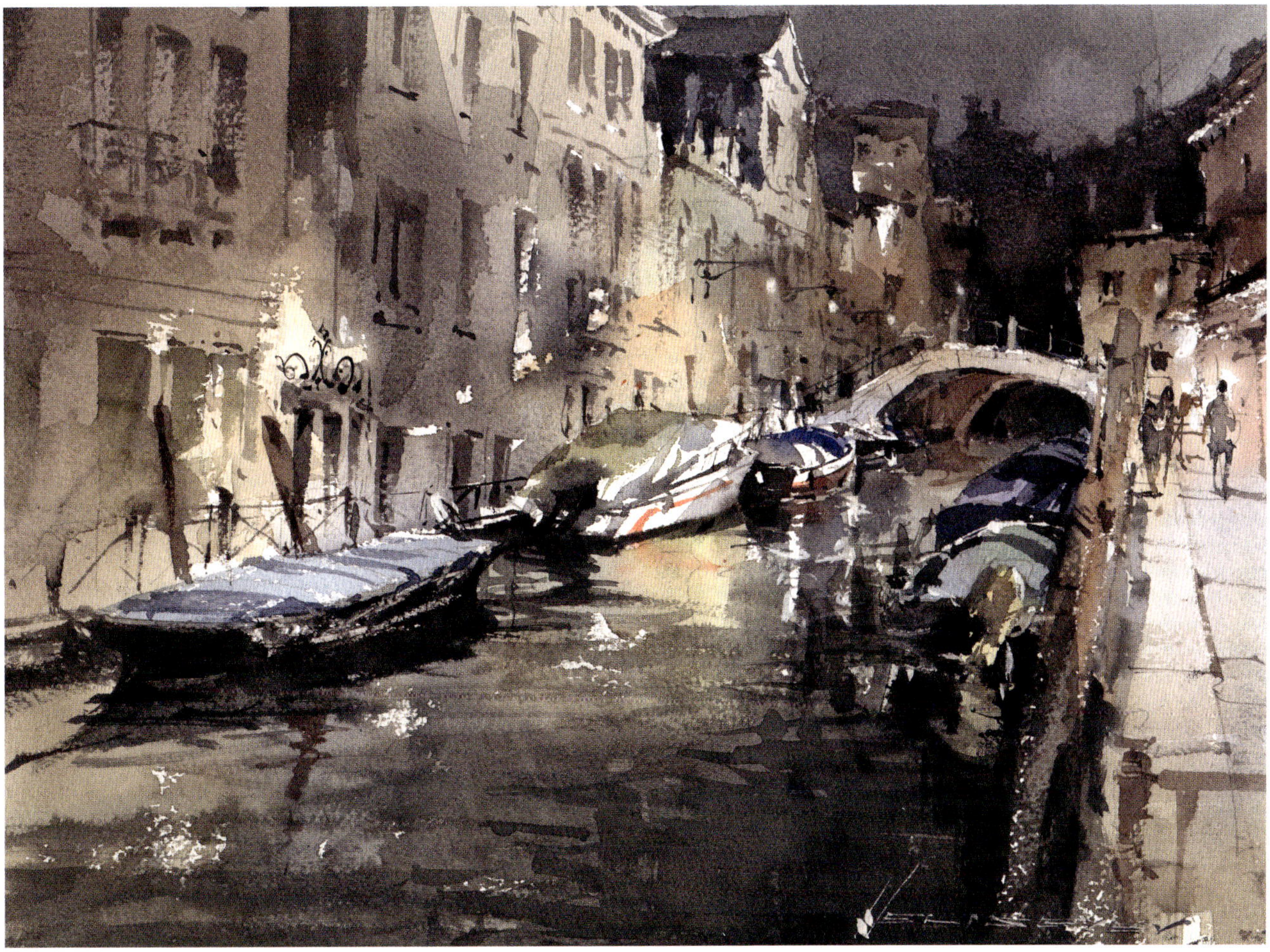

Venice Nocturne, watercolor, 10" × 14" | 26 × 36 cm

A similar principle applies to background objects, which are typically lighter than those in the foreground due to atmospheric perspective. These background elements are often painted after the initial wash, allowing for a deliberate and strategic approach to maintain the proper tonal sequence in the painting process.

When painting night views, strict adherence to the light-to-dark method becomes especially crucial. This is because night scenes often involve multiple sources of light, and following this method makes it easier to maintain control over all tonal values.

The application of titanium white opaque gouache at the conclusion of the watercolor process serves as a valuable tool for restoring lost highlights and adding final touches. However, it's important to exercise caution and avoid using it with significant coverage.

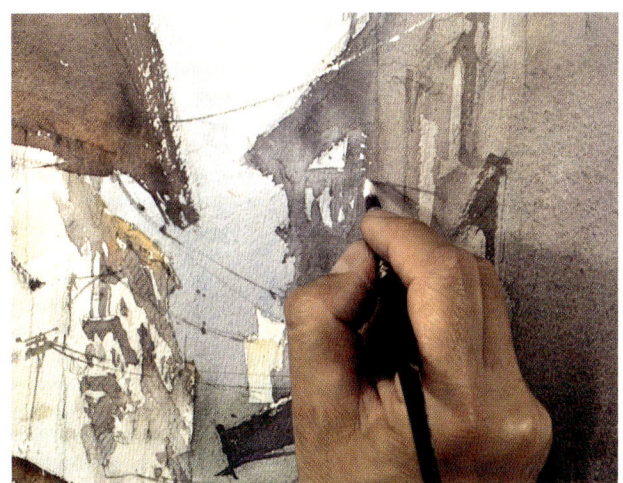

Finishing touches detail.

EXPLORING PRIMARY COLORS IN WATERCOLOR

As I continued my journey in watercolor painting over the years, I noticed that aspect of mixing colors in the painting had become second nature to me. I used it intuitively without much thought. However, using the scientific knowledge that every color around us is composed of three primary colors—yellow, red, and blue—helps to understand the theory behind confident color mixing. Unfortunately, when I attempted to mix pure colors in my studio, I found myself facing a predicament—all I seemed to create were muddy mixes. While I don't mind a little "mud" in my paintings (I'll address this later), I couldn't achieve the beautiful, transparent grays I sought.

After further experimenting, I realized that using pure primaries should be substituted with already factory premixed alternatives. So, instead of pure cadmium yellow, I used yellow ochre; instead of cadmium red, I opted for alizarin crimson; and in place of cerulean blue, I chose cobalt blue for the lit areas.

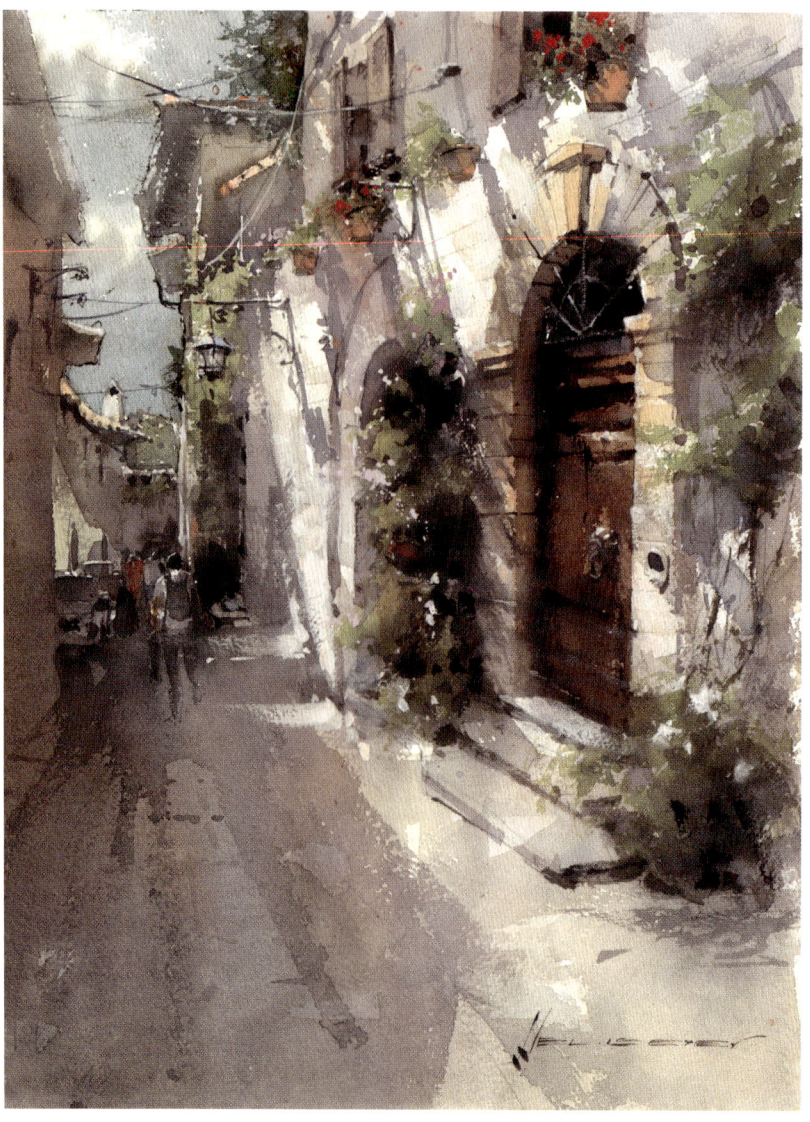

Assisi Street, watercolor, 20" × 15" | 51 × 38 cm

It's worth noting that these "new" colors were already premixed at the factory. Yellow ochre inherently contains some red compared to cadmium yellow, alizarin already contains blue compared to cadmium red, and cobalt blue has some red when compared to pure cerulean blue, which helped to blend them together seamlessly.

An important note is that alizarin plays a vital role as a buffer between yellows and blues. Mixing yellow ochre and cobalt blue directly would result in a green color, which isn't always desirable. Before adding blue to the yellow, I always introduce a bit of red, making the green less noticeable.

After mixing these new combinations of colors, I achieved the results I had been searching for (**A**). What's even more significant is that I could easily adjust the color temperature by varying the amounts of these colors on the fly, without the need for additional colors beyond the ones I mentioned. Considering the countless shades and temperatures of gray that surround us—some warmer, some cooler—these three colors proved versatile enough to deliver what I needed with the right proportion. However, there was one caveat: They weren't suitable for achieving really darker mixes, such as midtones and cast shadows.

It struck me that color mixing techniques were closely tied to the values or tones of the objects we aimed to depict. We already know that any brightly lit object can be broken down into three integral parts in terms of brightness: the lit areas (**B**), midtones, and cast shadows, with the latter being the darkest. What if we designated three sets of primary colors for these three areas on our palettes? Further experimentation led me to discover the need for additional colors to cover these darker areas.

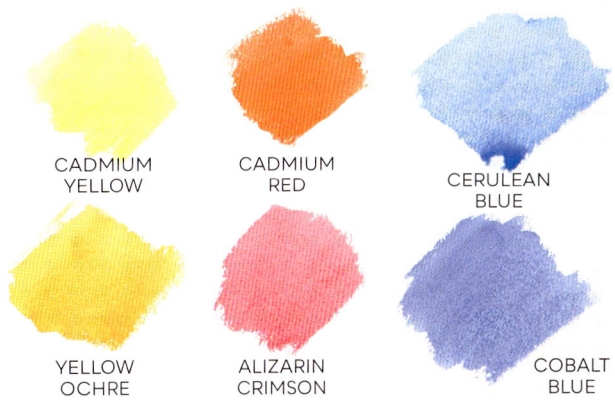

CADMIUM YELLOW   CADMIUM RED   CERULEAN BLUE

YELLOW OCHRE   ALIZARIN CRIMSON   COBALT BLUE

Lit area primaries.

A

Lit area mix.

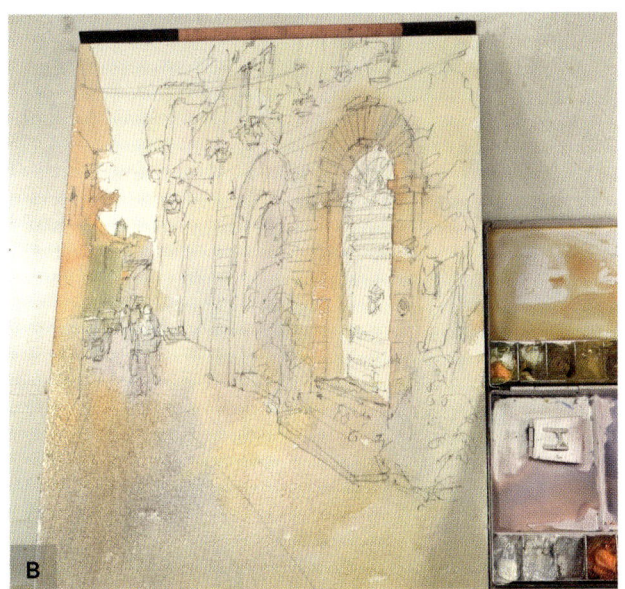

B

Use of primaries in first-stage painting lit areas.

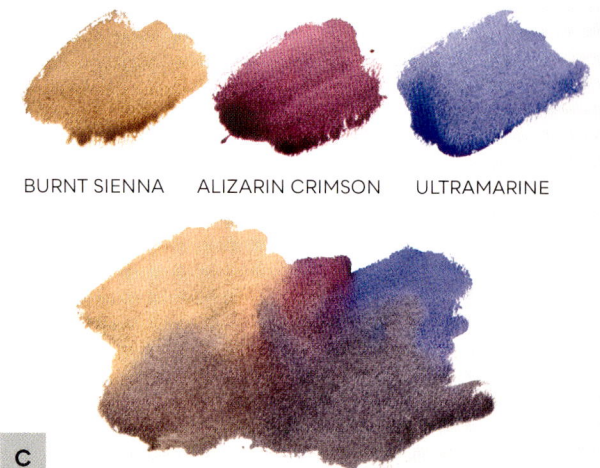

BURNT SIENNA   ALIZARIN CRIMSON   ULTRAMARINE

C

Midtones primaries.

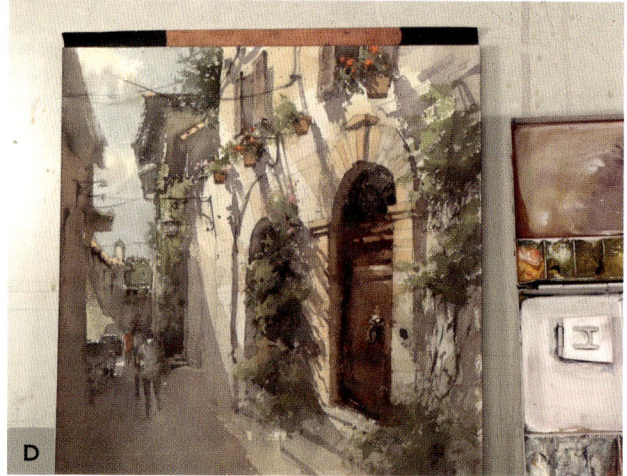

D

Primaries for cast shadows.

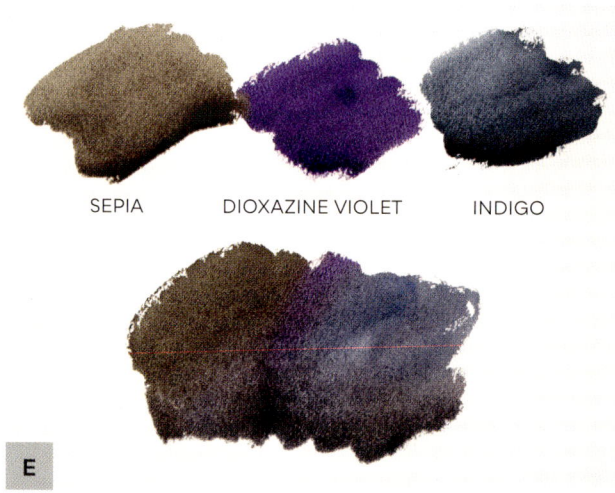

SEPIA   DIOXAZINE VIOLET   INDIGO

E

Cast shadows mix.

Now, let's delve into the specifics. To successfully mix midtones, I use burnt sienna for yellow, a mixture of alizarin crimson and dioxazine violet for red, and ultramarine for blue (**C**, **D**).

When we venture further into even darker values, I frequently turn to sepia, dioxazine violet, and indigo (**E**).

It's important to ensure that the three colors we mix have similar water proportions in each consecutive set to simplify the mixing process. Controlling the temperature becomes easier by adjusting the amount of pigment in the mixes instead.

"Do we only need nine or seven colors to encompass the entire spectrum of painting?" you might wonder. The response is a resounding "no." Indeed, many objects in our surroundings exhibit pure, unadulterated colors, like red shorts or blue bicycles, for example. It's imperative to have all these primary and other intense colors at our disposal on our palettes. By doing so, we can wield them as needed and juxtapose them with various shades of gray to accentuate the brilliance of these vibrant colors even further.

Scan to view a
video tutorial

The second aspect to note is that each red plays a vital role as a buffer between yellows and blues. When I'm mixing colors for tree foliage, I combine yellows and blues directly without use of red to achieve the exact shade of green I desire, without relying on factory-made green pigments (**F**).

After all is said, it's perhaps easier to understand the whole theory by using a table of colors as shown in the picture (**G**) where the columns signify the primaries and the rows the areas of darkness on the object.

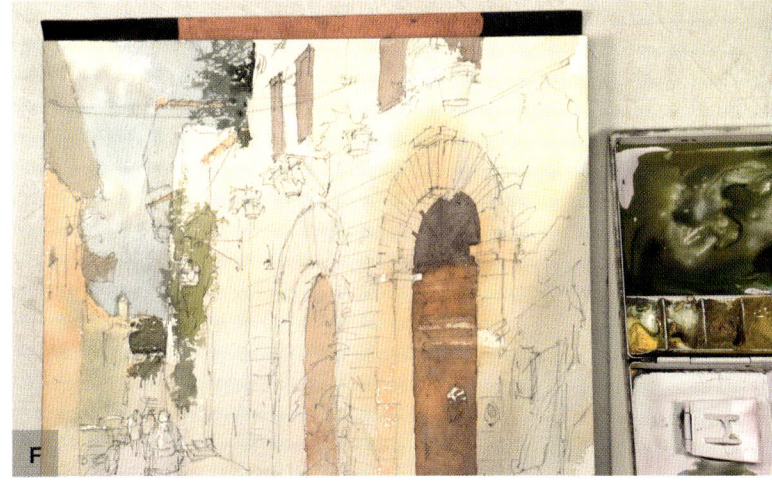

Mixing into greens detail.

	YELLOW	RED	BLUE
LIT AREA	YELLOW OCHRE	ALIZARIN CRIMSON + 10% DIOXAZINE VIOLET	CERULEAN BLUE + COBALT BLUE
MIDTONES	BURNT SIENNA + VAN DYKE BROWN	ALIZARIN CRIMSON + DIOXAZINE VIOLET	ULTRAMARINE
CAST SHADOWS	VAN DYKE BROWN + SEPIA	DIOXAZINE VIOLET	ULTRAMARINE + INDIGO

Color table.

COLOR MIXING DIRECTLY ON PAPER

Many times I've observed an abundance of muddled hues on my palette, transferring onto the watercolor paper due to a pervasive overmixing of various colors. To counteract these unfortunate outcomes, I make a conscious effort to blend my colors directly on the paper as much as possible.

While the act of mixing colors directly on watercolor paper is generally manageable, the challenge increases with smaller areas of coverage. In such instances, I find it more practical to resort to mixing colors on the palette.

It's crucial to work on a slightly inclined board. To maintain control over the direction of the washes, I always begin from the top of the board and gradually progress downward, allowing gravity to facilitate the mixing process.

The color mixing technique on paper also requires careful measurement of components in the mix. For instance, if the desired end result is a light and warm mix, yellow ochre should perhaps dominate among cobalt blue and alizarin crimson colors. I always create the initial original color mixes with water beforehand on my palette to ensure precision.

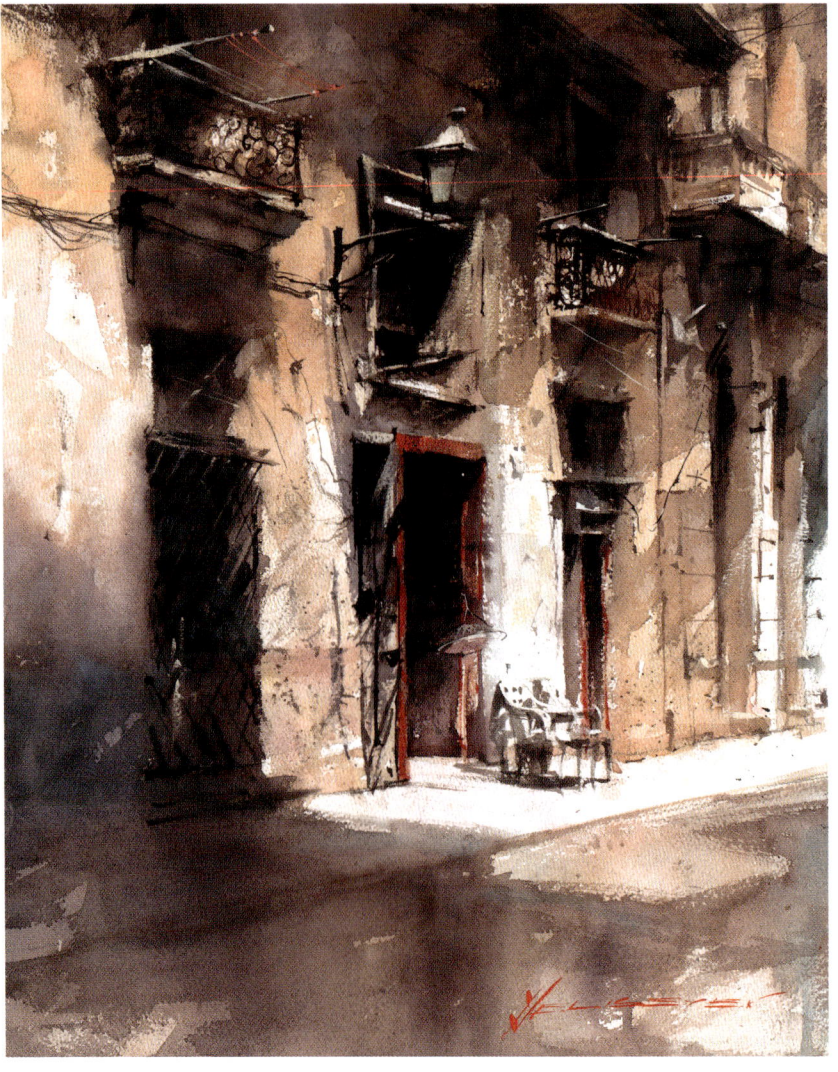

Two Chairs, watercolor, 21½" × 17½" | 55 × 45 cm

In the actual process of mixing, it's crucial to deliberately leave certain areas with varying degrees of mixing effort. This intentional approach aims to achieve a gradual gradation of color, allowing specific sections to be mostly undisturbed as the colors naturally blend during the drying process.

During this painting method, I employ a loose zigzag brush movement for color application to prevent a rainbow effect. Importantly, I keep the brush consistently in contact with the watercolor surface, essentially pushing the color in a particular direction. The subsequent addition of the second color is applied in the area of the first color, overlapping only where necessary according to artistic vision. This principle is also extended to the consecutive third color.

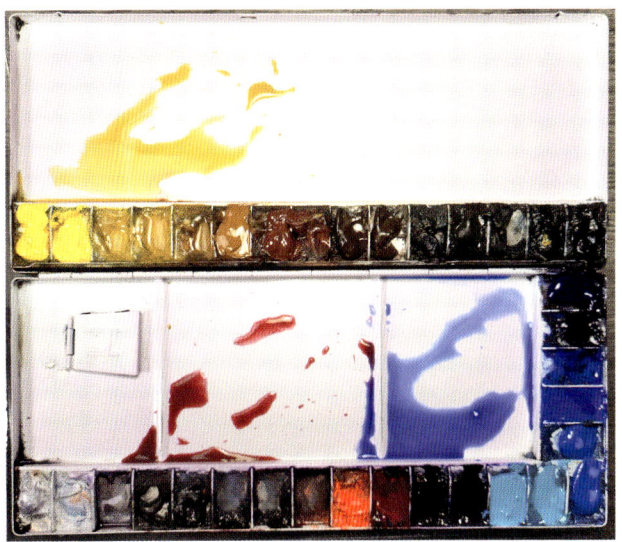

Palette color preparation.

Color mixing method.

Watercolor application dynamics.

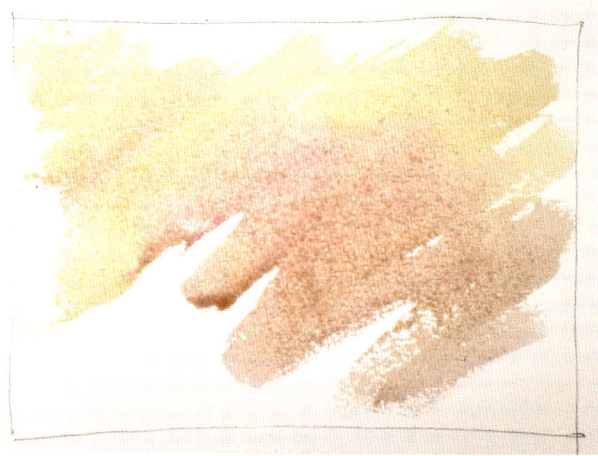

Mixing two colors.

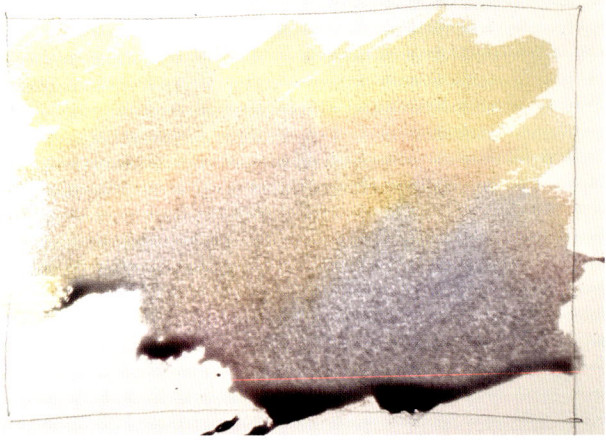

Color mixing three colors.

Color mixing with additive colors.

At this stage, it's relatively easy to adjust the results by introducing darker colors into the still-wet mix or by manipulating the color temperature in specific areas simply by depositing pigment onto the watercolor paper. It's crucial to carefully observe the wetness of the previously painted area and refrain from making any adjustments if the paper is semi-dry.

I have discovered that mixing on paper works exceptionally well in the initial stage of the watercolor process when covering large areas with watered down washes is essential. The looseness of the application not only serves this purpose effectively but also enhances the subsequent layers of paint, subtly alluding to the expressive and free nature inherent in the medium.

Scan to view a
video tutorial

I have observed that novice painters often lose control of the wetness by working slowly, resulting in what we refer to as blooming effects. When this occurs, it's better to leave it undisturbed and address these effects later after they have dried. A reliable way to determine if it's too late to add or adjust a wash is to examine the surface of the watercolor paper at an angle. If the surface has lost its shiny appearance and acquired a sort of satin finish, it is better to leave it untouched and avoid taking risks, regardless of the desire to make adjustments. Attempting to fix the washes may only result in a more distracting appearance.

This is a crucial moment to emphasize that timing is everything in watercolor. Before applying any washes to my paper, I precede it with thorough preparation work. I've noticed that, at times, almost half of my painting time is dedicated to preparing ingredients on the palette and color mixing before the start of actual painting.

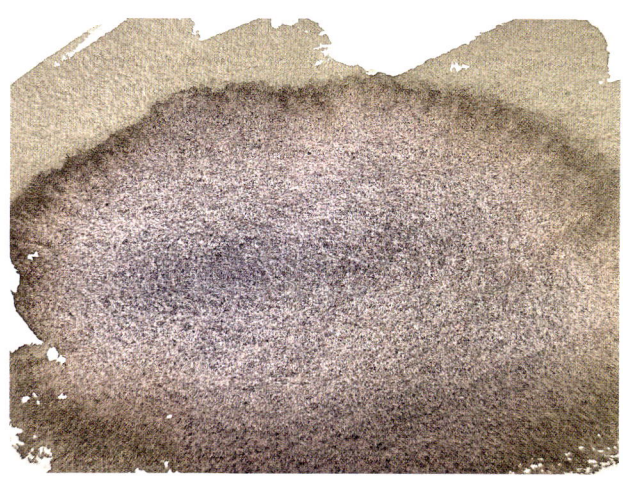

Blooming effect.

At this point, I remind myself that the strength of watercolor lies in its unpredictability, and what we refer to as "happy accidents" are an important part of the process. If I desired strict control over my painting, I would dedicate my time exclusively to oil paintings, where such control is more achievable due to the nature of the medium.

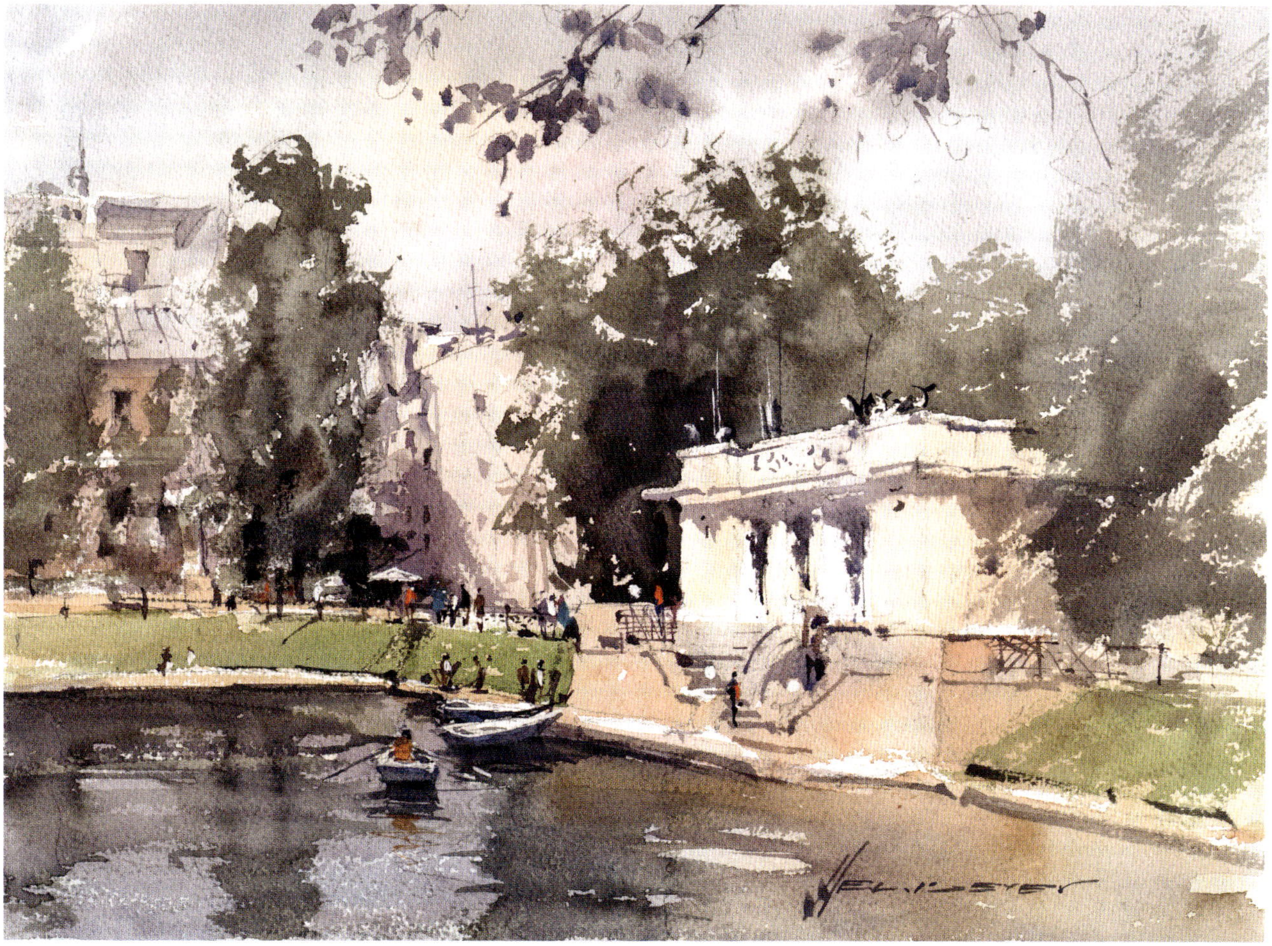

Patriarch's Ponds, watercolor, 10½" × 14½" | 27 × 36 cm

NAVIGATING THE THREE PLANES OF VISION

It's not a secret that landscape painters grapple with an almost boundless source of information when working en plein air or from photographs. This can indeed be a blessing, but more often than not, it turns into a problem, as the sheer volume of it becomes overwhelming.

In reality, our perception of reality is three-dimensional. However, the task of painting is to convey a two-dimensional representation on paper or canvas while creating the illusion of depth.

The fundamental and highly effective technique for dividing a landscape into planes is to envision three vertical flat surfaces neatly stacked in succession. Each of these surfaces represents a two-dimensional picture capturing a specific portion of the entire image. The farthest surface constitutes the background, portraying elements of the landscape that are most distant within the picture. The next plane closer to the artist represents the midground, encompassing the focal area and immediate surroundings as perceived by the artist. The nearest plane, closest to the artist, forms the foreground, containing all the immediate details and information.

This method is straightforward; we paint each plane as a flat surface without concerning ourselves with conveying three-dimensionality on each one. Just as 3-D glasses in a movie theater create the illusion of depth, stacking these three flatly painted planes against each other suffices to generate a sense of depth in the painting.

The background plane should employ a wet-on-wet painting technique, featuring soft edges, light washes, and muted colors to mimic atmospheric perspective—although the use of water bottle sprayers can be advantageous (**A**).

The midground plane, serving as the focus of attention, benefits from high contrast, chiseled brushwork, and intense color applications to draw the viewer's attention (**B**). These two planes alone can effectively create a sense of depth. But how does the foreground plane fit into the overall picture? In reality, we seldom pay attention to our immediate surroundings, focusing most of our attention on the midground, where the action unfolds. Therefore, we should reduce the level of detail in the foreground plane by using the drybrush method, implying a suggestive approach that distinctly contrasts with the background's appearance (**C**). The use of rough watercolor paper may be beneficial.

It's essential to acknowledge that each individual perceives the landscape differently and every artist brings their unique perspective and impressions to the canvas. Consequently, the placement of these planes may vary among artists, which is both normal and expected as long as they don't break the consecutive order of them. This diversity in perception is one of the reasons why even within a group of artists painting the same scene, the end results can be strikingly distinct, irrespective of their skill level.

Scan to view a video tutorial

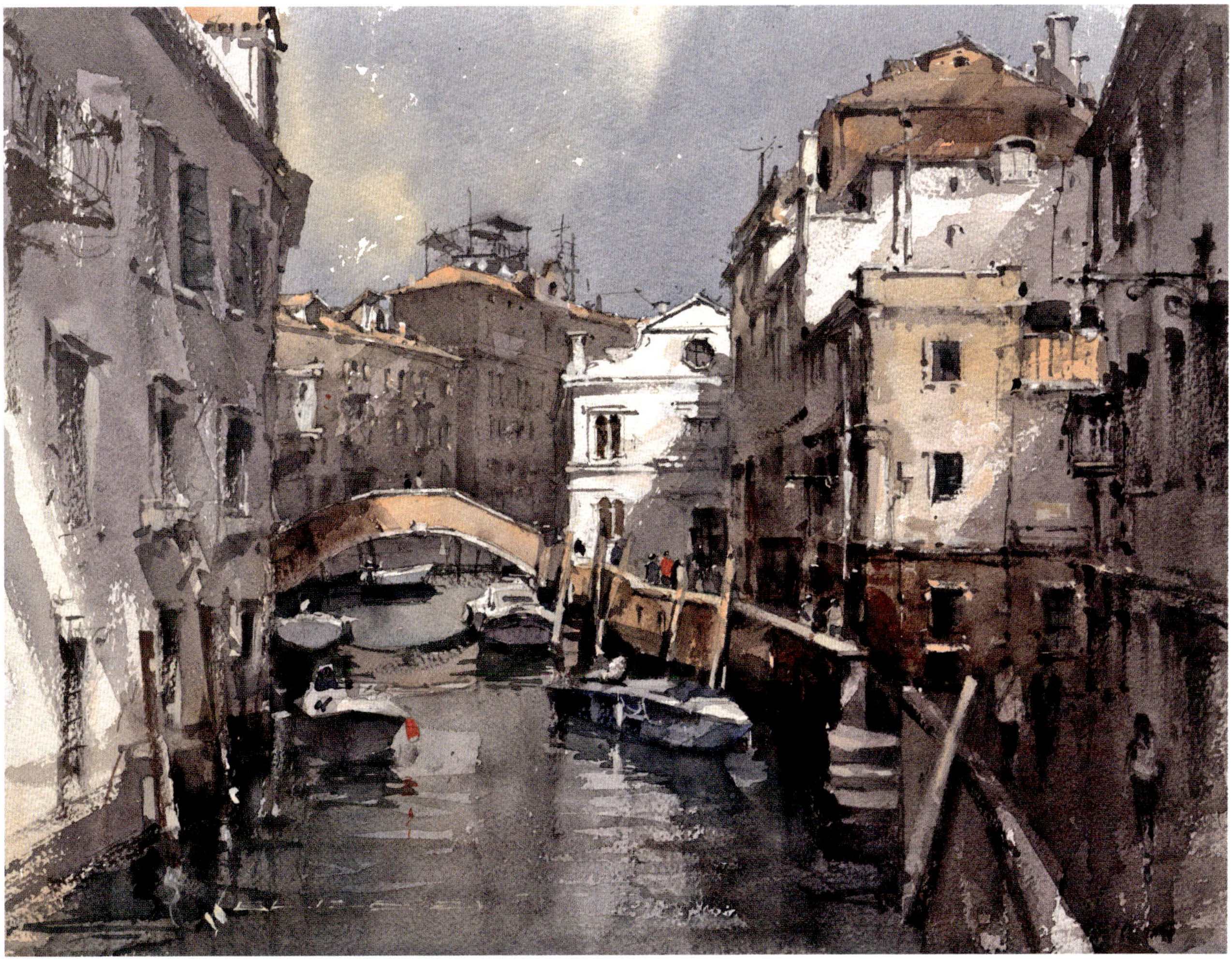

Venice, watercolor, 14" × 19" | 36 × 47 cm

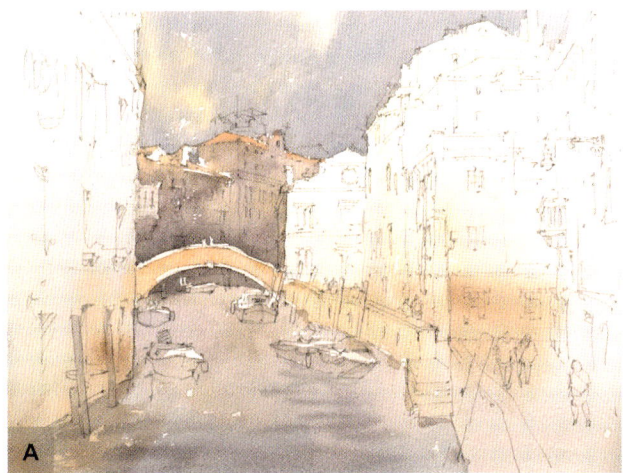

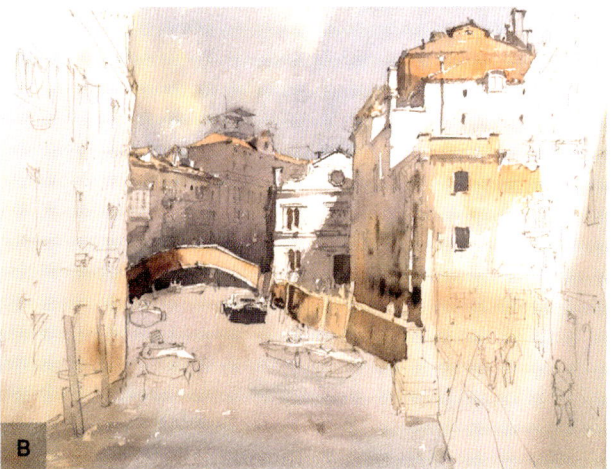

Back plane soft wash. Light washes are used to deemphasize contrast and color in the background plane. Please note the very low contrast between the background building and the sky. The colors used are mixed with a significant amount of water.

Middle plane accents. High contrast and bolder colors are being implemented in the midground area to draw attention to this plane. This area draws the attention of the viewer, similar to the center of a theater stage where all the action takes place, and it's lit accordingly brightly.

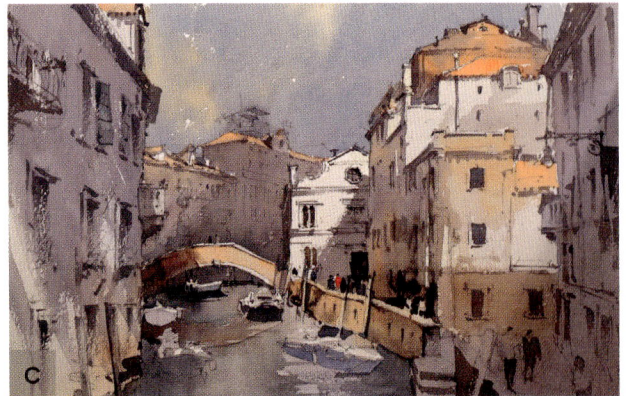

One important stage in finding the placement is the creation of a monochromatic sketch, be it grisaille or graphite pencil (see *Venice*, below).

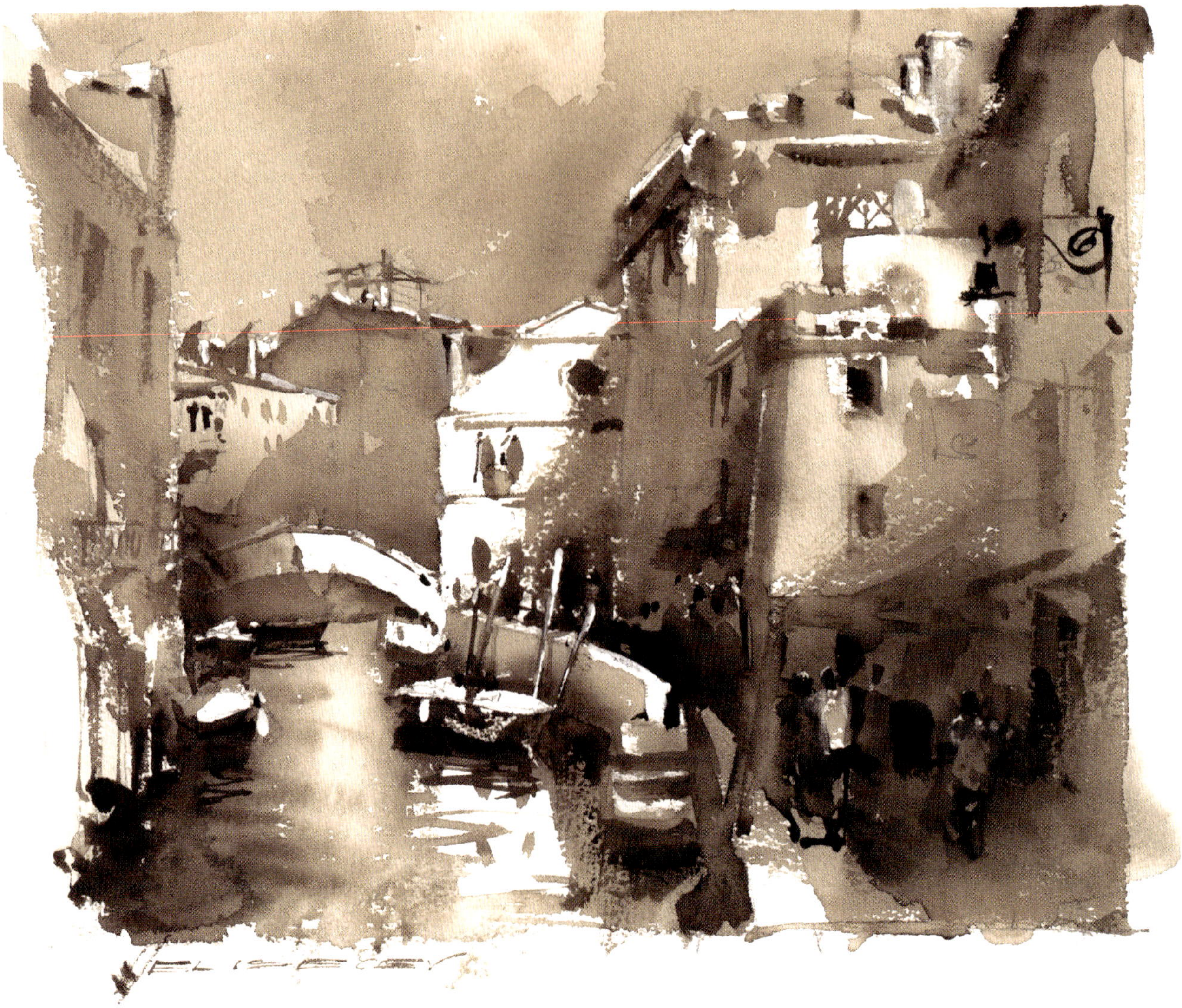

Foreground plane drybrush. The preliminary wash in the foreground area is applied before adding drybrush details. This step is taken to reduce the contrast in the foreground plane of the painting.

Venice, watercolor sketch, 9" × 11" | 24 × 28 cm

This sketch serves as a reference for the future full-color painting, not only as a value study but also by clearly displaying the separation of background, midground, and foreground planes with their respective brushwork execution.

COLOR DYNAMICS IN FOCAL AREAS

In "Identifying Focal Areas" (p. 122), I explore the significance of high contrast as a means to emphasize and isolate specific elements, thereby capturing the viewer's attention within the artwork. Additionally, the deliberate use of color can serve as an effective technique to direct focus toward key areas in the painting.

While some artworks employ vibrant colors across the entire surface, this approach is more fitting for decorative pieces where focal points may be less crucial or entirely absent.

Truth be told, I encourage artists not to shy away from embracing the concept of "mud" in their work. Using subdued, grayish shades with minimal color intensity can offer a unique advantage. These washes, despite having limited color information, establish an ideal backdrop for subsequent applications of more pronounced and accentuated colors. This approach serves to restrict and guide the viewer's attention toward specific points of interest within the painting.

Imagine a precious stone set against the backdrop of a black evening dress—its radiance stands out distinctly. Now, envision that same jewel amidst a spectrum of vibrant hues in evening attire; its brilliance might get lost amid the multitude of colors. A similar effect occurs when a color, seemingly identical, is surrounded by an array of intensely bright tones, drowning in a sea of colors all vying for attention within a painting. This creates an unfocused and chaotic visual experience.

In such a scenario, it becomes evident that even within chaos, the human brain naturally gravitates toward a specific focal point. It's impractical for an individual to absorb the entirety of a scene by looking in various directions simultaneously. As fine art aims to delve into deep human thoughts, experiences, and emotions, I strive to establish a singular focal area in my paintings as much as I can.

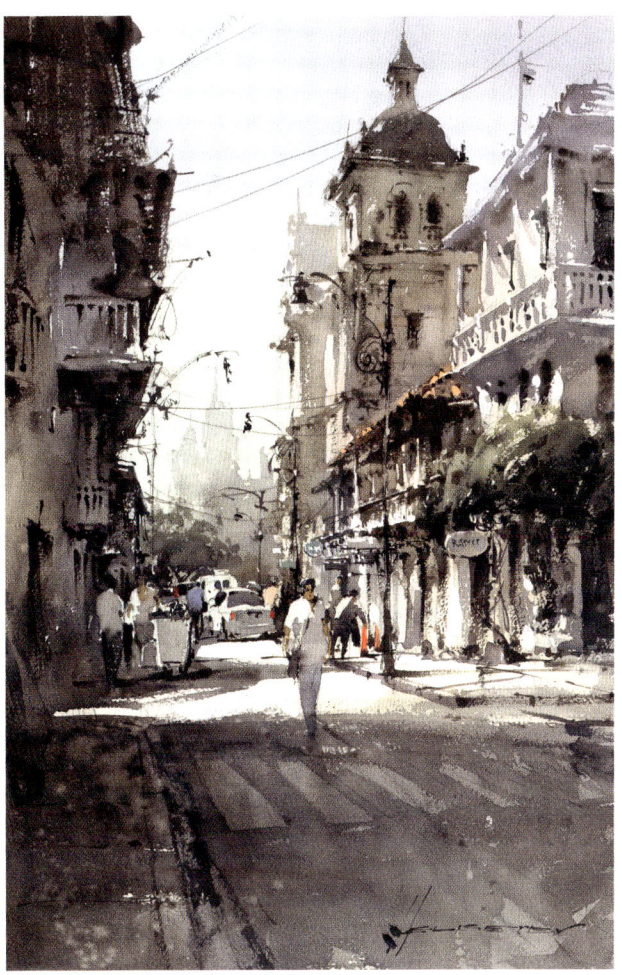

Cartagena Light, watercolor, 22" × 15" | 56 × 37 cm

Drawing from my experience as a scenic painter, I find ample opportunities to improvise and use colors meaningfully. For example, strategically placing a human figure clad in a vibrant shirt can serve as a focal point; a colorful car might command attention in a larger space; or introducing brighter, more intense green foliage can narrow the vision in one direction in a landscape painting. Each decision in the placement and intensity of colors must contribute to the creation of a meaningful and engaging visual narrative.

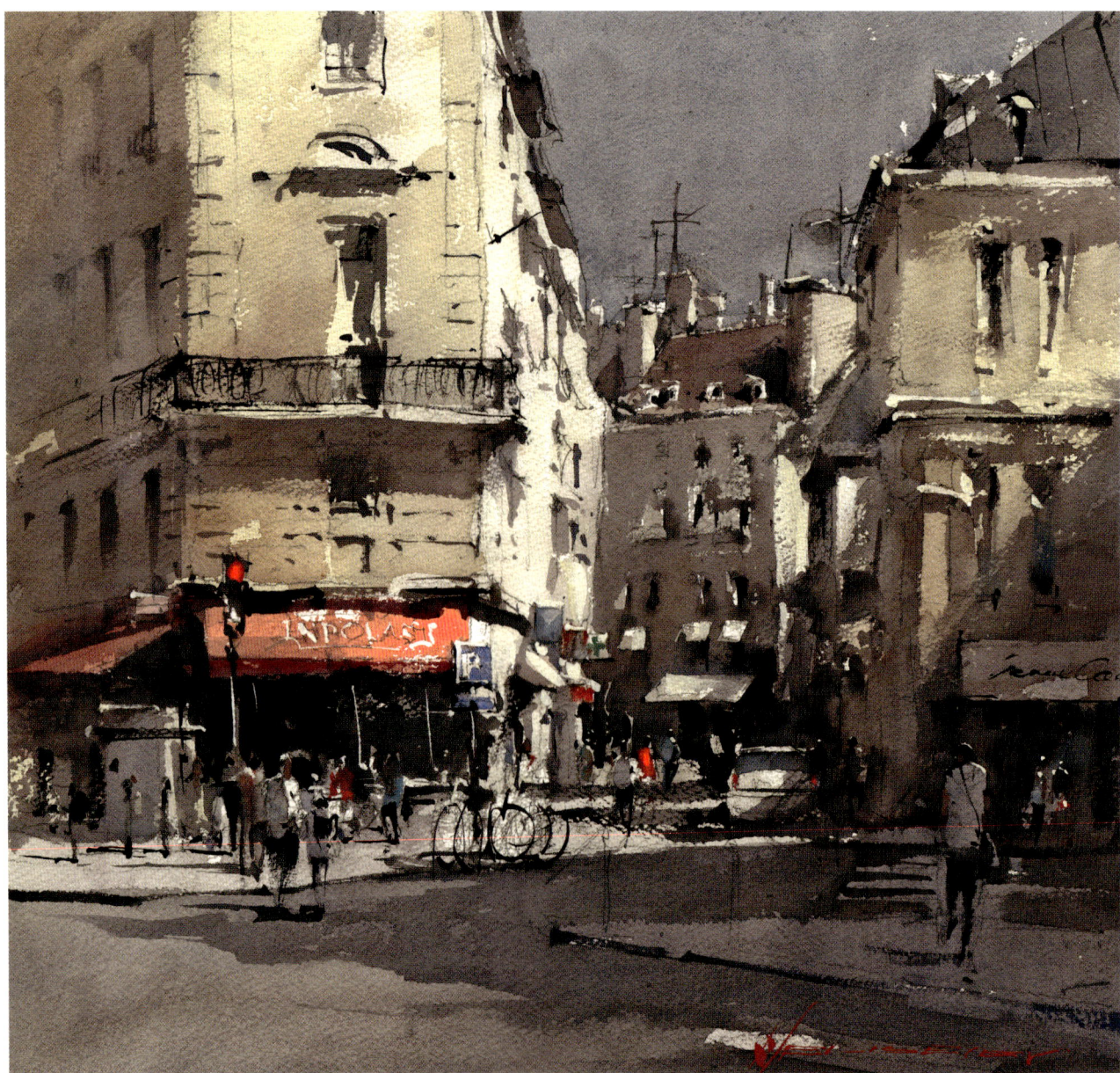

Paris Café, watercolor, 14" × 15" | 36 × 38 cm

I want to emphasize that a crucial task for artists, regardless of their subject matter, is to discover effective ways to establish a vibrant and accentuated area that complements the tonal values in the painting. By strategically isolating the focal point, which includes careful consideration of color, I now have the freedom to refrain from excessively amplifying the contrast in the painting while still maintaining its relevance. This allows for a more nuanced and controlled approach to achieving visual impact.

It also indicates the necessity of finding ways to diminish the brightness and intensity of colors in less critical areas. This can pose a challenge for less experienced painters who may be primarily replicating elements from a reference image or reality painting en plein air. The difficulty arises because substituting the authentic elements with subdued versions in the painting is not only a test of imaginative color conception but also a challenge in achieving harmonious color unity within the artwork.

As a practical approach, I typically select a few colors that captivate me in their unaltered form when combined in adjacent areas. To achieve the desired effect, I dilute the other colors with extra water during the mixing process, creating a lighter appearance. Additionally, I can reduce color intensity by incorporating grey mixes into the palette.

BALANCING GENERALIZATION AND REFINEMENT

Generalization and refinement stages are not bound by specific timings for implementation, except perhaps during the initial stage of watercolor when the entire surface is almost entirely covered with the initial wash. After that, it's up to the artist's vision and ideas, which are formed in the artist's mind before picking up the brush. I have observed that in my painting process, there could be multiple interconnected stages for simplification and refinement. The reason for this is that in every particular painting, there is a unique chain reaction of these stages, which does not repeat and depends on the artist's vision and the desired level of detailing.

I can assert that without the general stage, or what we can refer to as the unification stage, further refinement becomes difficult, and vice versa.

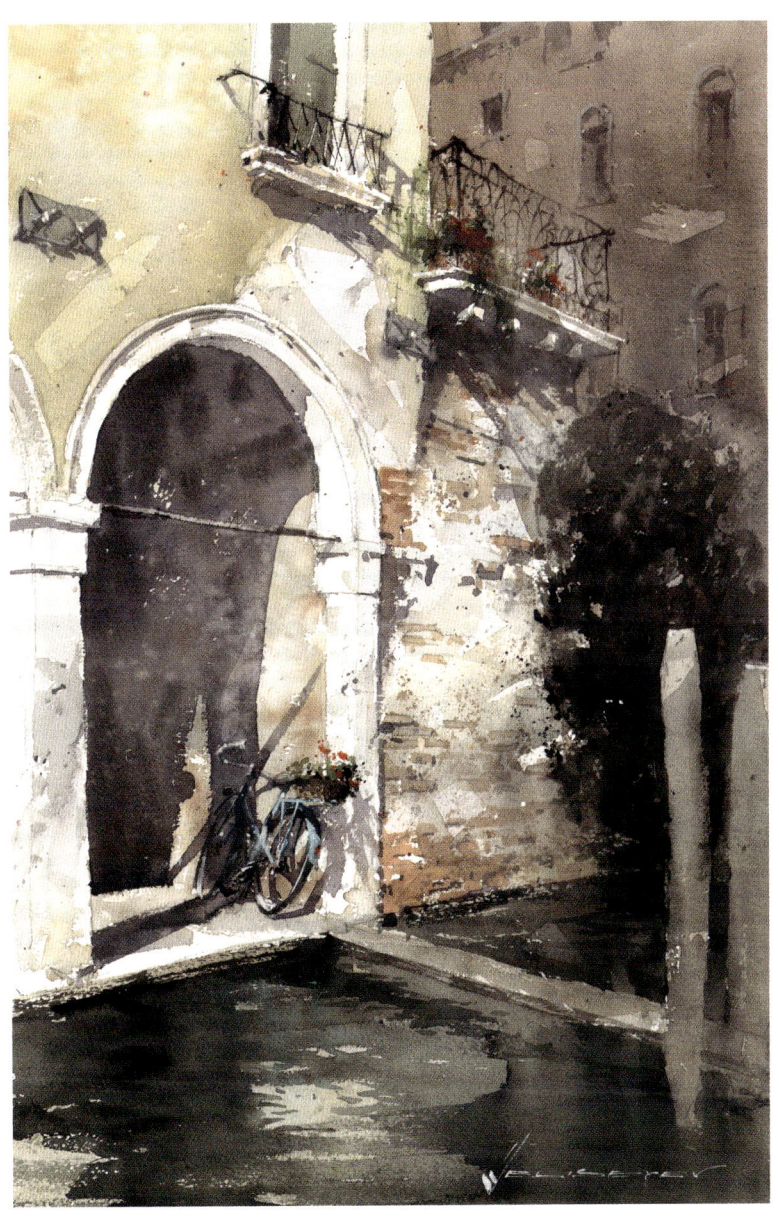

Venice Arches, watercolor, 21½" × 14½" | 55 × 37 cm

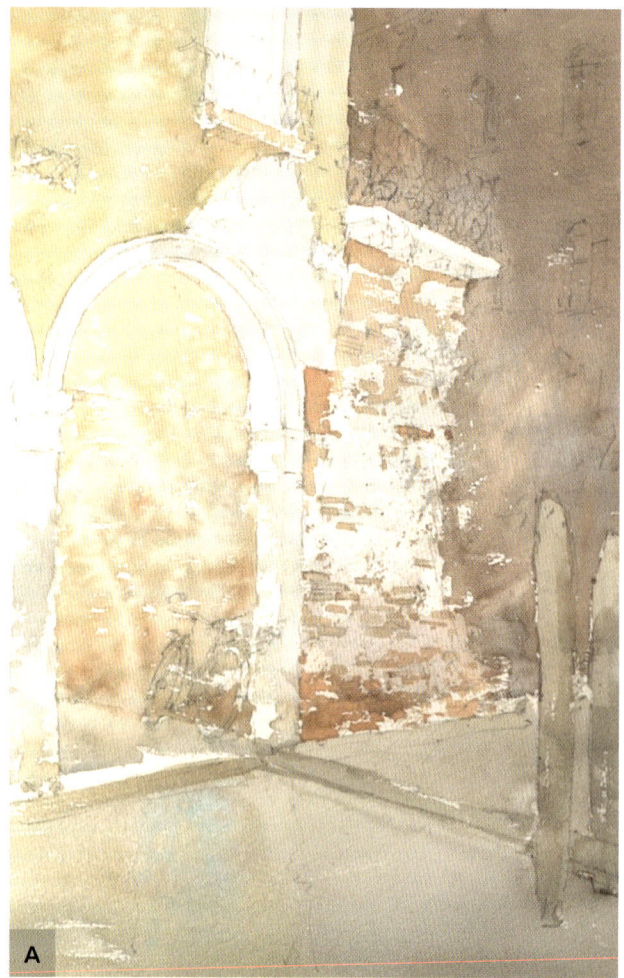

A

Generalization stage with brick isolation.

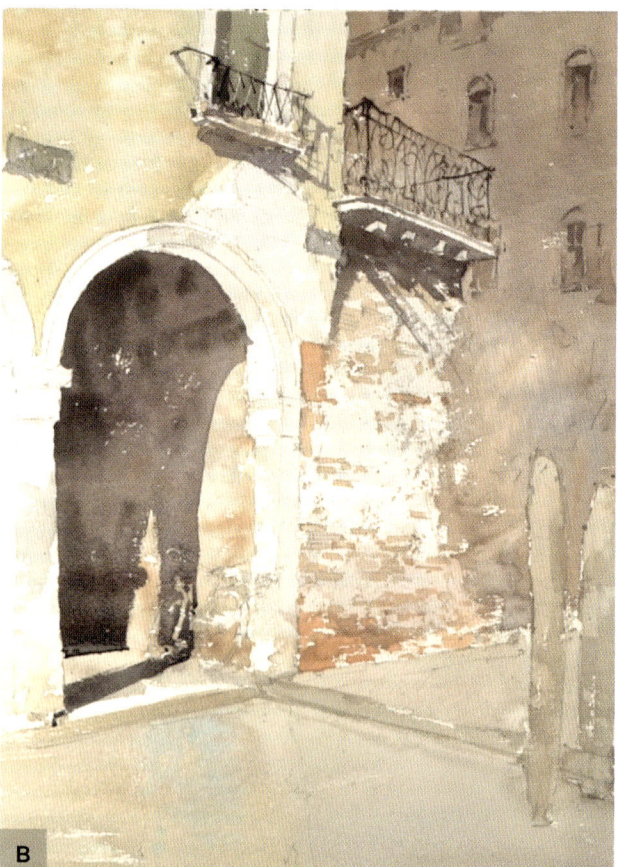

B

Midtone generalization.

As I mentioned, my approach to preparing watercolor paper for further development involves covering the paper with a single wash of paint as shown in (**A**). The color of this wash varies according to the elements in the picture. I make an effort to apply the wash continuously, avoiding halting at the boundaries of the elements as much as possible, but it's dependent on the subject matter at hand. In (**B**), it's apparent that considering intricate placements of elements with different colors calls for their separation based on color. The color might gradually change its temperature, unifying elements in the picture along the way during this initial stage. If I were to stop painting at this point, the result would resemble an abstract representation of reality which is yet unfinished.

The decision to continue with additional general washes or delve into detailing specific parts of the image is at artist discretion. Often, I observe beginners immediately focusing on detailing different parts of the painting. This can pose challenges in later stages, as combining these detailed sections may prove difficult, resulting in a disjointed final result. To avoid this, I find moments within the refinement process to connect different parts of my painting, ensuring cohesion.

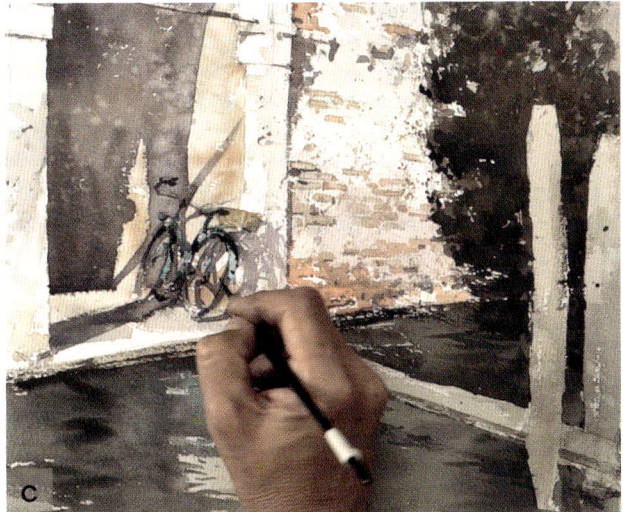

Detail of the bicycle.

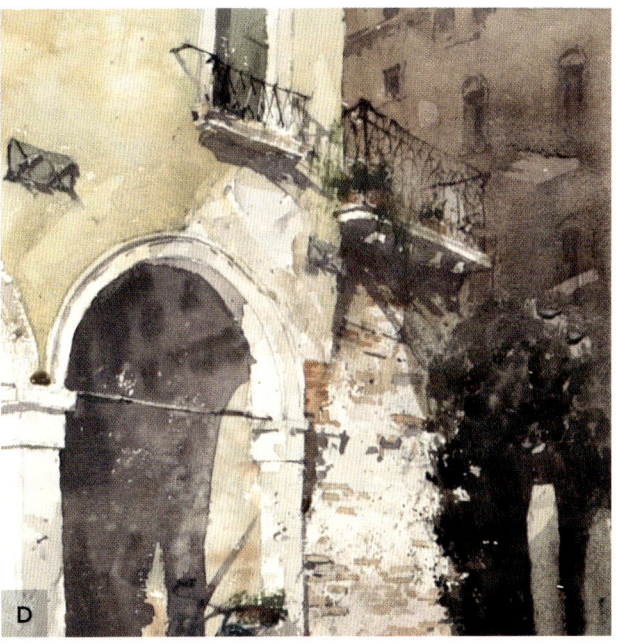

Brick detail.

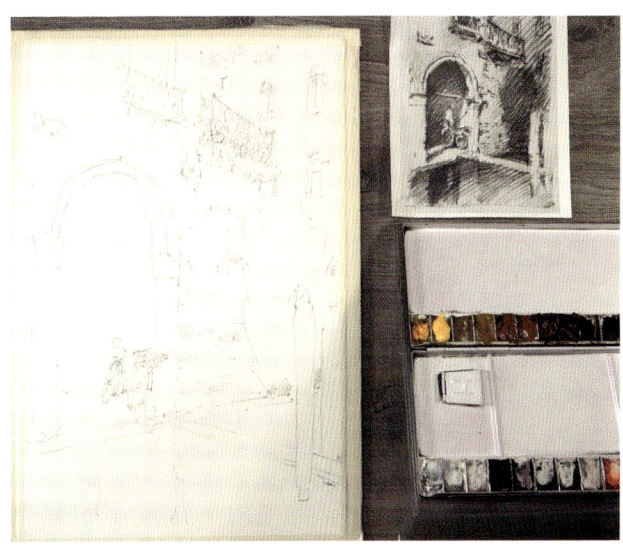

Pencil layout and sketch.

The pictures above and top right (**C, D**) show different stages taken to complete the watercolor.

I've observed that beginners often struggle with perceiving the scenery in general terms, and this difficulty can be a significant challenge to creating compelling watercolor paintings. It seems that humans, by nature, are inclined to focus on details, as the ability to distinguish details and objects has been crucial for human survival. However, in the context of painting, mastering the skill of seeing the basic environment void of detail, in general terms, is essential. The preliminary sketch may greatly help envisioning this in a monochromatic manner.

When I approach a scenery I intend to paint, my first focus is on the direction of light, a fundamental aspect for understanding the interplay of light and shadows in the painting. I make a mental note of the illuminated areas versus the darker ones and their placement within the overall composition. At this point, I cease to see individual objects and instead perceive abstract shapes that will collectively form the pattern of values in the painting. Squinting at the scenery proves to be a valuable aid, helping me filter out nuanced shades of gray.

Scan to view a video tutorial

IDENTIFYING FOCAL AREAS

In "Navigating the Three Planes of Vision" (p. 114), I mentioned that focal areas usually occur in the middle plane of vision, flanked by the foreground in front and the background plane at the back of the scenery. Where exactly focal areas occur in the middle plane is up to the artist. First, I look into the rule of thirds to avoid placing it in the center of the middle plane as much as I can. But what is the significance of focal area, and why do we even need it? In real life, human vision works so that it can focus on one thing at a time. When we find ourselves in unfamiliar territory, our eyes scan the area to identify points of interest if you're a tourist, danger zones if you're in a dangerous territory, or simply what's ahead of us when doing our routine chores. The key word here is "focusing" on something. Photographs, on the other hand, often focus on everything, making them less engaging and devoid of emotion. After all, the camera is just a tool. So, when artists start painting things "realistically," the results often fall short of ideal. I've noticed that after a certain time of painting outdoors, I get tired and slip into a copying mode. After all, it's difficult to concentrate for a long period of time, especially when outdoor conditions are less than ideal.

That's why I recommend preparing a sketch quickly, and the process is described in detail in "Developing Sketching Techniques" (p. 32). When on location or painting from a photo or using sketches as a reference, I study it for a while without touching a pencil or paintbrush. I ask myself questions by simply observing the scenery: Why would I like to paint this scenery? What captured my attention the most in it? Is it the object or the mood of the scenery, or is it the object or the light on it at this particular time? As I mentioned earlier, I usually avoid painting

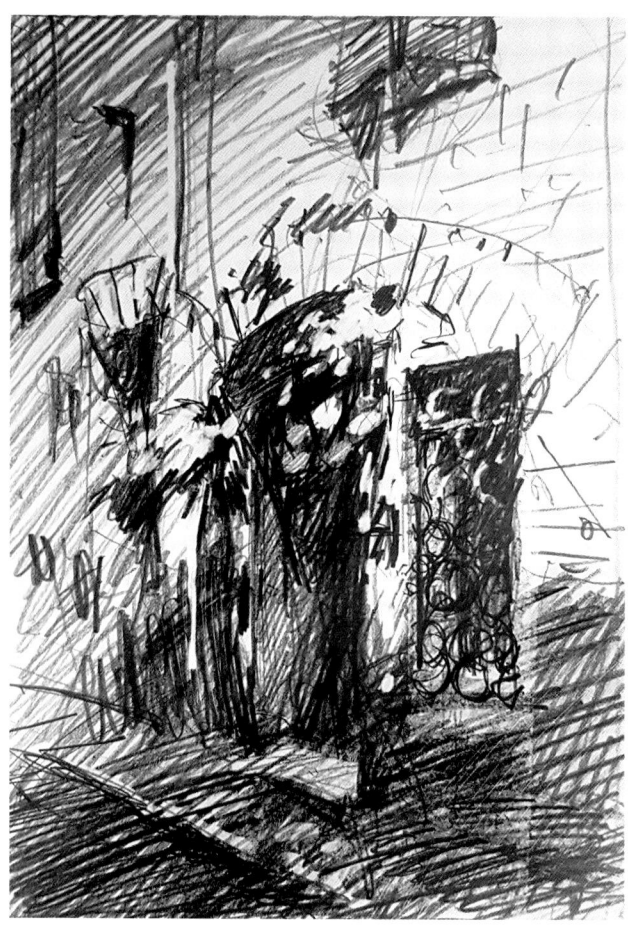

Assisi Door, watercolor and graphite sketch, 4½" × 6" | 16 × 11 cm

well-known landmarks, as they are already "discovered," and my way of painting involves a method of discovery, which is to try to uncover a new perspective on the ordinary scene or structure and deliver it on watercolor paper or canvas. After answering these questions, I typically work on my sketch, which will serve as a reference for the future painting, incorporating these findings (see *Assisi Door* sketch, above).

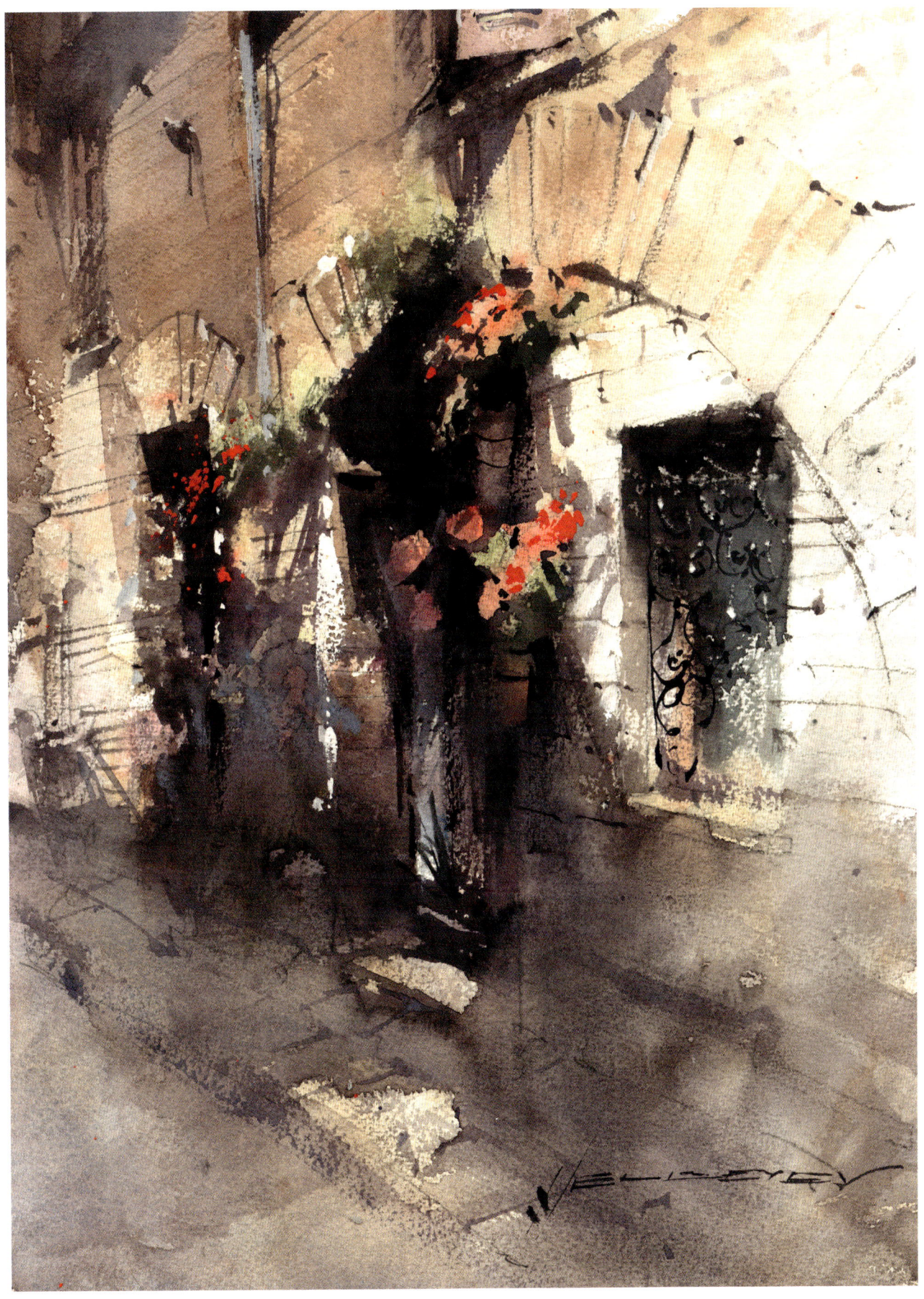

Assisi Door, watercolor, 22" × 15" | 56 × 37 cm

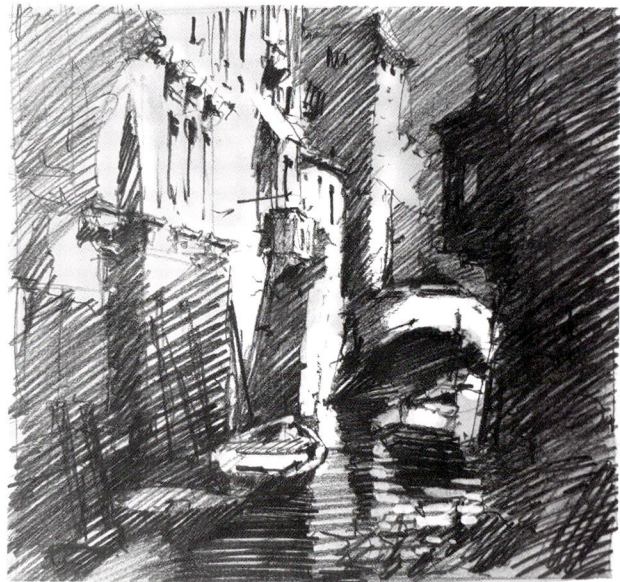

Venice Bridge, watercolor and graphite sketch,
8" × 9" | 20 × 22 cm

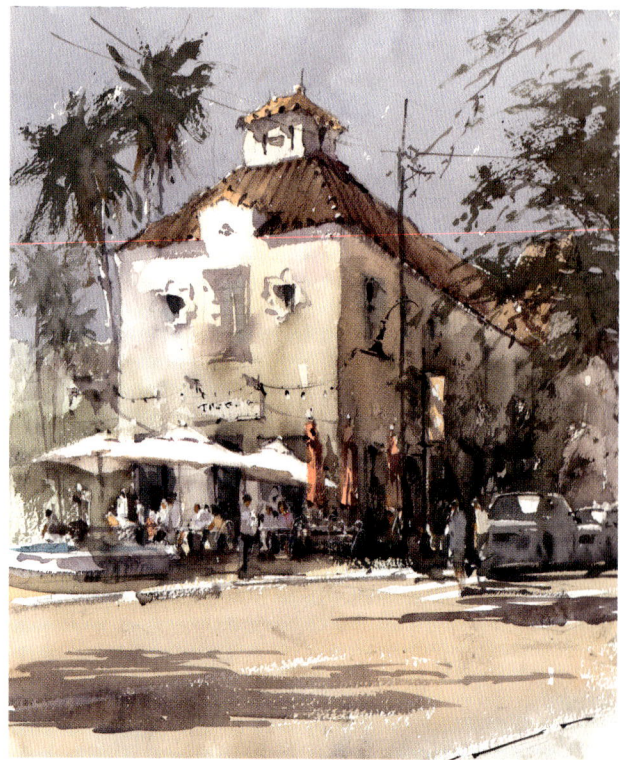

Outdoor Café, watercolor, 16½" × 13" | 42 × 35 cm

The simplest way to isolate focal areas is to bring high contrast to that specific area, where the brightest bright and the darkest dark adjacent areas will be located. The human eye will be drawn to that area in the painting and then scan everything else. Keep in mind that the actual brightest and darkest areas can be located elsewhere in the painting, but they should not be in direct contact with each other. The word "adjacent" is key here (see *Venice Bridge* sketch, left).

Another way to highlight focal areas is to use color selectively, employing the most intense colors there. That's one of the reasons why I sometimes use muted and muddy colors throughout the painting. When I use a bit of brighter and more intense colors in the focal area, it's easily isolated and identified.

As was mentioned earlier, most of the time, I use the focal area along the line or a sequence of hierarchies of focal areas to enhance my composition. If the line is more or less horizontal, the result is a more static image (see *Winter Path* sketch, opposite top).

A diagonal line through the painting leads to a dynamic and more dramatic image. It doesn't matter how small the area is; as long as it's there, the painting will be enhanced. To compare it to a theater stage, where the lighting focuses on the action in the scene while everything else is dimmed, the same principle is applied to the painting's surface when you "artificially" use paints and water to illuminate the focal area.

When I identify the main area of interest, I prepare the sketch, focusing in part on this area. Most often in real life, this area is not artificially lit by some magical light. It's lit inside my mind, and the task of enhancing it lies in my ability to reinterpret the scenery. Again and again in this book, I urge you not to simply copy what you see, but to start processing it in your mind. It's very hard to compete with a camera. Most humans on this planet have a tool to snap and copy a picture of what lies in front of them: a smartphone. Artificial intelligence is another tool to create visually stunning images without much effort. One thing these tools cannot do is feel and convey the depth of vision that humans possess. That's why I'm a big proponent of trying to create my paintings with lasting feelings deeper than postcard eye-candy or primitive human emotions like anger, joy, or fear.

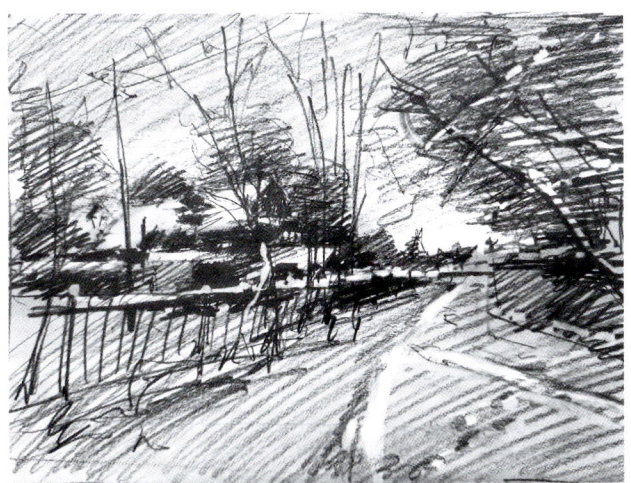

Winter Path, graphite sketch, 8" × 11" | 21 × 27 cm

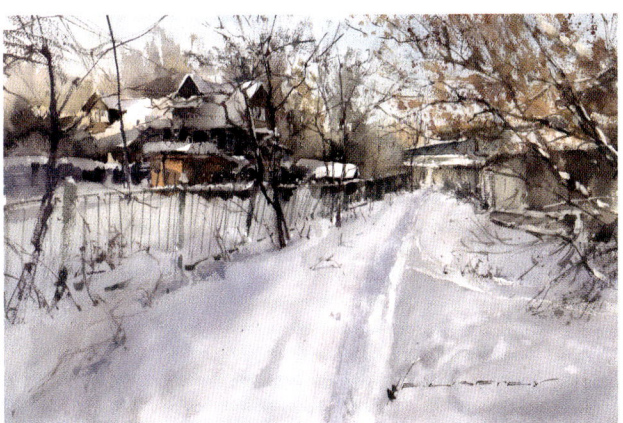

Winter Path, watercolor, 14½" × 22" | 36 × 56 cm

To effectively manipulate the focal point, I propose revisiting the cube placed upon the surface (**A**), previously discussed in "Rendering Objects in Light" (p. 30).

It becomes evident that the highest contrast naturally forms adjacent to the cast shadow on the ground, being the darkest region on an otherwise well-lit surface. However, what if I aim to relocate this high-contrast focus to the top corner of the cube? Allow me to demonstrate that this can be achieved without resorting to mere replication of reality. By subtly darkening certain surfaces, I can shift the contrast to the desired area.

Firstly, by applying a slightly darker hue to the sky, I draw more attention to the upper section of the cube. Secondly, I exercise my artistic license to darken the surface of the ground, introducing a touch of creative alteration. Lastly, I would deepen the midtone at the cube's apex. As you can observe, the objective has been accomplished without defying the laws of physics while successfully relocating the focal area to its intended position (**B**).

Scan to view a video tutorial

A

Cube under light.

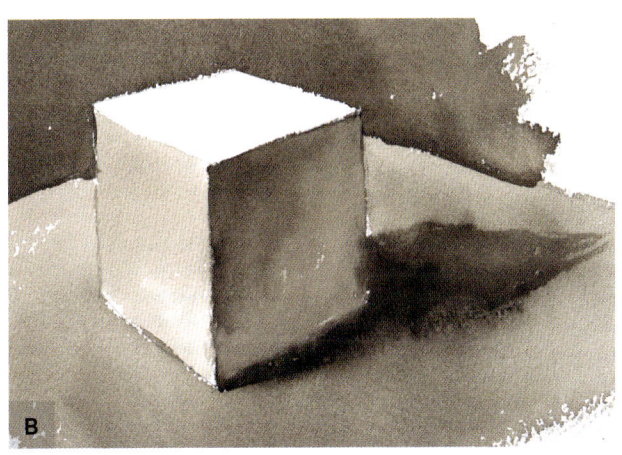

B

Cube focal area.

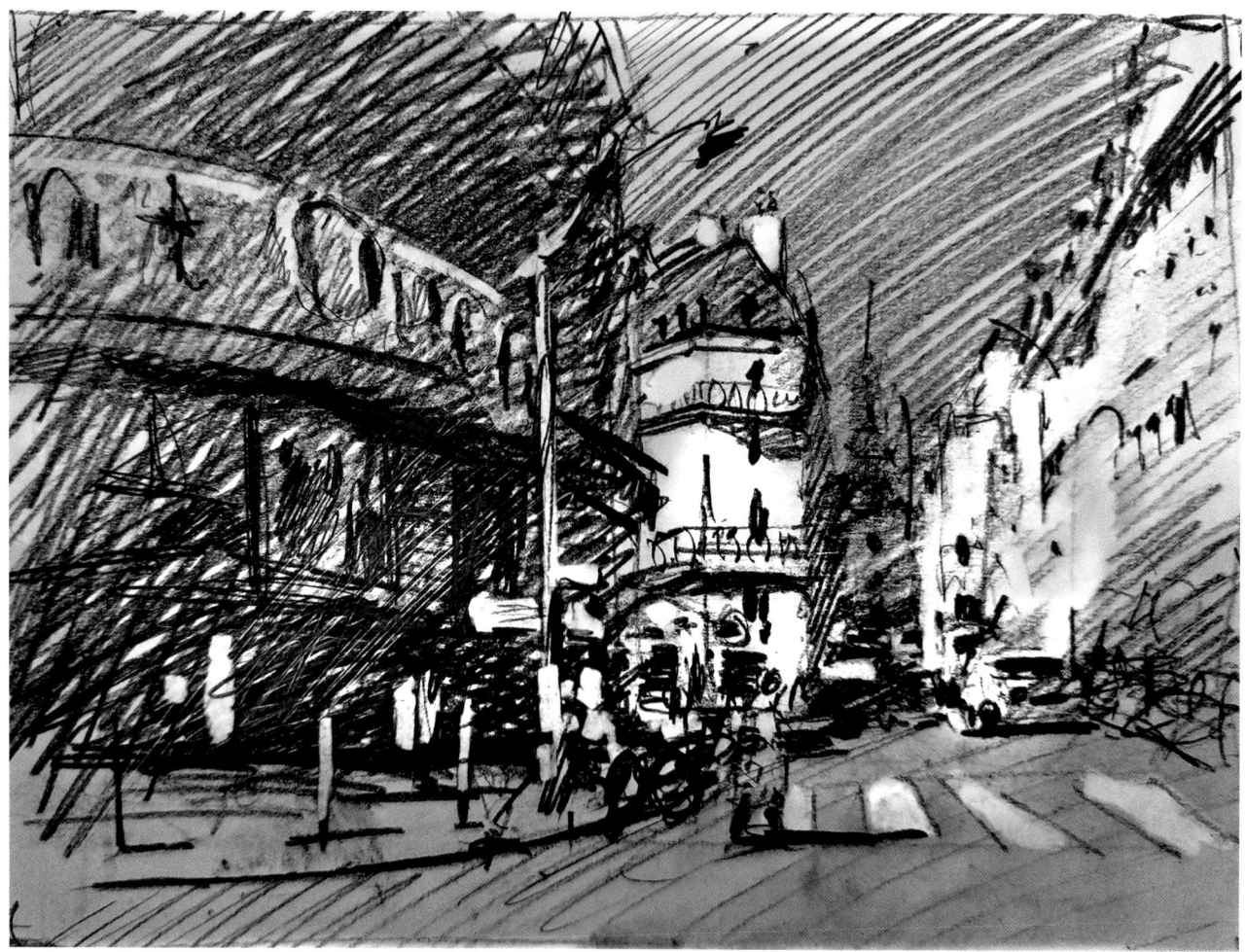

Gaumont Opera, graphite sketch, 5" × 7" | 13 × 18 cm

As mentioned earlier, high contrast in a painting between different elements or adjacent lit areas in an object will draw the viewer's eye to that area. In other words, it's the darkest dark area adjacent to the brightest area in the painting. Sometimes, a painter encounters too many contrasting areas in real life, and the immediate task is to organize them by importance and reduce the significance of secondary ones. This is where the rules of omission come into play, as the painter must remove a lot of information, especially when painting outdoors or from photographs. It's worth noting that what is considered important varies from one painter to another, and each must decide for themselves. This is a significant challenge for beginner painters, as they often end up mindlessly copying everything they see, resulting in a poor replica of reality.

When I paint, I keep a previously done sketch in front of me. It not only helps me stay focused on original intensions but also guides me to the unfinished look of secondary areas, rather than referencing them from reality. In practical terms, as mentioned before, the darkest area must find its way into the focal area, but it's important to note that the darkest area can also be located in the secondary areas leading to dramatic presentation. The key word here is contrast in the focal area. As long as the darkest area is surrounded by accompanying tonal values that reduce the contrast, it's okay to have the darkest areas throughout the painting as well (see *Gaumont Opera* sketch, above).

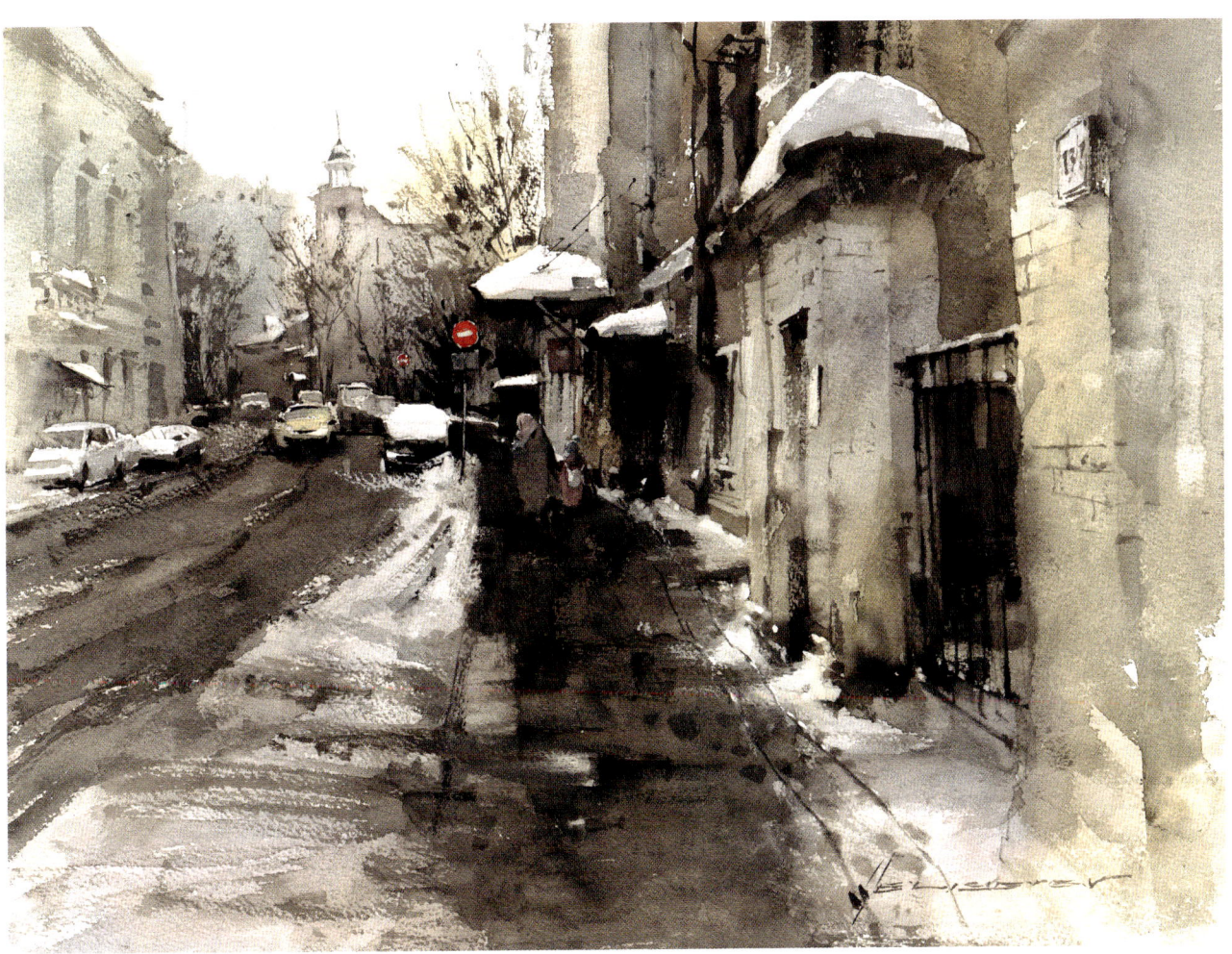

School Time, watercolor, 18½" × 14" | 35 × 47 cm

We must also consider the role of color in the focal areas. When I look at paintings with excessively intense colors throughout its surface, I sometimes find myself lost in them without a clear understanding of what the painter is trying to convey. It's akin to a story with no clear narrative, hardly a fascinating read. The most intense colors should be near or in the focal areas helping to draw the eye to them. Sometimes, a small red dot is all a painting needs to achieve that finished look. This could be anything in the scene, such as a red or blue shirt, a car, or a brightly painted door. The challenge often lies in the secondary, subdued areas. The artist must replace bright and intensely colored real objects with interpreted variations of them. The ability to mix gray and sometimes muddy washes is essential and requires significant skill because we are now in a creative zone that is hard to teach and provide rigid rules for. The relevant information can be found in "Exploring Primary Colors in Watercolor" (p. 106).

Watercolor brushwork techniques also play a role in enhancing the focal points we are discussing here. In the "Navigating the Three Planes of Vision" section (p. 114), we already discussed watercolor application techniques that help identify and enhance focal areas.

Regarding the practical aspect of placing our focal areas in the painting, compositionally, I would like to refer you to the rule of thirds, which I find highly effective for determining placement. Another important tip is to position the area somewhat closer to the horizon line (HL). When we move toward a certain point in real life, we tend to focus on that area the most, so it makes sense to place the center of attention there. I would avoid placing the area of interest at the extremities of the painting surface, as it may appear accidental at best and give the impression that the artist is not handling the process with clear intent.

USING UNIFYING WASHES

Unifying washes serve as an excellent painting technique for softening secondary areas of a painting. During the painting process, I sometimes encounter situations where these areas attract too much attention due to their excessive color vibrancy and tonal contrast.

The concept behind applying a unifying wash on top of multiple elements in the painting is a highly effective method to further deemphasize areas around the focal point. It's important to note that the unifying wash need not cover all secondary areas in the painting; it's most effective in selected portions, often creating an intriguing sense of mystery while concealing and softening edges in the most affected areas.

Moreover, unifying washes can also serve as a color gradation technique. For example, one might begin with a very light yellow ochre, gradually transitioning to burnt umber, and ultimately finishing with dark violet, typically in the lower corner of the image leaving the focal areas unchanged. It's essential to highlight that the painting surface should be inclined from top to bottom to ensure the effectiveness of the wash and maintain control throughout its application. In the watercolor of Banjole village, I even had to invert the watercolor board to minimize the exposure of the stones in the lower right corner (**A**).

As you can observe, this painting employs more than one unifying wash to tackle multiple problematic areas.

Another unifying wash was needed in the background area as well (**B**). Typically, I initiate the wash from the top of the intended area on inclined surface with a very light wash or even clear water, progressively intensifying its darkness by adding more pigmented mix. Before applying the unifying wash, I prepare these mixes in advance, ranging from light to dark. There are no predefined recipes for determining the size or darkness of the wash; it hinges on the specific results I desire. For instance, in *Italian Café* (opposite top), you can see a very dark wash early in the process, and if you compare

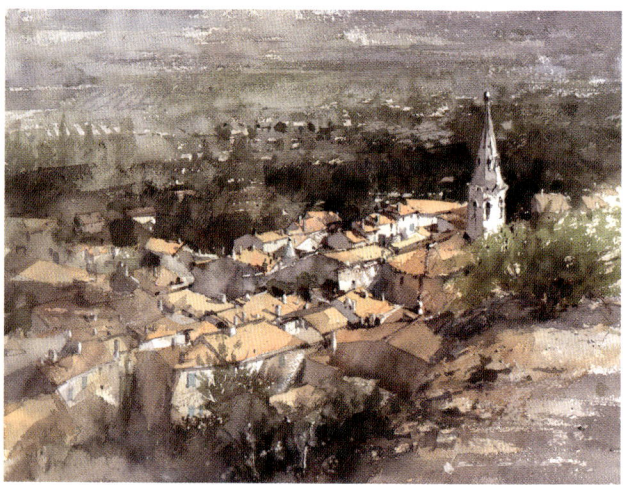

Provence Town, watercolor, 14" × 19" | 36 × 48 cm

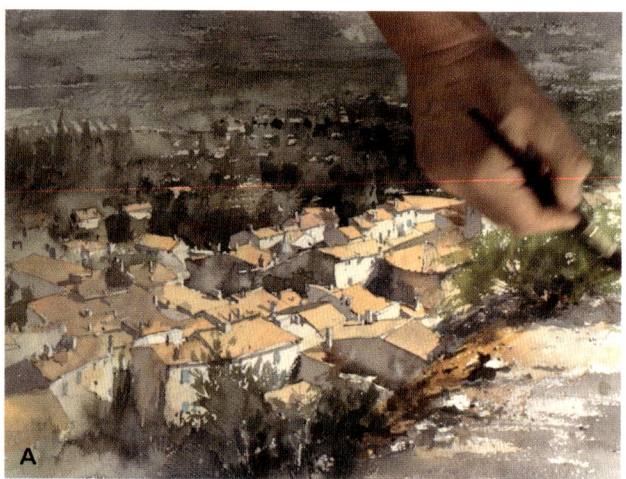

Inverted board, unifying wash application.

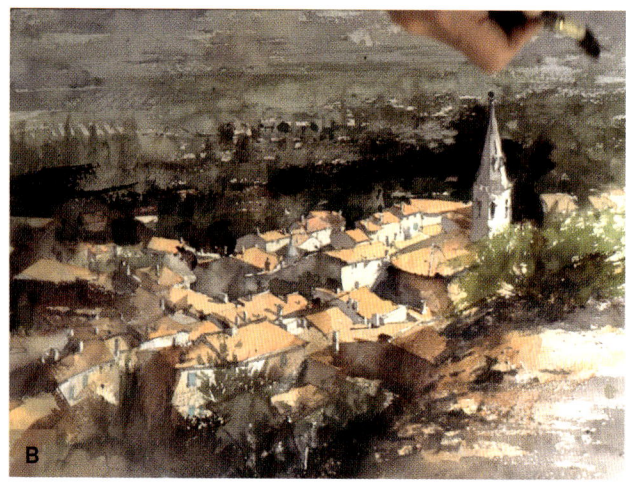

Inverted board, tower highlight.

the sequence of images (**C–F**) with the final result, you'll notice how much darker the initial washes are. I delve further into this in the following chapter. You may also notice that in this image in the lower right corner, there were no elements to unify with a wash. I intentionally selected this image for a step-by-step demonstration to illustrate that the wash serves the purpose of unifying the dark area as a whole, leaving little need for further development in that region.

It's also worth noting that I break the uniformity of the wash by leaving spots that are unpainted, trying to create an impression of accidental leftovers. This technique adds to the allure of watercolor in the immediacy department and also removes an impression of the heavy-handed application.

Using unifying washes comes with a risk since it's possible to darken the image excessively, reaching a point of no return. Watercolor tends to lighten as it dries, so it's necessary to apply slightly darker washes than initially appears necessary. I often tell my students that while unifying washes can elevate a good painting into a great one, they can also destroy a fine painting if not applied with care. Therefore, I recommend that beginner painters focus on mastering total control of watercolor application before attempting this technique.

It's crucial to keep in mind that the unifying wash is typically applied when the painting is nearly complete and already has three underlying washes. The fourth wash atop them must be executed with great care.

I should note that although I occasionally finish my paintings with a unifying wash, I usually prefer to apply it before the final touches, which may include adding opaque whites in the areas of lost highlights and dark watercolor lines. The unifying wash can potentially smudge these details and render them ineffective.

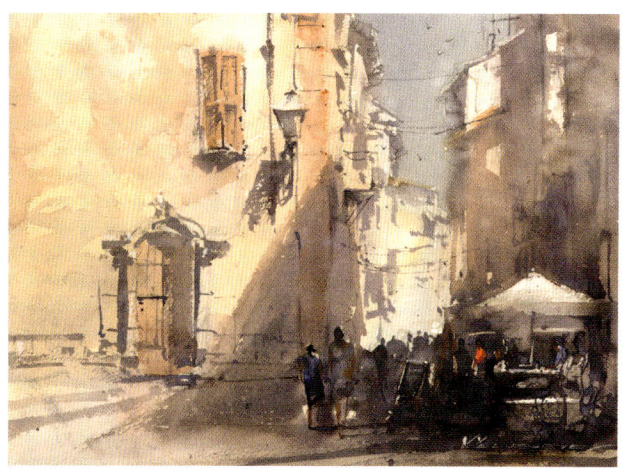

Italian Café, watercolor, 10½" × 14½" | 27 × 37 cm

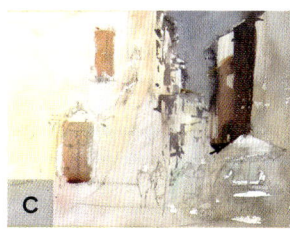

Sequence of dark washes, step one.

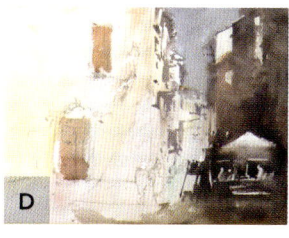

Expansion of dark wash, step two.

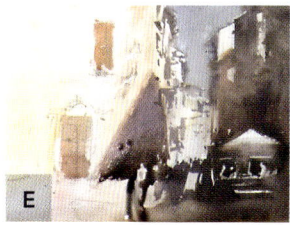

Dark wash, step three.

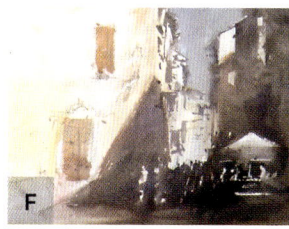

Dark wash, step four.

Scan to view a video tutorial

PAINTING THROUGH THE LINES

In "Layering vs. Wet-on-Wet Techniques" (p. 70), I provide a detailed description of the practical method of painting through lines. This section instead primarily focuses on the conceptual aspect, explaining why it's desirable to implement this technique in painting.

Every now and then, I encounter the phrase "paint through the lines," and almost every time, I employ the method without much thought. The significance lies not only in understanding how to cover watercolor paper with paint but, more importantly, in comprehending how to mentally approach the depiction of various elements in the painting.

The idea that pencil lines are used to delineate various objects on paper is an abstract method, considering that the lines themselves do not exist in this world and are invented by humans as a means of communication. When I draw a line on my paper to depict an object, I am merely describing its form, outlining surfaces, or marking the borders between different objects. Simultaneously, we can perceive objects as separate elements only if there is a difference in tone or color between them. To discern that difference, we need light to objectively judge them. If I turn off the light, the objects visually disappear.

With that being said, it becomes evident that we essentially paint the light on the surfaces of objects, and pencil lines serve as a vague reference for their form and placement. They function solely as aids in the painting process.

When working with watercolors, I minimize the use of pencil lines, opting instead for a paint-loaded brush to convey the three-dimensionality of objects. This preference arises from the brush's ability to use the painted area as a means of expression, diverging from the reliance on lines. The picture below demonstrates that the windows and architectural details were predominantly implemented with the minimal and loose aid of defining lines.

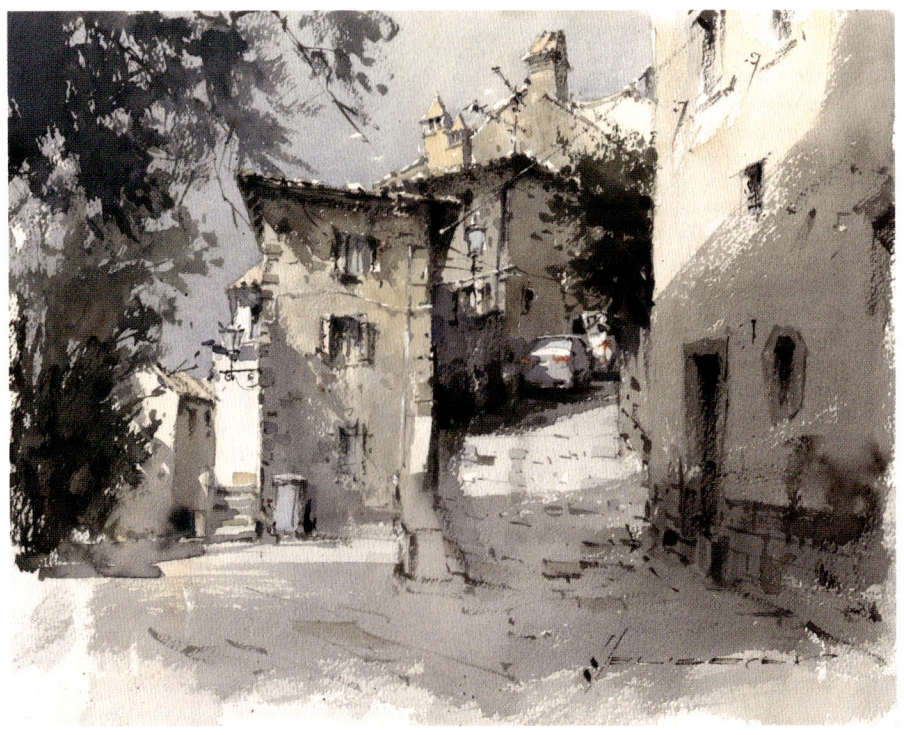

Cortona, watercolor, 11½" × 15" | 29 × 38 cm

Initial wash.

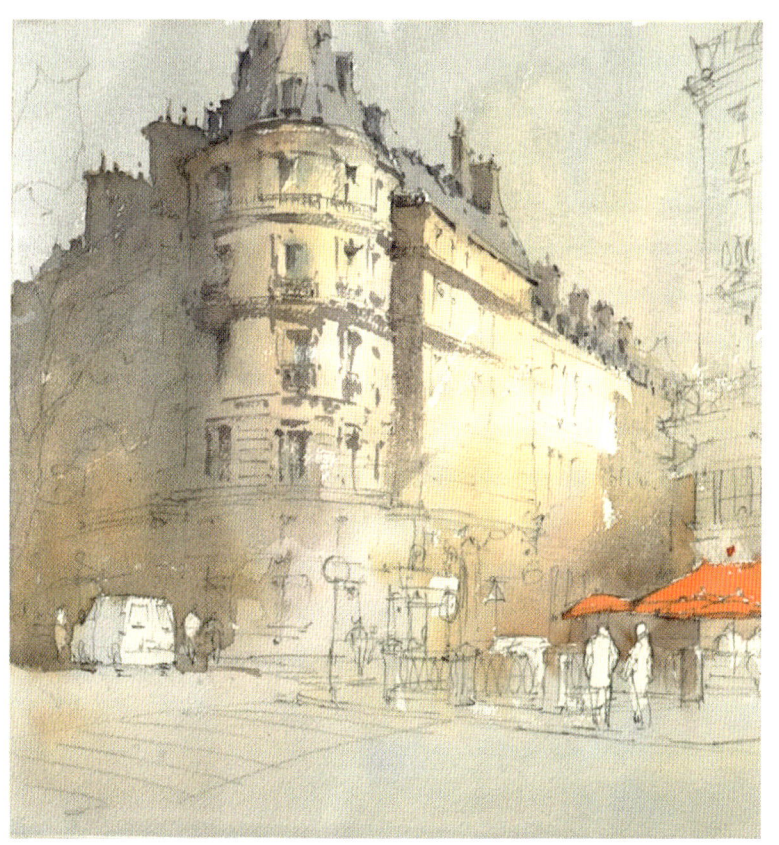

Brushwork detailing.

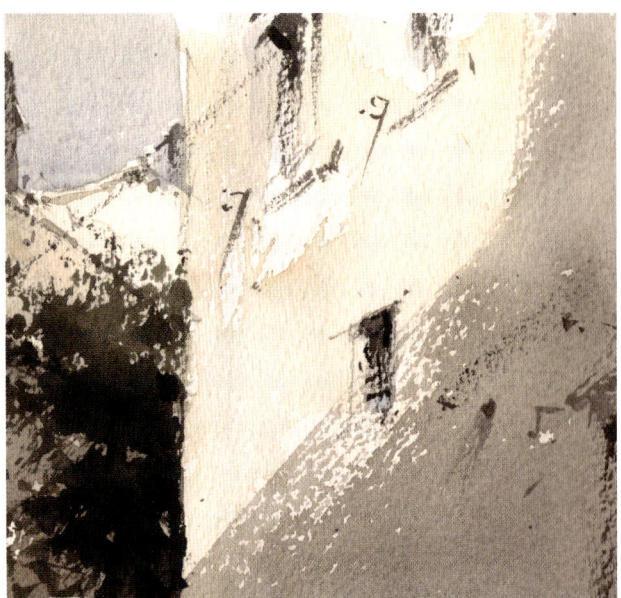

Cortona, window detail.

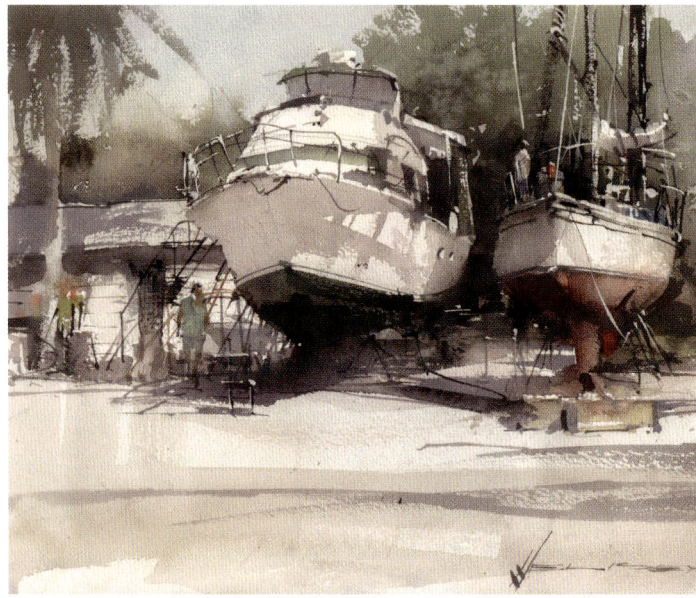

Cortez Dry Dock, watercolor, 10½" × 14" | 27 x36 cm

I've observed that excessive use of lines in my paintings constrains my brush movement, particularly when detailing objects. Over time, I've learned to completely forgo detailing objects in pencil. This shift allows me to move away from the notion of merely coloring the area between lines, enabling me to concentrate fully on describing the three-dimensional physics of elements within the picture.

Another crucial aspect is the skillful implementation of hard and soft edges in the painting. In this regard, the pencil line plays a detrimental role when there is no actual line between objects, and only a subtle and gradual value change exists between elements that need to be presented. These atmospheric effects often manifest in the distance of the background plane or during foggy conditions. The physical challenge arises from the difficulty in removing graphite pencil lines after they bond with the watercolor surface, particularly following the use of water on top of them.

The first wash that covers the whole painting and describing the lit areas throughout the image mostly is a coverage of all elements and is painted with quite loose reference to the lines identifying them and only as a means of color variations. It is only later that pencil lines serve as a reference for start and finish of darker areas of midtones. It's also important to note that when we unify our lit and dark areas in the painting, we start ignoring the line boundaries and

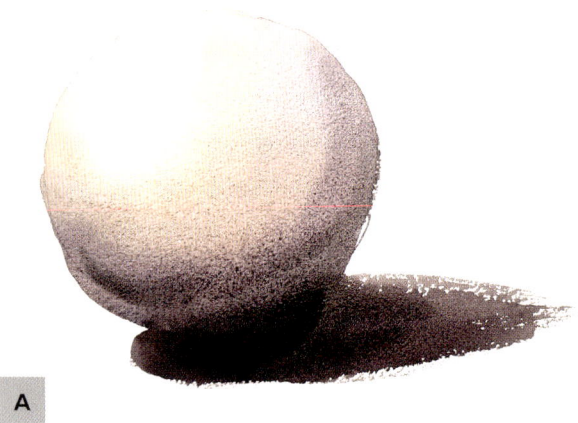

A

Seamless transition in the dark areas.

paint right through them, as evident in (**A**), in the area separating midtone from the cast shadow.

All in all, it becomes apparent that the artist must use lines sparingly, only in places where the complexity of the depicted form may pose significant challenges to paint and potentially delay the watercolor application process. I have already emphasized in this book how timing in watercolor is crucial and specific to the medium, and making minimal use of lines is essential and necessary; they should be considered only as loose references most of the time.

HARMONIZING LIGHTS AND DARKS

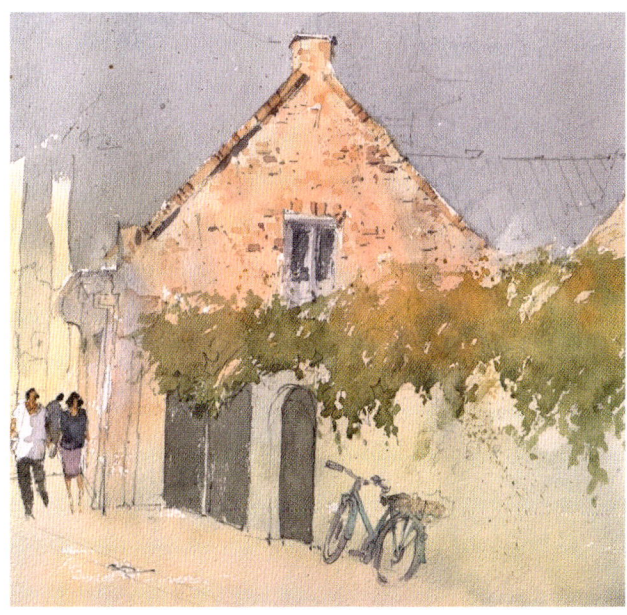

Unifying lights.

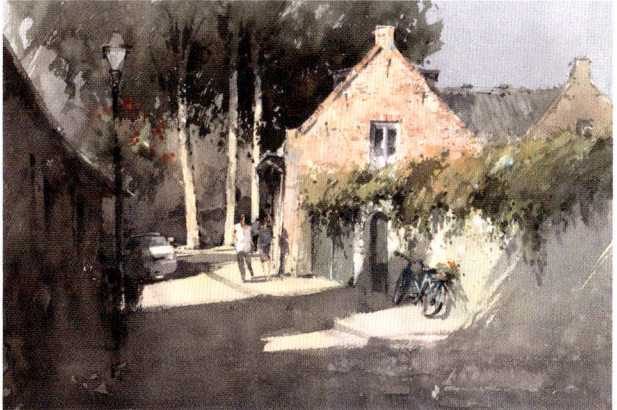

Oirschot Town, watercolor, 14" × 21½" | 36 × 54 cm

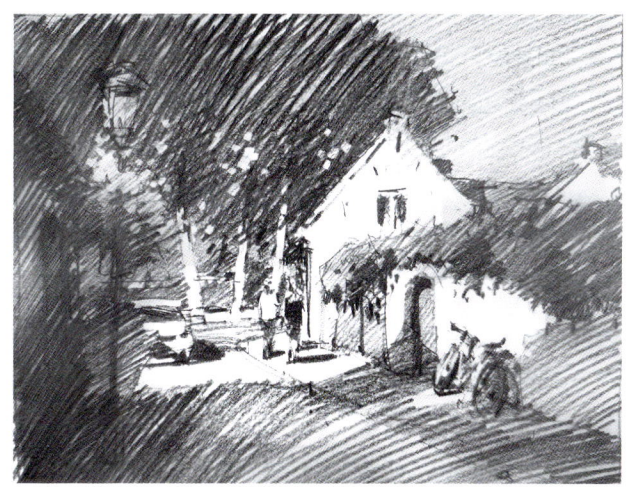

Oirschot Town, graphite sketch, 8" × 10" | 20 × 25 cm

One of the significant visual appeals arises from the sense of unity and an uncluttered appearance in scenic paintings. Rather than depicting a myriad of attention-craving details, I am trying to identify areas with the highest contrast between light and dark during the painting detailing process, all the while ensuring not to disrupt the tonal unity.

While working on the small-sized sketch, I identify large areas that remain largely undeveloped due to its compact size and rapid execution. I strive to incorporate this appearance into the final painting. The sketch also clearly illustrates the balance between general light and dark areas in a unified manner. I find it necessary to frequently squint while looking at the target of depiction, filtering out unnecessary details. This helps me perceive reality as a collection of simple shapes, providing a framework to which details can be added.

When observing a brightly lit wall, I imagine that intense light would naturally bleach out finer details in real life. Consequently, in my painting, I strive to reflect this by avoiding an overly detailed rendition and instead capturing the essence of the strong light's impact on the surface.

The same phenomenon occurs in the dark areas of midtones and cast shadows, where a significant amount of detail tends to be obscured due to the limited presence of light. To enhance the appearance of unity, I consistently blend the borders between midtones and their corresponding cast shadows. The substantial assistance in unifying the darker elements stems from the fact that, in reality, every midtone gives rise to a corresponding cast shadow, making it relatively straightforward to identify and paint each element accurately. As previously discussed in this book, considering that, all else being equal, cast shadows are darker than the midtone, it suffices to seamlessly continue the dark wash of the midtone and intensify it in the cast shadow area without interruption. This approach effectively creates a unified and harmonious integration of dark tones throughout the composition.

To further blend the dark or light elements together, I often use a unifying wash over the detailed areas. This technique helps minimize their prominence and darkens the entire area as a cohesive whole.

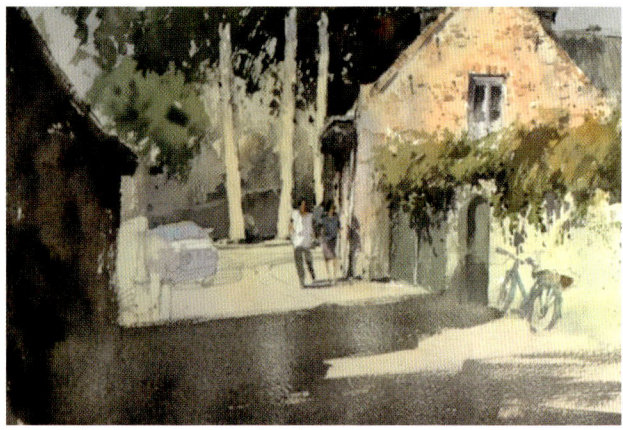

Midtones and cast shadows.

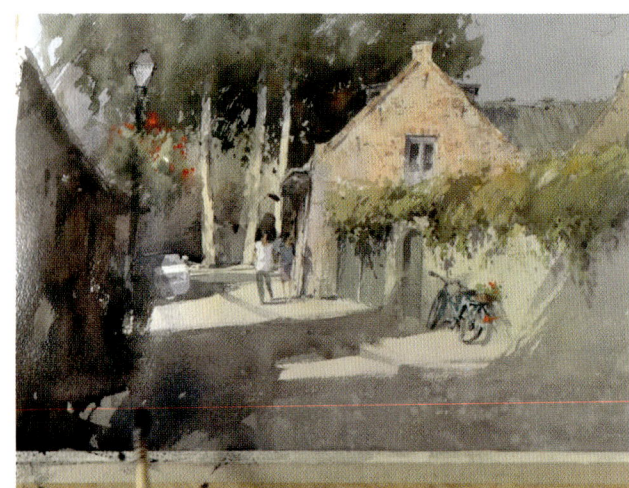

Unifying darks wash.

PORTRAYING ATMOSPHERIC LIGHT

When painting outdoors, observing the subtle shifts in natural light throughout the day can be challenging. One of the most pronounced transformations takes place during what photographers refer to as the "golden hour." This magical period occurs when the sky is clear, and the sun hovers just above the horizon, casting a warm, sometimes nearly orange hue on all illuminated surfaces. This atmospheric phenomenon doesn't occur in the morning, and its occurrence is linked to the unique properties of our planet's atmosphere.

As a nonscientist, I won't delve into the technical details of why this happens. Instead, I'll focus on examining the resulting effects on the subjects affected by this phenomenon. Notably, if we examine the cast shadows during the late day golden hour, we can easily discern a fascinating contrast in color temperature. These shadows tend to lean toward the cooler end of the spectrum, occasionally adopting a chilly ultramarine tone.

Conversely, in the morning hours, a completely different atmospheric phenomenon unfolds. During this time, lit areas may exhibit a somewhat cooler appearance, and intriguingly, the resulting cast shadows take on a warmer quality. This interplay of light and shadow, influenced by the time of day, adds depth and nuance to the outdoor painting experience.

The golden hour and early morning light serve as stark contrasts that vividly showcase atmospheric phenomena. It's crucial to recognize, however, that after noon, the shift in light color is gradual and often imperceptible. Despite this subtlety, I conscientiously consider the time of day when painting, adjusting my palette accordingly.

In the realm of en plein air painting, I apply this invaluable knowledge, opting to paint what I understand rather than laboriously capturing every color nuance in reality. The most neutral light prevails when the sun is at its zenith, yet this time isn't optimal for artists. The shortest cast shadows and a somewhat flattened scenery result, minimizing the painter's advantage.

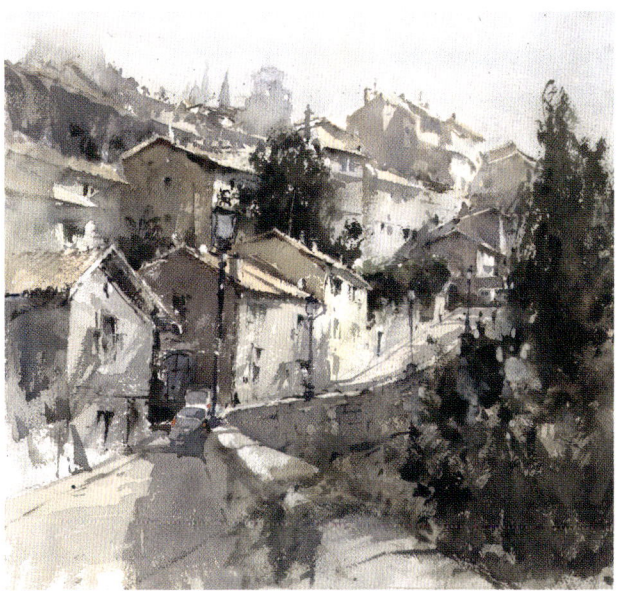

In Cortona, watercolor, 14" × 15" | 35 × 38 cm

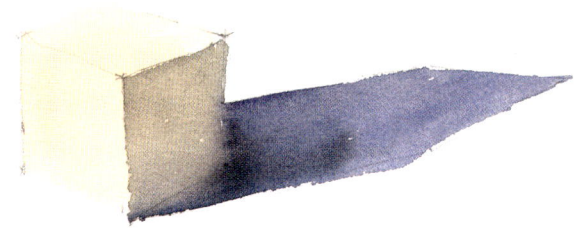

Golden hour color temperature.

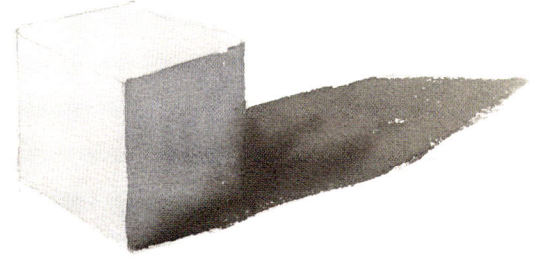

Morning light color temperature.

In the realm of fine art, where conveying the impression of a scene takes precedence over mere factual representation on paper, these atmospheric quirks offer a unique opportunity. They provide a deeper insight into the character and distinctive appearance of a given scene. Recognizing and enhancing these anomalies becomes pivotal.

Just as correct perspective and skillful light distribution contribute to a painting's authenticity, the choice of light color adds the final layer of fundamental realism. This subtle touch has the power to emotionally resonate with viewers, as they perceive the painting's remarkable truthfulness on a fundamental level.

Given this, I seldom purposefully pursue atmospheric effects at their extremes in my personal work unless they play a crucial role in unveiling the subject's character. My suggestion is to focus on adjusting the overall color balance in the painting from the outset, considering the desired outcome. I've found that warmer, earthy tones resonate more closely with human nature. These hues evoke a sense of security and home, harkening back to traditional settings illuminated by firepits and fireplaces.

Conversely, colder palette paintings exude a contemporary, clean aesthetic, evoking a sense of coldness. However, it's essential to note that heavily skewed paintings toward one end of the color temperature spectrum may result in an unbalanced and disharmonious impression. To mitigate this, I often seek areas within the painting to counterbalance the dominant color with its opposite counterpart, creating a harmonious interplay that enhances the overall visual appeal.

In delving into the discussion of shadow colors, it's crucial to recognize that these hues are not static but undergo subtle shifts as they approach their source. One notable influence is the blue tint from the sky, which can impart a bluish cast to the shadows. As previously explored in the chapter on light distribution and cast shadows, shadows are not only darker than adjacent midtones but also tend to appear cooler, with the exception of their immediate proximity.

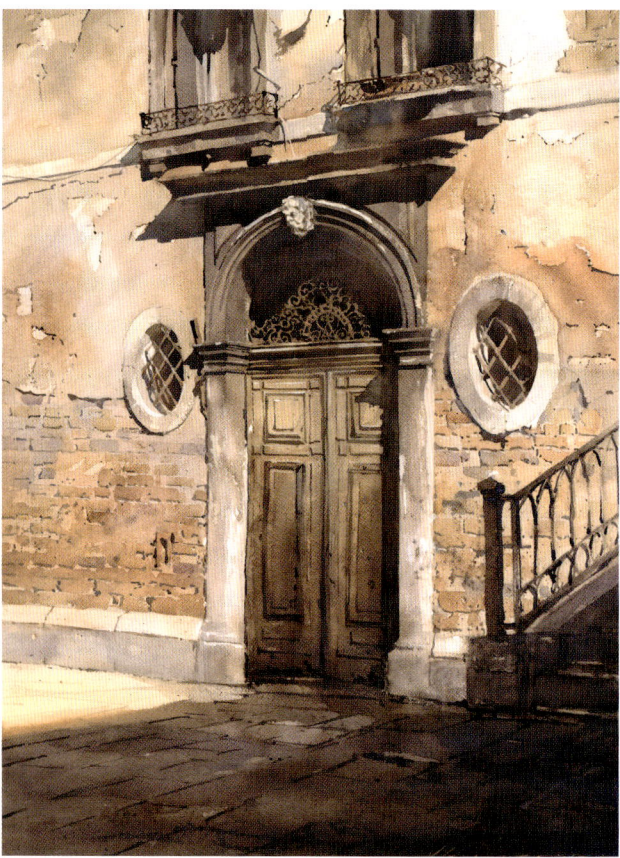

Doors of Venice, watercolor, 28" × 21" | 72 × 54 cm

This phenomenon occurs because the light blue rays struggle to reach these shadowed areas, resulting in a warming effect on the color palette. To counteract this, I frequently employ sepia or other dark browns to neutralize the blue cast, restoring a more balanced and realistic tonal quality to the shadows. This nuanced approach ensures a more accurate representation of the interplay between light and shadow in the depicted scene.

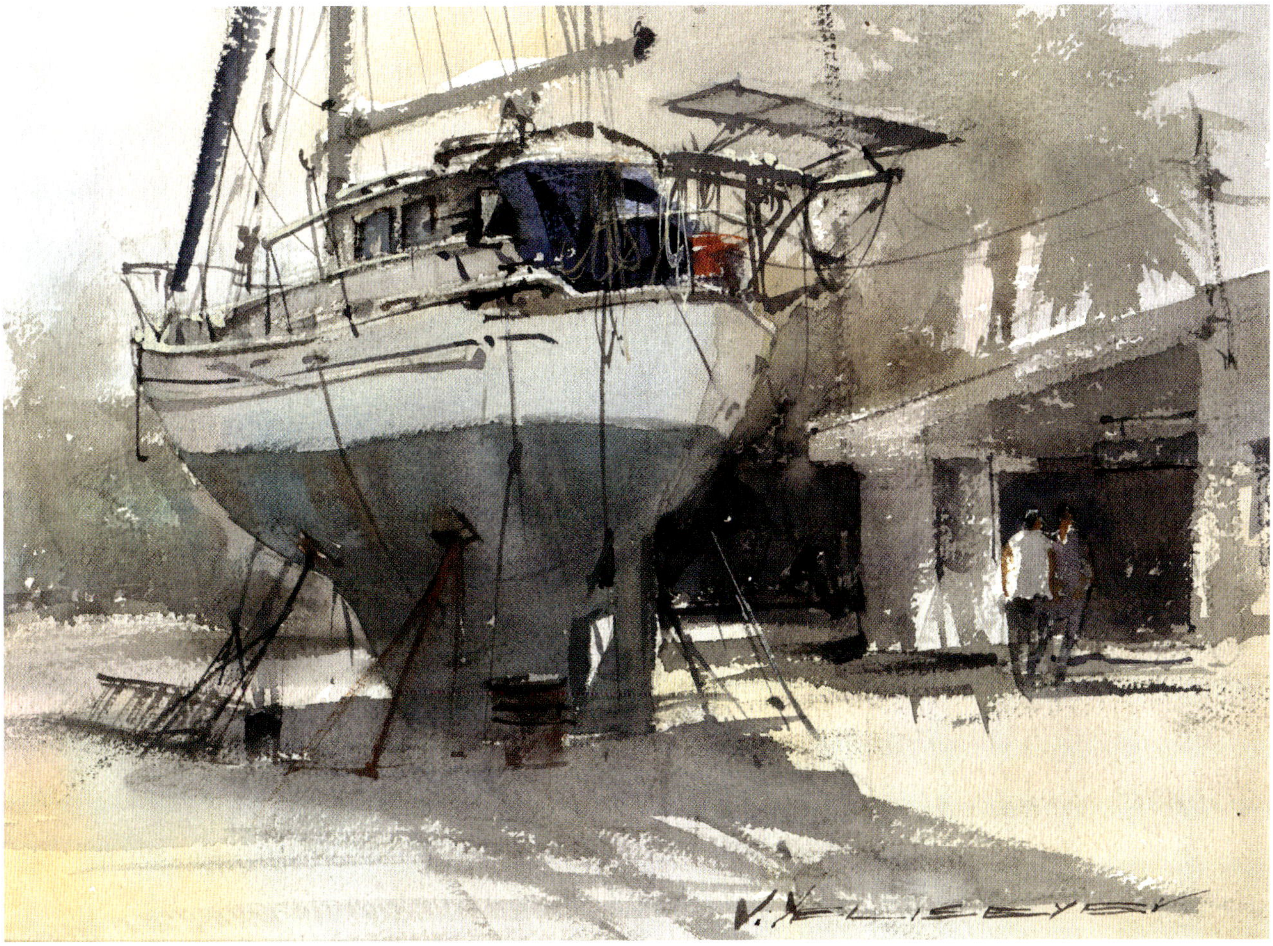

Dry Dock, watercolor, 10½" × 14½" | 27 × 37 cm

Undoubtedly, the most influential factor on color is the underlying base color of the objects themselves. The most challenging aspect of the painting process lies in capturing their true appearance under various atmospheric light conditions. However, armed with this knowledge, one can make informed judgments about color and potentially save valuable time and effort in the color mixing process. This understanding serves as invaluable guidance, facilitating a more accurate representation of the complex interplay between objects and their surrounding atmospheric conditions.

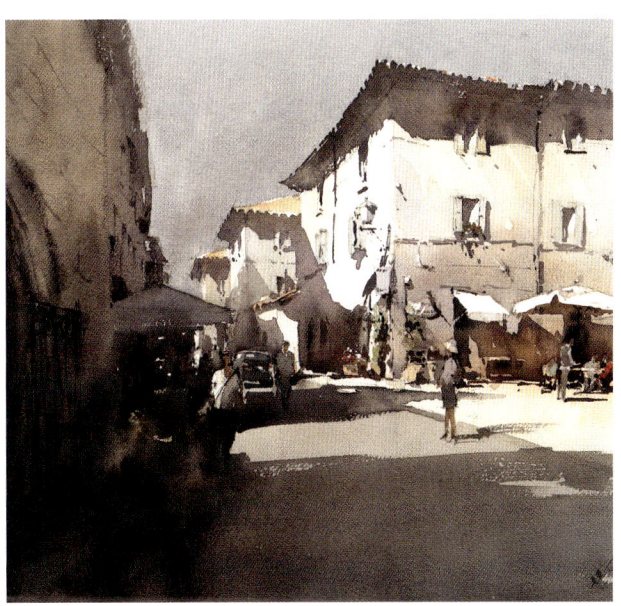

Orvieto (detail), watercolor, 15" × 22" | 37 × 56 cm

MANAGING HARD AND SOFT EDGES

Skillful manipulation of the edges in a painting requires vision on the part of the painter to enhance the overall impact of the artwork. I usually strive to identify the reasons for edge manipulation before applying them in my watercolors.

The most apparent reason for softening an edge is to enhance the sense of depth in the background plane of a scenery.

In my paintings, I frequently leverage this atmospheric phenomenon of distance edge softening to heighten the perception of depth. Only after establishing this natural softening effect do I consider manipulating it to a greater or lesser degree based on my artistic goals. I have employed this technique to create a three-dimensional illusion, even when working with objects possessing minimal depth, such as the Roman plaster bust of Seneca.

Observing the back of the bust's head reveals a noticeable contrast in edge softness when compared to the front, especially in the focal areas of the face. This deliberate manipulation of edge softness serves to guide the viewer's focus on the facial features and enhance the overall visual impact of the artistic composition.

Another application of the edge manipulation technique occurs within the same plane of vision when I aim to de-emphasize specific parts of the subject in front of me. This method proves effective in isolating focal areas within an otherwise flat plane that possesses approximately equal amounts of detail across its surface. By strategically creating hard edges with high contrast, I can guide the viewer's eye toward the artistically designated area, establishing a narrative that adds depth to the overall perception of the painting. This intentional manipulation of edges serves as a powerful tool for storytelling and enhancing the visual impact of the artwork.

When faced with the challenge of painting intricate areas featuring extensive stone or brick walls and deeply set windows, maintaining the monolithic appearance of the wall can be tricky amidst contrasting details. To preserve the unity and avoid

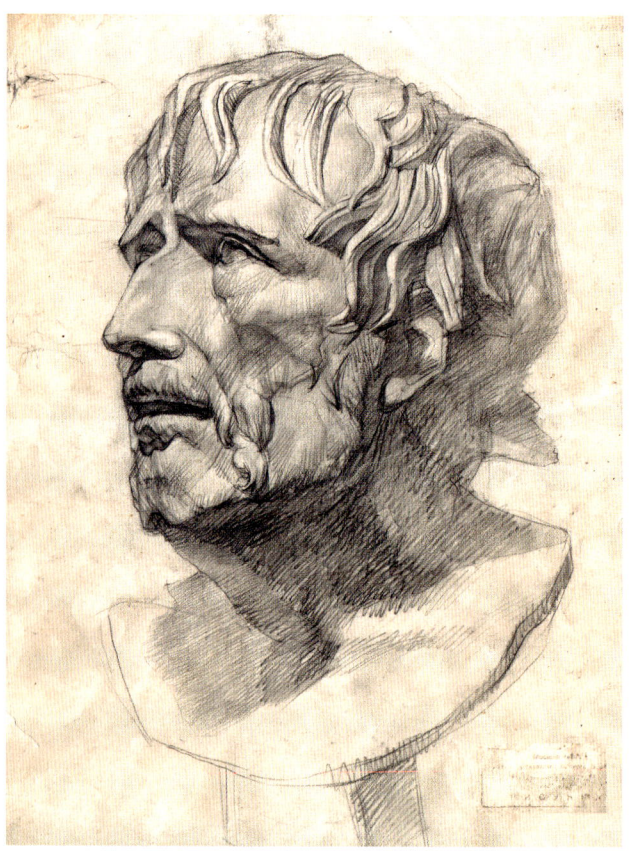

Seneca Bust, graphite pencil on paper, 17½" × 13" | 45 × 34 cm

overwhelming the surface with too many details, I employ a technique where I paint the intricate elements and, just before they fully dry, delicately wash out parts of them using a brush saturated with clear water.

The key to this approach lies in timing—waiting just long enough so the washed areas remain visible, but in a subtle, ghostly manner. This technique suggests there's more to the scene than meets the eye, creating a playful yet cohesive appearance. Some parts of the detailing remain clearly visible while blending into the underlying wall, offering a nuanced balance. The decision of where to soften edges and which details to leave intact is subjective and relies on the artist's vision and the direction of light within the scenery. This approach allows for a dynamic and artistic exploration, emphasizing the importance of creativity in the process.

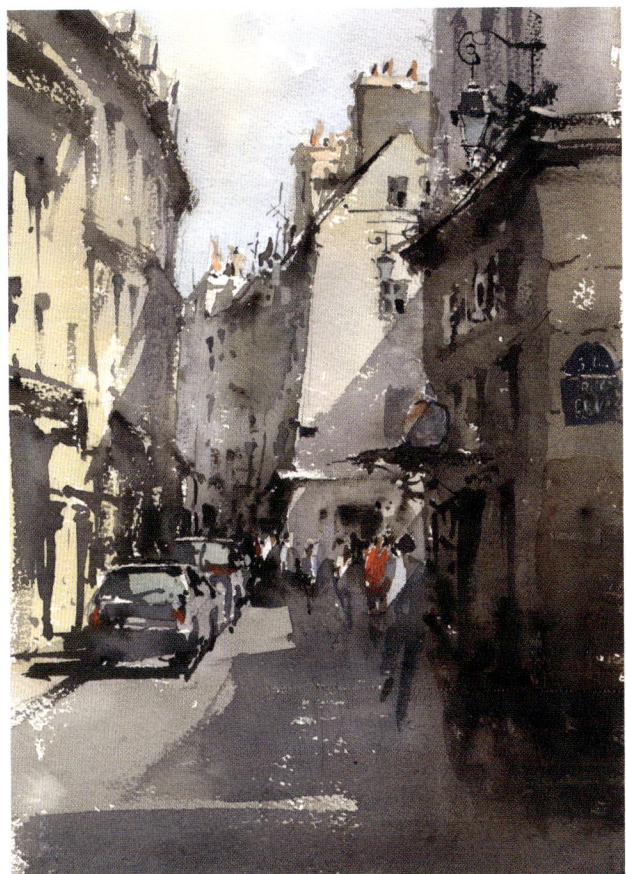

Paris Street, watercolor, 14" × 9½" | 35 × 24 cm

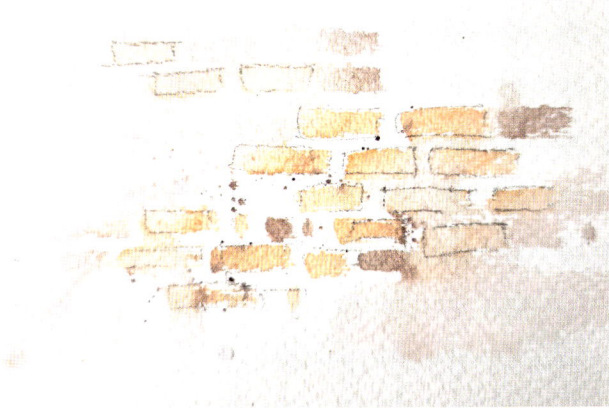

Softening brick edges with water wash on top.

A highly impactful application of edge manipulation comes into play when the goal is to infuse a sense of mystery into the painting. This involves the deliberate softening, which can extend to color blending, tone blending, or a combination of both, in the areas between distinct objects within the artwork. This technique is particularly potent for breaking away from an etched and illustrative appearance, introducing an element of intrigue and subtlety.

The same principle applies to tonal gradations, where I work toward eliminating clear separations between objects. For instance, if there are multiple objects making up a background, softening or altogether eliminating the borders between them enhances their collective role in supporting the foreground object.

Another phenomenon that comes to mind is when elements situated in dark areas are not very pronounced, and I often do not paint them entirely, as in the windows of *Paris Street* watercolor. In the image *Winter Park* on page 51, the branches are washed away by the front-lit winter sun. In my experience, this effect occurs only in specific areas directly in front of the sun.

This natural occurrence creates a captivating play of light and shadow, enhancing the realism of the scene. By carefully observing and replicating this phenomenon in art, especially in specific areas where the sun's direct influence is strongest, artists can imbue their work with a heightened sense of authenticity and dynamic lighting.

The reflections from a bright light source on glass and metal surfaces provide another example where soft and broken edges can be successfully implemented. This technique is frequently employed in oil paintings, given its ease of implementation. In watercolor, achieving a similar effect is possible by softening the edges using a wet sponge or stiff synthetic brush fibers on a completely dry painted surface.

Manipulating the softness of edges in watercolor painting allows for the attainment of a delicate and mysterious quality. When combined with light effects, this approach can ultimately result in watercolors that are sensitive and engaging, breaking away from a postcard-illustrative and analytical appearance.

Scan to view a
video tutorial

UNDERSTANDING TONAL VALUE KEYS

If you've ever observed paintings that stand out for their unique brightness, especially in specific areas like snow-covered landscapes, without the presence of deep, dark shadows, then you've likely encountered what we term a high-key painting. Conversely, artworks that are notably dark, with even their brightest elements lacking significant luminosity, fall under the category of low-key paintings.

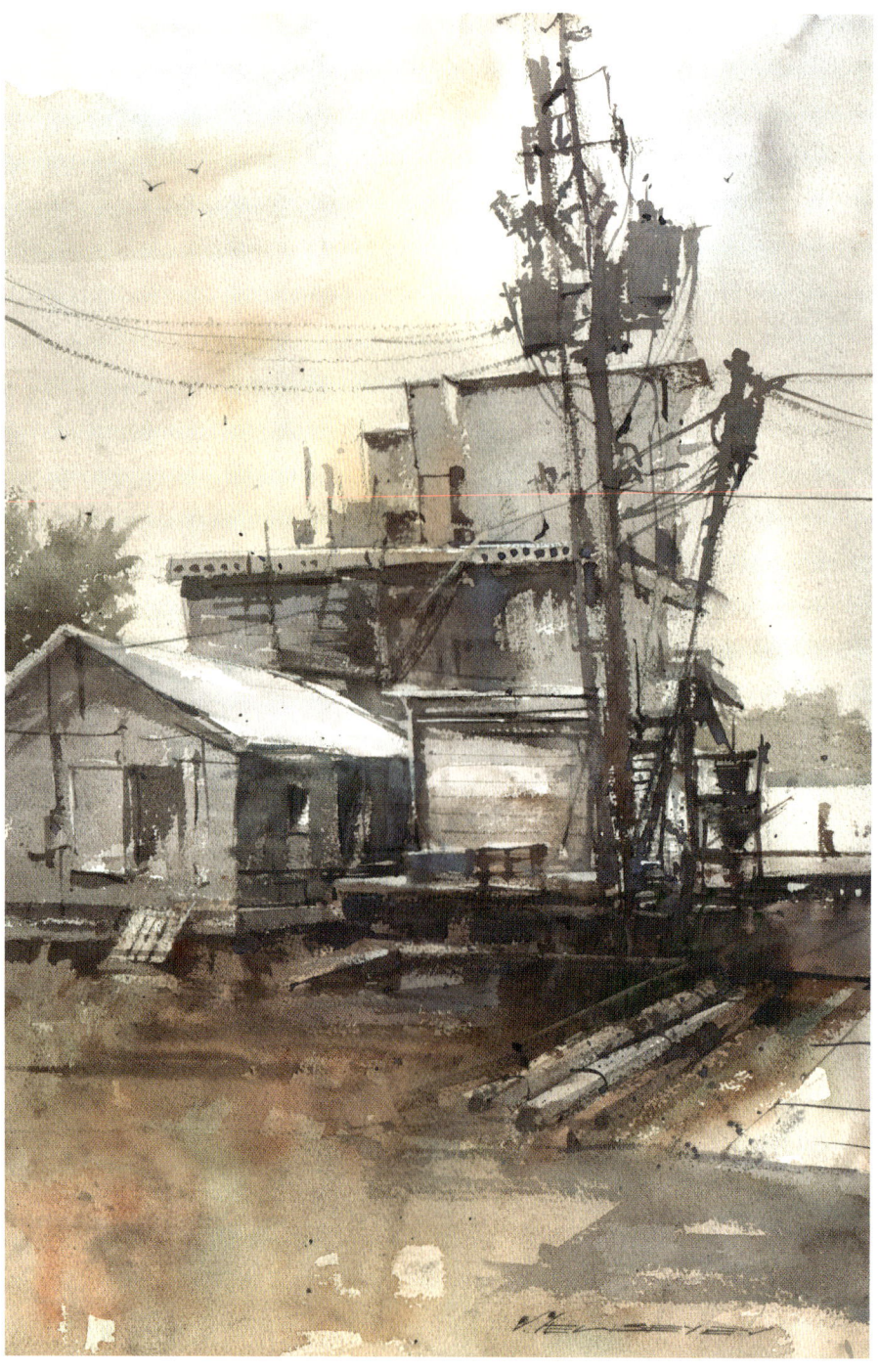

Apalachicola, watercolor, 21½" × 14½" | 55 × 37 cm

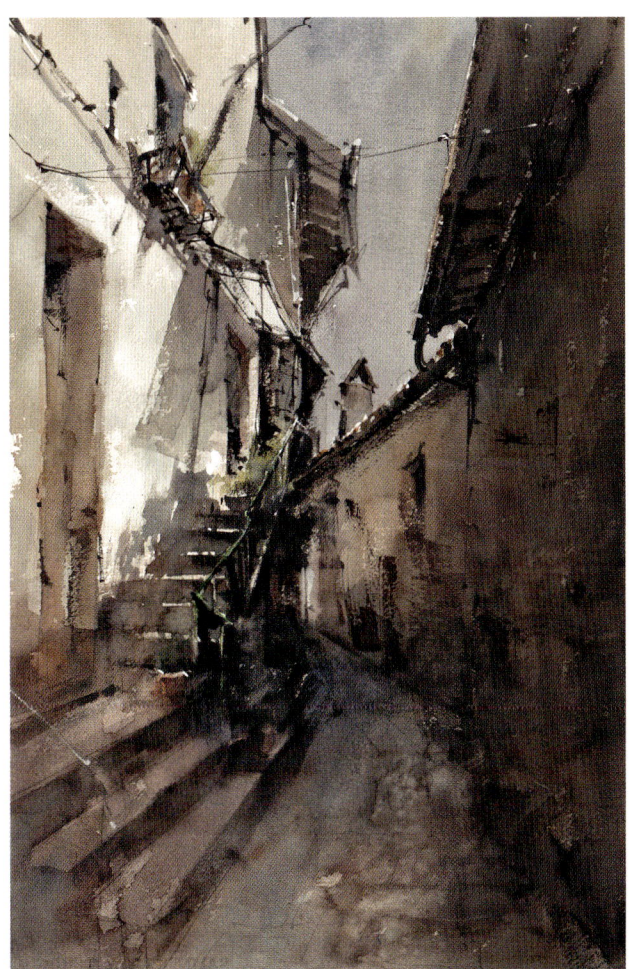

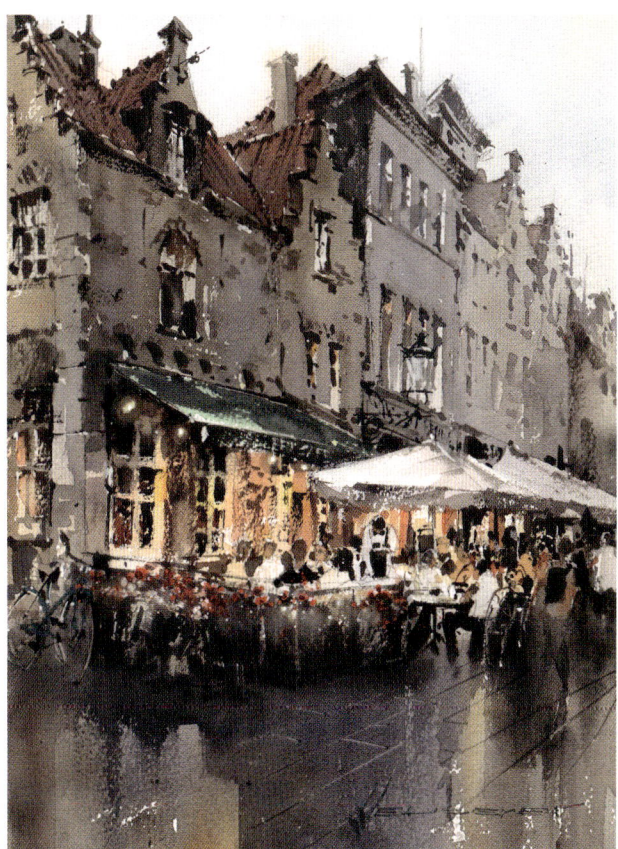

Nightlife in Bruges, watercolor, 14½" × 10½" | 37 × 27 cm

Stroncone, watercolor, 21½" × 14½" | 55 × 37 cm

The ultimate decision to tilt a painting toward either end of the tonal spectrum lies in the artist's deliberate choice of values that align with a specific artistic vision. Personally, I refrain from intentionally adjusting the overall balance unless the subject matter necessitates it. For example, a foggy scene inherently lends itself to a lighter presentation in a painting, while night scenes tend to take on a low-key appearance due to the prevalence of shadows over light.

Regardless of the shift in fundamental tonal values, one critical principle must be upheld: the relative relationship of tones between adjacent areas.

Every painting holds the potential for a positive impact on the viewer when all its components align harmoniously in terms of the relationship between lights and darks. It's imperative for any painter to cultivate their artistic perception by honing in on these intricate relationships within the composition. By effectively solving this visual puzzle, the end result will exude a natural and believable quality, irrespective of the actual values employed.

This underscores the significance of beginning the artistic process with a quick sketch, serving as a valuable reference for the intended values, especially when preserving the final aesthetic is crucial. The preliminary sketch acts as a guiding framework, ensuring the coherence and fidelity of the intended visual impact throughout the painting process.

My approach typically involves selecting tonal values that closely mirror those found in the actual scenery. This choice simplifies the progression of my work, allowing for seamless referencing to real-life values without the need for constant adjustments between light and dark spectra.

BACKLIT VS. FRONT-LIT PAINTINGS

The consideration in my artistic process involves taking note of the sun's position relative to the subject I aim to depict. Two fundamental scenarios unfold: one with the sun behind me, casting a brilliant illumination on the objects in front, and the other with the sun ahead, enveloping the elements facing me in shadow. Discerning the sun's location is a straightforward task—simply observing the ground and tracing the direction of cast shadows provides a clear indication, whether these shadows extend toward or away from me.

I've observed that paintings illuminated from the front tend to exhibit a heightened sense of three-dimensionality and brightness. This is attributable to the viewer being able to perceive the majority of the object surfaces illuminated. However, a noteworthy challenge arises in highlighting and isolating the most crucial aspects of the painting when every element is equally bright. To address this, I've developed a technique of employing unifying washes to tone down peripheral areas, simultaneously intensifying the darkness of midtones and shadows in the focal regions. This method serves to create a focused and compelling image, guiding the viewer's attention to the essential elements of the composition.

In the realm of backlit sceneries, where shadows prevail and illuminated areas are primarily on the secondary sides and tops of objects, the challenge lies in preventing the scene from appearing overly flattened. In such scenarios, the use of intricate silhouettes for elements becomes paramount. To enhance the three-dimensional quality of a backlit view, I incorporate the principles of aerial perspective. Distant elements in the composition exhibit lower contrast and appear considerably muted compared to closer elements.

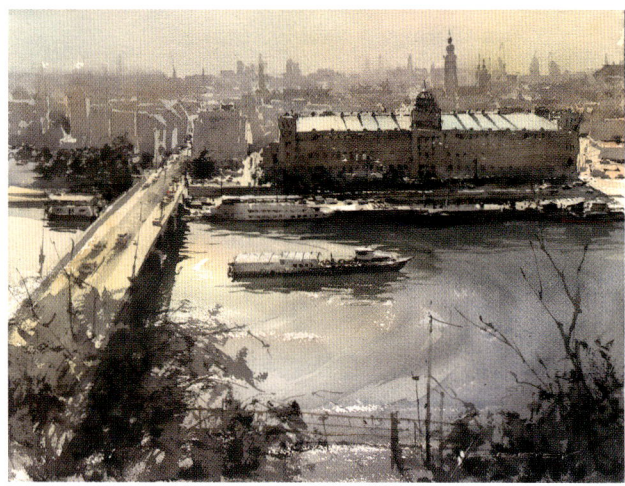

Prague View from Above, watercolor, 14" × 19" | 36 × 48 cm

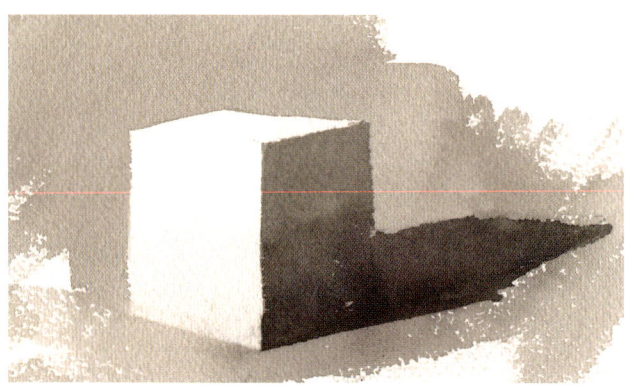

Front-lit cube.

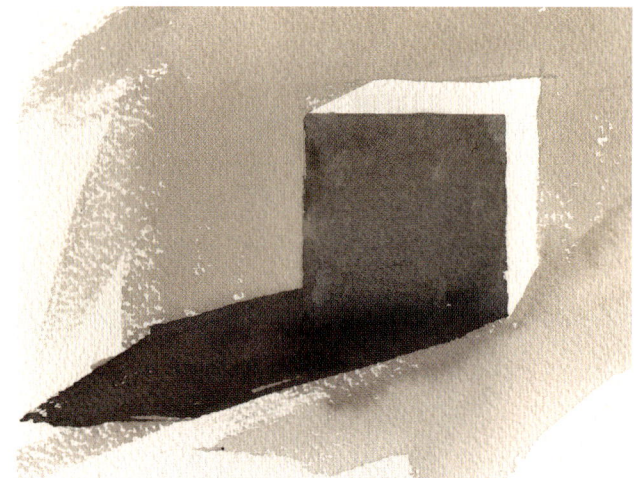

Backlit cube.

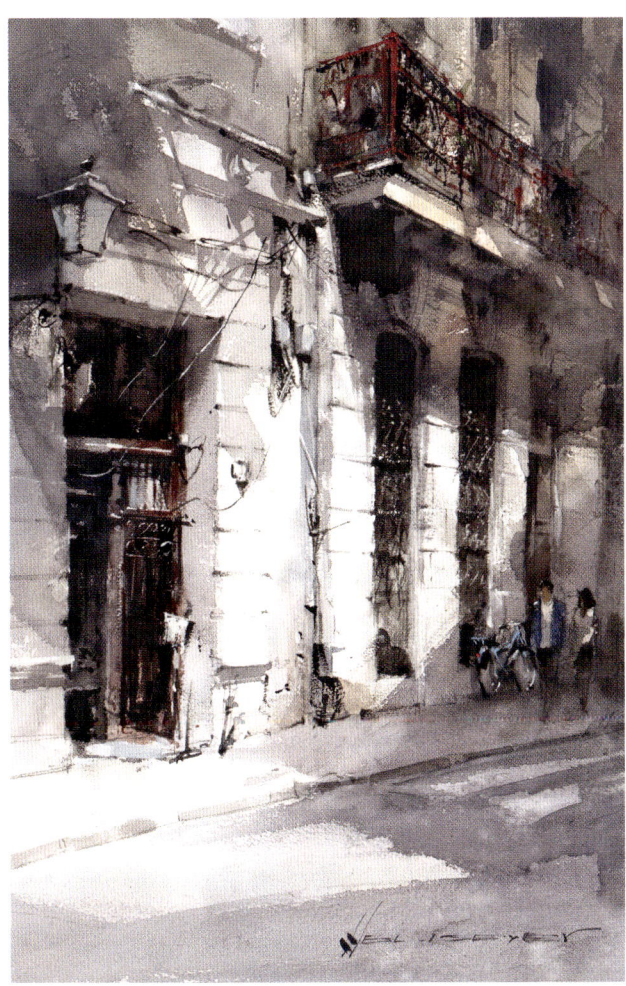

Havana Doors, watercolor, 21½" × 14½" | 55 × 37 cm

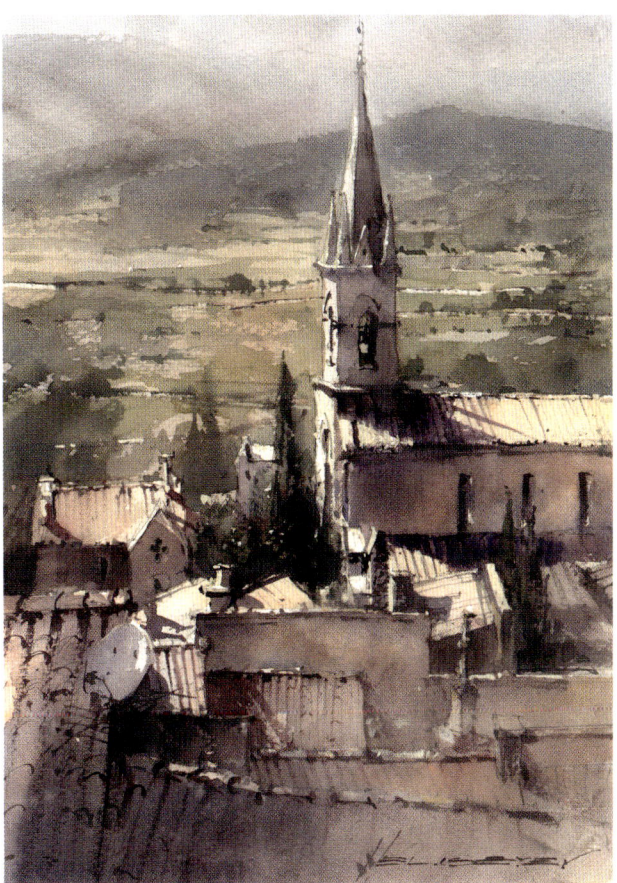

Provence Town (detail), watercolor.

This atmospheric influence serves a dual purpose—it not only enhances the three-dimensional perception but also aids in isolating focal points. The surrounding dark areas naturally frame the focal elements, and with strategic illumination, specific parts of these elements can stand out amidst the shadowy backdrop.

It's important to note that backlit views inherently possess a dynamic quality. The dark cast shadows directed toward the viewer create a powerful and moody atmosphere within the painting, adding an extra layer of depth and intrigue to the overall composition.

Regardless of the direction from which light emanates in my paintings, the ability to skillfully manipulate it remains of utmost importance to enhance the overall impression of the scenery. In the section dedicated to "Rendering Objects in Light" (p. 30), I delve into the fundamental physics and principles governing the distribution of light across surfaces. It's crucial to grasp that these principles remain consistent irrespective of the light's direction. Armed with this understanding, artists can easily manipulate light to create compelling and stunning results, often surpassing the visual impact of reality.

However, a key caveat is the need for caution in avoiding the mixing of incompatible and contradictory directions of daylight within the same painting. Cohesiveness in the portrayal of light is vital for maintaining the visual integrity of the artwork and ensuring that the chosen lighting conditions harmonize seamlessly to create a convincing and aesthetically pleasing work of art.

RESCUING A FAILING PAINTING

During my art classes, I often observe a common inclination among some students to restart their paintings somewhere in the middle or even closer to the beginning of the process when things don't go as planned. I understand that this desire stems from the frustration of the painting not turning out as intended, leading to a loss of direction in the creative process.

One of the most frequent scenarios is when a student makes an accidental mistake in their work, and it appears so distracting that there's a strong urge to correct it at any cost before moving forward.

In such situations, I advocate for continuing the painting process despite the perceived mistake and trying not to dwell on it. More often than not, when the painting is completed, these areas don't appear as bad as initially feared. In fact, they may even enhance the overall appearance of the artwork with the typical imperfections that make watercolors so charming and attractive.

The challenges become more profound when dealing with mistakes on a global scale in a painting, such as the sky appearing too dark or losing highlights due to heavy washes over them. It's crucial to understand that in these situations, when the painting doesn't go as planned, we must adapt to the new reality. This often requires us to reevaluate our initial ideas about the painting's final appearance and start improvising. This can be a difficult adjustment for some painters who prefer to maintain strict control over their work.

In such cases, my advice remains consistent: Do not abandon the painting—continue the work. The advantage of this approach lies in the fact that the painter may find themselves exploring uncharted territory, which can lead to increased creativity and new artistic possibilities.

When faced with challenges related to small imperfections, I make a deliberate choice to disregard those areas and continue painting as if nothing had occurred.

It's important to bear in mind that the strength of watercolor lies in its immediacy, and, interestingly, some small imperfections can actually enhance the overall appearance of the artwork in the end. Regrettably, beginner painters often struggle to progress beyond these minor imperfections and feel compelled to proceed only after fixing them. This inclination may be rooted in our educational traditions from childhood, where we were taught that mistakes must be corrected to move forward.

Watermill (opposite) displays some imperfections in the sky area, yet they barely detract from the overall appearance of the artwork. In fact, they contribute to the notion that the work was executed swiftly. There have been numerous occasions when I felt grateful that these imperfections didn't deter me from completing the painting. In reality, I've come to appreciate their presence in my artwork.

In *Venice Bridges* (p. 146), there are noticeable imperfections on the right side of the painting, particularly in the area of the wall. The intention was to depict a tree right against the wall on the right side of the painting, but it dried too light. While it could have been easily corrected by applying another layer of paint to the wall, I made the deliberate choice to leave that area untouched. I decided to embrace it as a discolored greenish patch on the wall, allowing it to become a part of the painting's character.

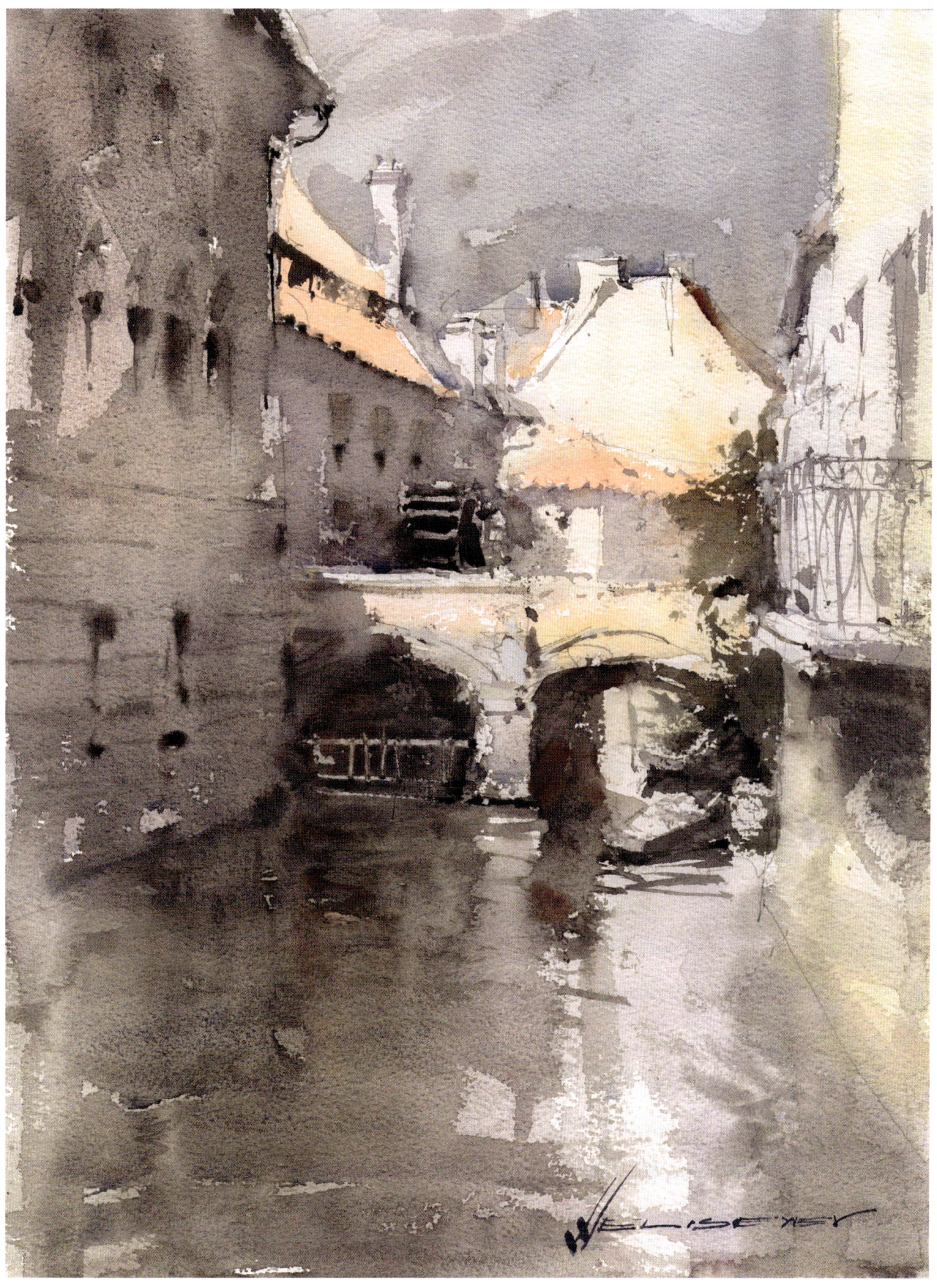

Watermill, watercolor, 15" × 11½" | 39 × 29 cm

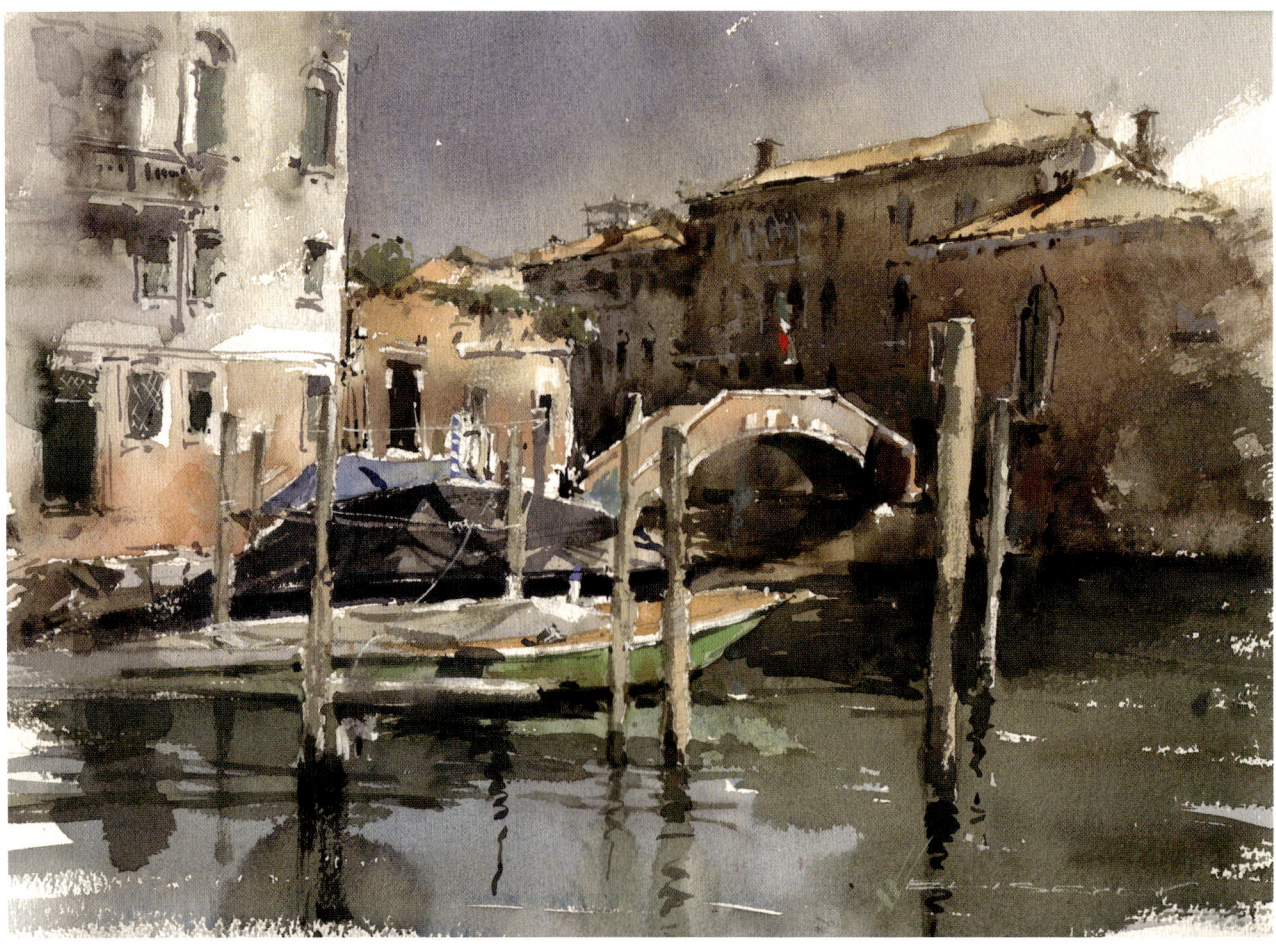

Venice Bridges, watercolor, 12" × 17" | 31 × 44 cm

As I've mentioned before, mistakes in art can lead us to change our course of action as we work toward completing a piece, all while offering valuable learning opportunities throughout the process. The act of creating a painting is inherently intuitive and can be challenging to predict, much like life itself. In life, we often strive to anticipate our next moves, yet we are consistently met with unforeseen circumstances. Instead of giving up, we endeavor to overcome these challenges, and in the process, we find satisfaction in resolving them along the way. This parallel between the creative process and life's journey is both intriguing and rewarding.

Addressing mistakes in the drawing department on the other hand is essential, and they should be corrected as soon as they are discovered. I'd like to outline common errors that are particularly noticeable to the viewer, with a focus on drawing skills.

The most frequent mistakes I observe, especially among beginners, pertain to perspective and proportions. After completing the pencil layout, it's crucial for the artist to pause and take a critical look before applying watercolor. Correcting these kinds of mistakes becomes significantly more challenging later in the painting process.

ADDING FINISHING TOUCHES

The process of finishing touches involves employing short brushstrokes with dark or white paint, along with the addition of dark or light lines to accentuate the dynamics and edges of the brightly lit parts of the elements in the picture.

The implementation of dark or light brushstrokes is easy to understand, as they enhance local contrast in any given area when needed. I often employ the drybrush technique there to create synergy with the previous layer of paint. This technique is particularly useful in areas of focal significance. I strive to be very painterly when implementing this technique to further enhance the loose quality of the painting and break off stiff edges where needed. This is the time to break away from realism and showcase the actual human-created appearance of the brushstrokes, as if emphasizing that it's just a painting and not a representation of reality.

I try to convey a sense of color in these brushstrokes, but due to the multiple layers already involved in the area, they tend to appear dark, which is acceptable considering their small size.

Lines are another powerful technique to enhance the appearance of the painting. It's crucial to avoid a monotonous look in the lines, introducing breaks and a dry-brushed appearance for a more natural effect of light on them.

The key advantage of the sword brush is its ability to smoothly transition the line from wide to thin, creating a natural and effortless appearance.

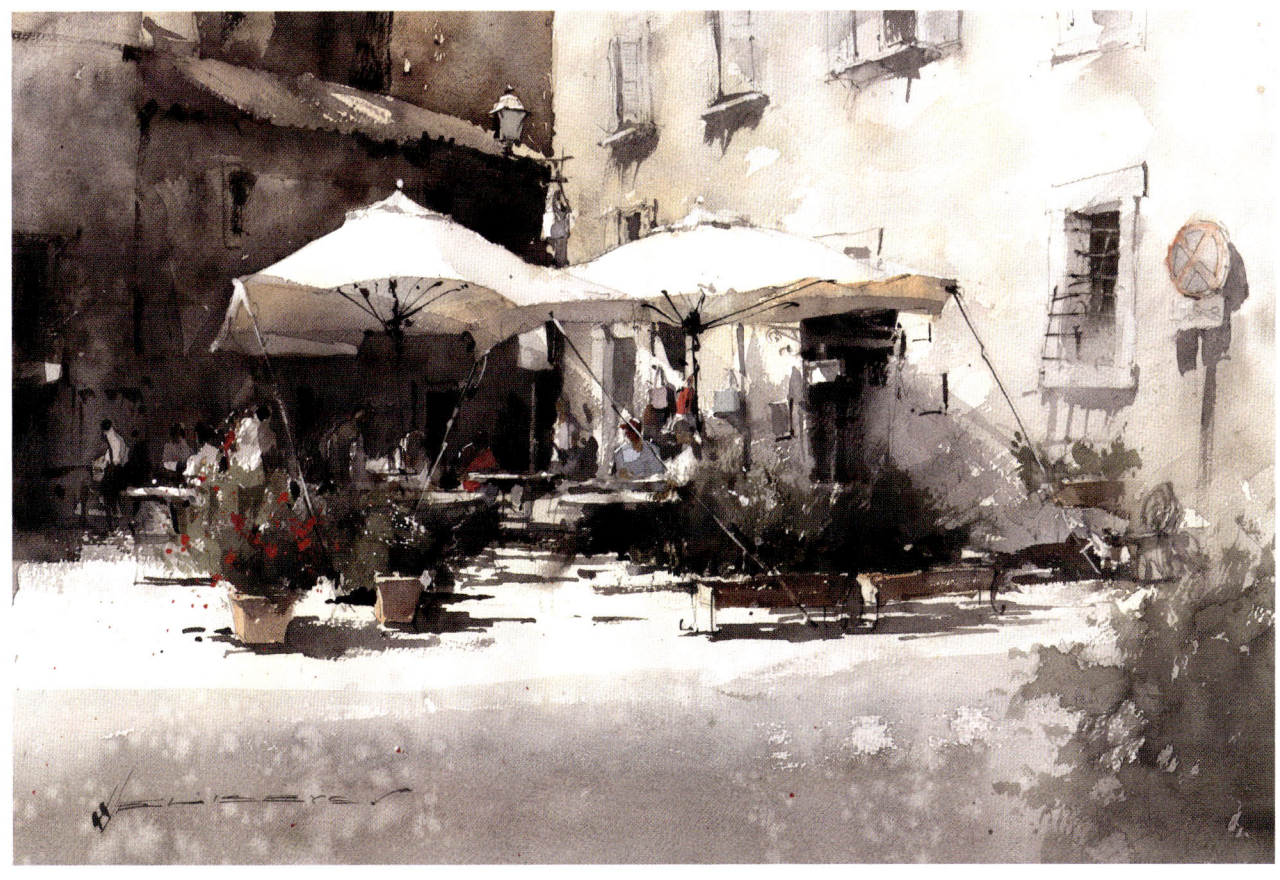

Orvieto Café, watercolor, 14½" × 21½" | 37 × 55 cm

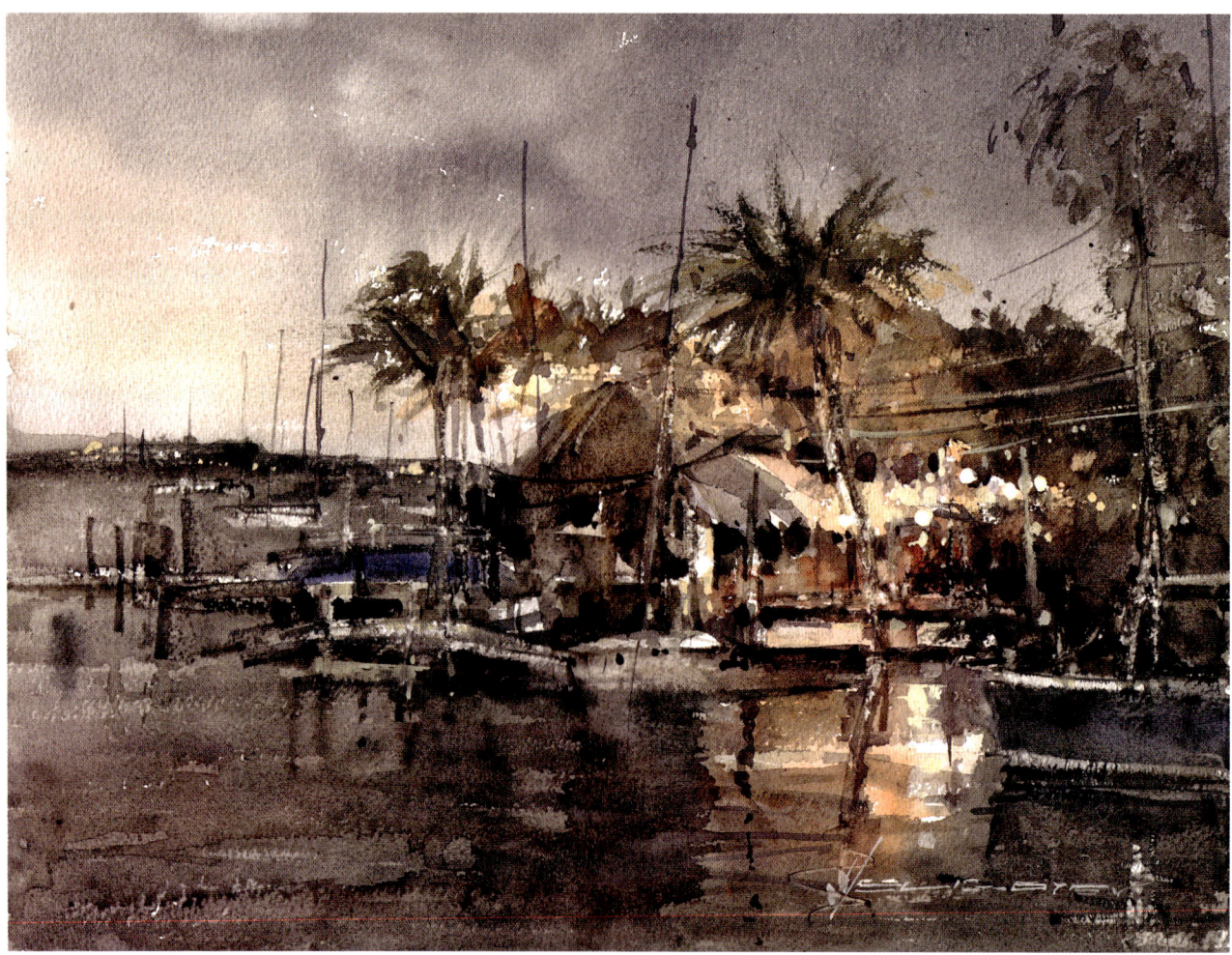

Tiki Bar, watercolor, 11½" × 15½" | 29 × 40 cm

The most effective method is to apply titanium white lines on a previously painted dark background and vice versa. These gouache highlights should be sparingly applied as individual spots where reflections occur, especially on highly reflective objects like metals and glass within the painting. I also recommend mixing gouache with a touch of yellow ochre, imparting a slightly warmer tone to the bright reflections. Additionally, these spots can be effectively employed in night scenes to accentuate light sources such as streetlights.

It's crucial to note that the use of gouache should be reserved for the final stages of the painting process, since applying any subsequent wash over gouache can lead to a smeared appearance.

The use of white gouache can be replaced with a scratching technique, which often yields more natural-looking results in watercolor paintings. This technique is thoroughly explained in the section "Splattering and Scratching Effects" (p. 84).

In instances where a painting exhibits excessively inaccurate edges, employing white or dark lines can be an effective method to rectify them during the final stages of the process. These lines serve as a corrective measure, helping to define and sharpen edges that may have become indistinct or imprecise. This technique allows for nuanced adjustment, enhancing the overall clarity and structure of the painting.

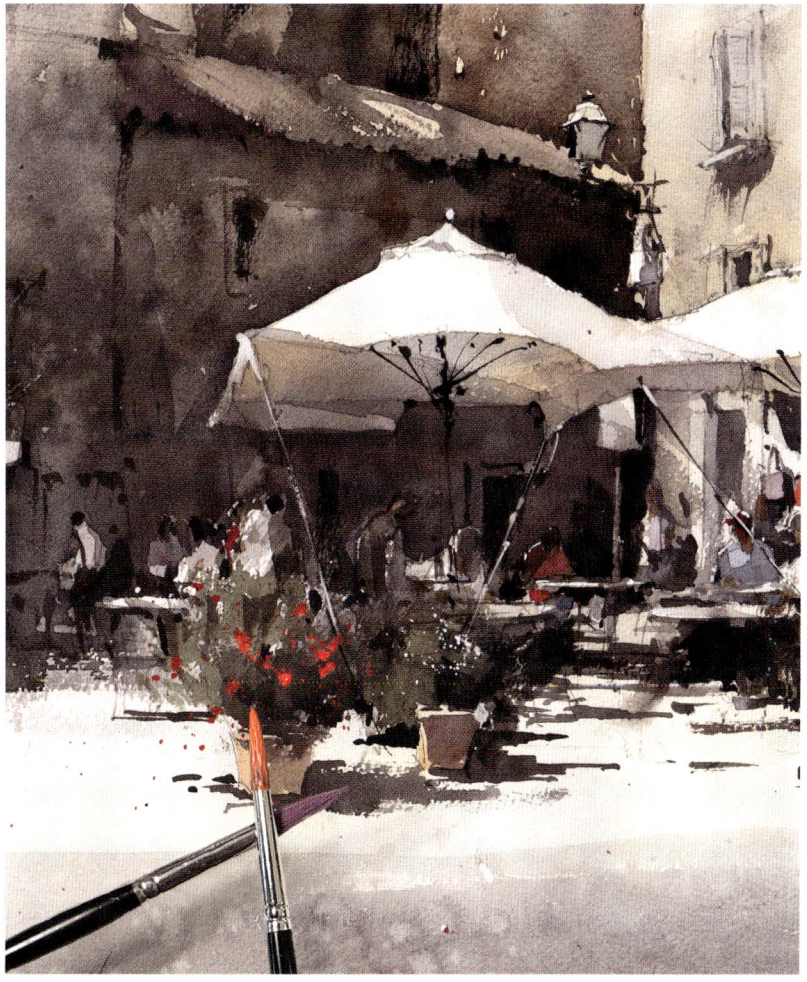

Orvieto Café, detail.

The same gouache, when mixed with various colors, can yield a wonderful sense of small flowers when splattered onto shrubs or lawns as needed at the end of the painting process. This technique allows for the creation of nuanced colors, such as light pink, which can be challenging to achieve with watercolor alone. Mixing gouache with watercolor produces a heavier, thicker mixture that is well-suited for controlled splattering in compact areas.

Scan to view a
video tutorial

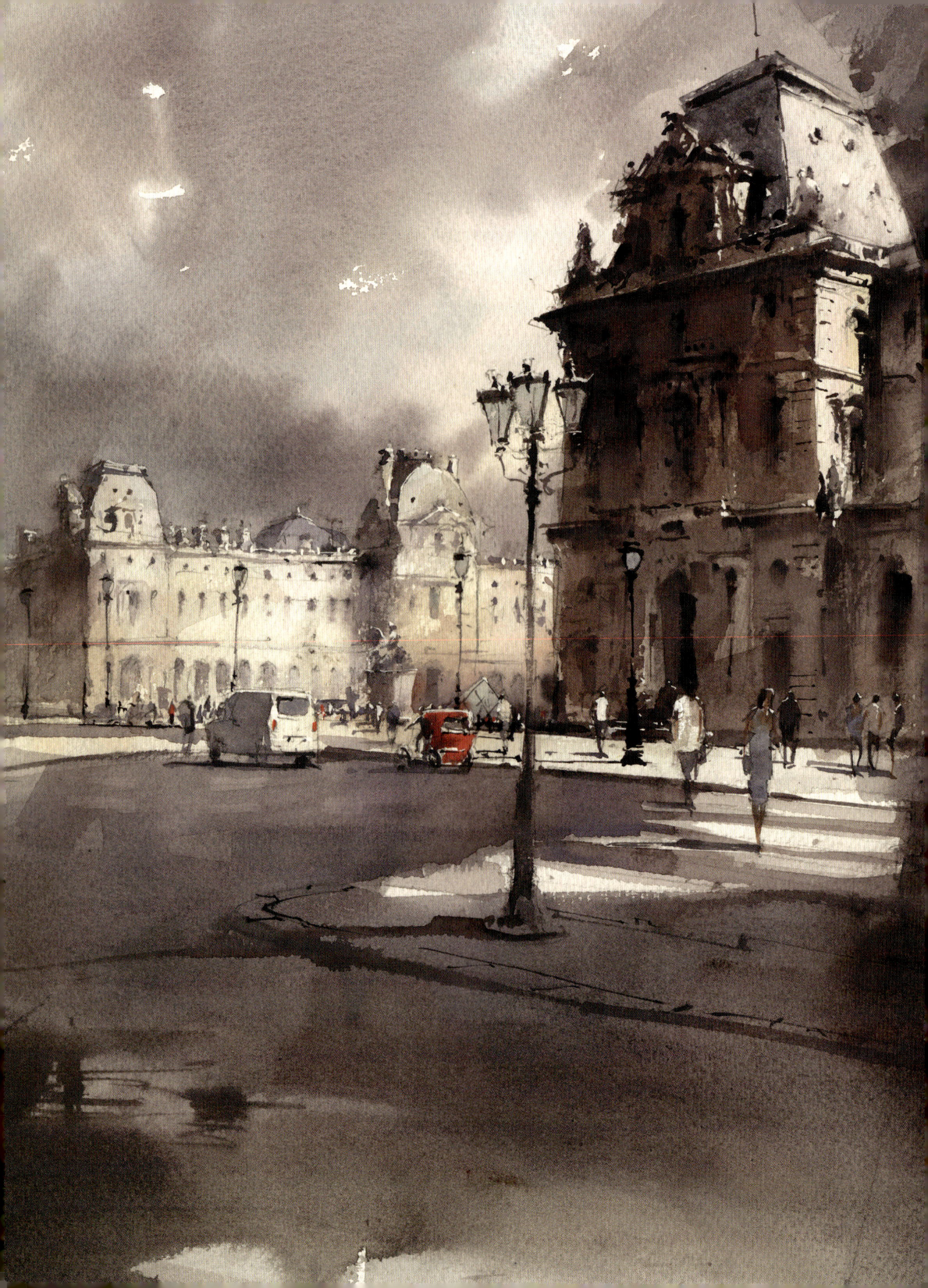

RESOURCES

BOOKS

Baetjer, Katharine & J. G. Links. (1989). Canaletto. The Metropolitan Museum of Art.

Hirshler, Erica E. & Theresa A. Carbone. (2013). *John Singer Sargent: Watercolors* MFA Publications/ Brooklyn Museum.

Martineau, Jane & Andrew Robinson. (1994). *The Glory of Venice, Art in the Eighteen Century.* Yale University Press.

Ormond, Richard & Elane Kilmurray. (2006). *John Singer Sargent: Figures and Landscapes, 1874–1882.* Yale University Press.

Ormond, Richard & Elane Kilmurray. (2014). *John Singer Sargent: Figures and Landscapes, 1908–1913.* Yale University Press.

Petrova, Evgenia. (2016). *The Four Seasons: Works from the Collection of the Russian Museum.* St. Petersburg: Palace Editions – State Russian Museum.

Ranson, Ron. (1989). *Watercolor Impressionists.* North Light Books.

Schmid, Richard. (2009). *The Landscapes.* Stove Prairie Press.

Spate, Virginia. (2001). *Claude Monet: The Color of Time.* Thames & Hudson.

Van De Wetering, Ernst. (2004). *Rembrandt: The Painter at Work.* University of California Press.

Vygodsky, L.S. (1978). *Mind in Society: Development of Higher Psychological Processes.* Harvard University Press.

Warrell, Ian & Franklin Kelly (Eds.). (2007). *J. M. W. Turner.* Tate Publishing.

MAGAZINES AND NEWSLETTER

Artists Magazine
artistsnetwork.com

Outdoor Painter
outdoorpainter.com

Plein Air Today
outdoorpainter.com/plein-air-today-newsletter

PleinAir Magazine
https://tinyurl.com/3at8j5dz

The Art of Watercolour
artofwatercolour.com

Watercolor Artist
artistsnetwork.com/magazines/watercolor-artist

LEARN MORE ABOUT VLADISLAV YELISEYEV

To learn more about Vladislav, his artwork, and his classes (both online and in person), visit:

- Website: yeliseyevfineart.com
- Instagram: @vladislavyeliseyev
- Facebook: @vladislav.yeliseyev, @ArtistYeliseyev
- YouTube: @VladislavYeliseyev

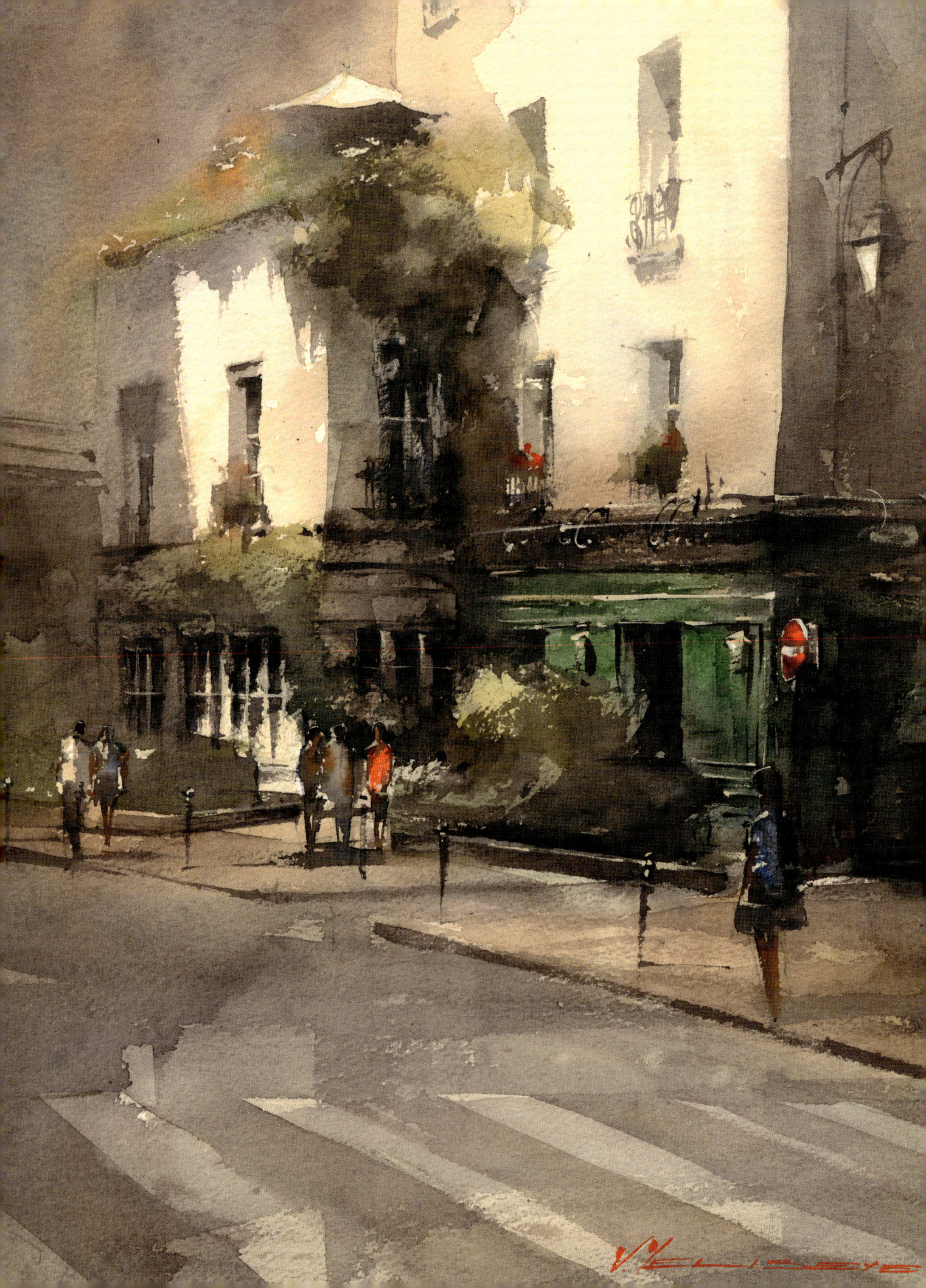

ACKNOWLEDGMENTS

This book would not have been possible without the guidance of the art teachers I had the good fortune to learn from in my early years. They helped shape my vision of fine art and introduced me to the technical foundations of watercolor painting.

I would like to thank all my students, whose curiosity and feedback sparked the idea of writing this book to help streamline the watercolor learning process. I'm especially grateful for their insightful questions, which helped me identify key challenges that readers might face and shaped the structure and focus of this book.

I also acknowledge the influence of Lev Vygotsky's concept of the "zone of proximal development," which provided deep insights into the learning process between students and teachers.

Special thanks goes to the editorial team at Quarto and Rockport Publishers for their dedication and support in bringing this book to life.

ABOUT THE AUTHOR

Vladislav Yeliseyev is a highly respected master watercolor artist, architectural illustrator, and sought-after workshop instructor. Originally from Russia, Vlad earned a bachelor's degree in Classical Art from the Moscow School of Art and a Master's in Architecture from the Moscow Institute of Architecture before immigrating to the United States, where he established himself as a leading watercolorist. He is a Signature Member of the National Watercolor Society, the American Impressionist Society, and the Florida Watercolor Society, and has been invited to participate in many plein air and landscape events as both a teacher and a juror. Vlad's work is included in private and corporate collections worldwide and has been awarded Best in Show, First Place, Collector's Choice, and other honors. His articles have been published in *Watercolor Artist*, *Plein Air Magazine*, *The Art of Watercolour*, and other publications, which have also featured his work on their covers. Through his international workshops and online classes, Vlad shares his passion for capturing the beauty of landscapes with expressive brushwork and a masterful command of light and color. He lives in Sarasota, Florida.

◀ *Café in Green*, watercolor, 16" × 12" | 40 × 31 cm

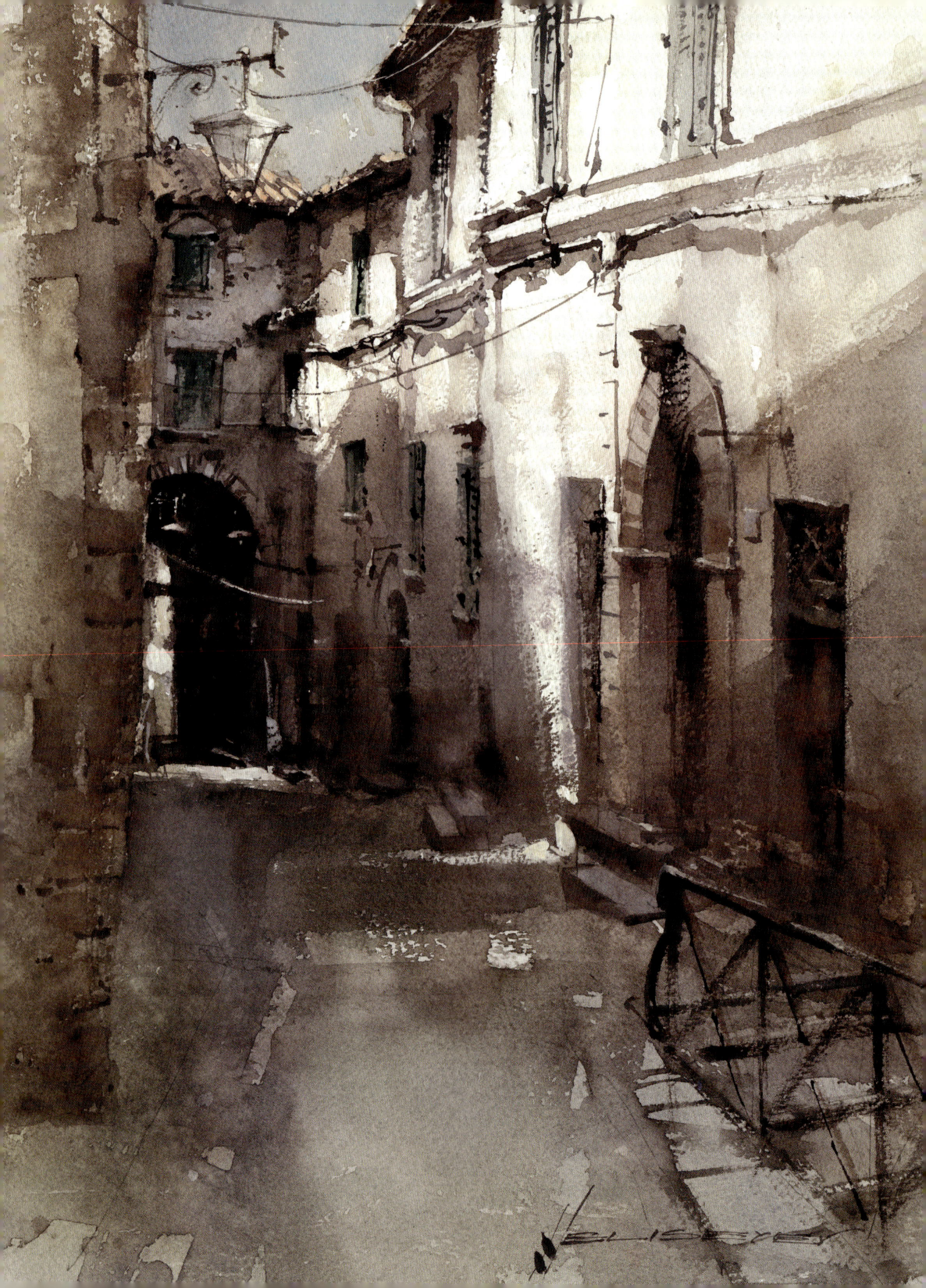

INDEX

ALSO IN ROCKPORT'S
FOR ARTISTS SERIES

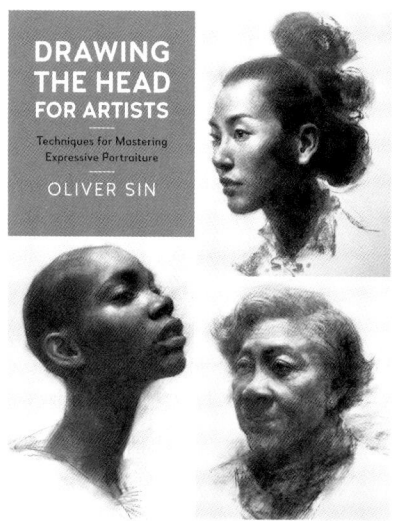

Drawing the Head for Artists
978-1-6315-9692-6

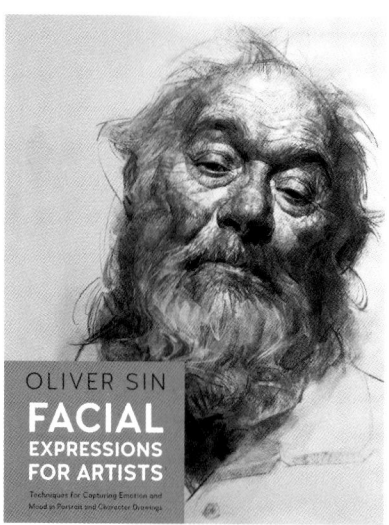

Facial Expressions for Artists
978-0-7603-8240-0

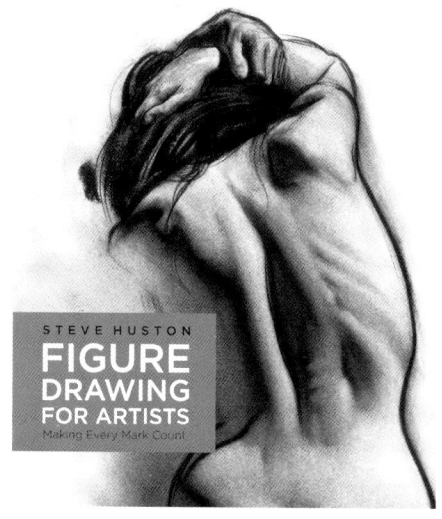

Figure Drawing for Artists
978-1-6315-9065-8

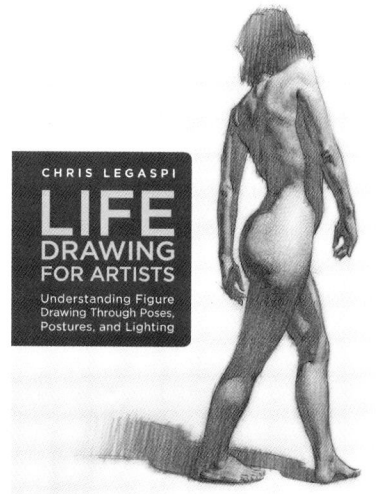

Life Drawing for Artists
978-1-6315-9801-2

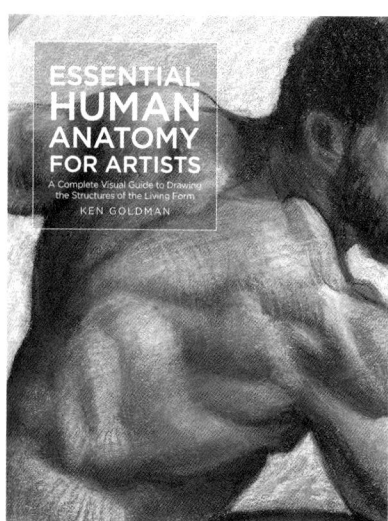

Essential Human Anatomy for Artists
978-1-6315-9959-0